MW00790556

GOOD MORNING LORD

STARTING EACH DAY WITH THE RISEN SON

ADRIAN ROGERS

Published by Innovo Publishing, LLC
www.innovopublishing.com
info@innovopublishing.com
1-888-546-2111

Providing Full-Service Publishing Services for Christian Authors, Artists & Ministries: Hardbacks, Paperbacks, eBooks,Audiobooks, Music, Screenplays, Film & Courses

GOOD MORNING, LORD: STARTING EACH DAY WITH THE RISEN SON
By Adrian Rorgers

ISBN: 978-1-61314-767-2

Cover Design: Houseal Creative with Innovo Publishing, LLC
Interior Layout: Houseal Creative with Innovo Publishing, LLC

Printed in the United States of America
U.S. Printing History
Third Edition: 2021

preface

Cause me to hear Your lovingkindness in the morning, for in You do I trust; cause me to know the way in which I should walk, for I lift up my soul to You.

PSALM 143:8

How did you sleep last night? Deep, pleasant slumber, uninterrupted by troublesome dreams? Fitfully? Tossing and turning as you replayed yesterday's turmoil? Did you sleep the sleep of the perpetually exhausted, worn from life's burdens? Perhaps you did not sleep at all as you considered an important impending decision.

It doesn't matter. Whether you are well-rested or red-eyed, you need to be with God this morning—every morning—to be reminded of His love and faithfulness, to receive direction for the day, and to lift your soul in worship.

The book you are holding provides beautifully crafted devotions from trusted pastor, author and teacher Adrian Rogers. Pastor Rogers would, of course, point you to scripture first—to time alone studying God's Word, listening for His voice, and meditating on His instructions. He would point you to prayer—deep communion with your Father through the power of the Holy Spirit. He would point you to praise—giving glory to the Lord Jesus Christ as your Savior.

So it is with humility that this little book, *Good Morning, Lord*, is offered to you as an accessory to your time alone with God.

The most important thing is to get alone with Him consistently and expectantly. After all, His mercies are "new every morning." (See Lamentations 3:23.)

What we need is not great faith but faith in a great God.

ADRIAN ROGERS

January

1

> Yea, though I walk through the valley of the shadow of death, I will fear no evil; For You are with me; Your rod and Your staff, they comfort me.
>
> **PSALM 23:4**

Years ago, some men were on a leaky old ship in the middle of a rough and stormy sea, fearful for their lives. One went to see the captain and said, "Captain, are we safe?" He said, "Well, I'll put it to you this way: the boilers on this ship are very weak and may explode at any moment. Also, the ship is very old and she's taking on water. To be honest, we may have an explosion or we may sink. We may go up or we may go down. But," he continued, "at any rate, we're going on."

And that's the way we are as we face this new year. Jesus may come—we may go up. We may die—we'll go down and then go up. But at any rate, we're going on...even though we don't know what this year will bring.

Before the old map makers had the modern instruments we have, they would draw maps for as far out as they had explored. They didn't know what was beyond. You see on old maps: "Beyond this, there may be dragons." They'd never seen a dragon, but they didn't know what was out there. They were afraid of the uncharted. And that is the way many of us feel about the future.

ACTION POINT Face this new year by squaring your shoulders, lifting your head, and saying "I will fear no evil, for You are with me." if you have not done it yet, the greatest thing you could do to begin this year would be to give your heart to Jesus Christ. This would be the beginning of a brand new life, the first day of an eternal life! Are you willing to openly and publicly acknowledge Christ as your personal Savior?

January 2

So they said, "Believe on the Lord Jesus Christ, and you will be saved, you and your household."

ACTS 16:31

If you are not saved, your first step in this new year must be to give your heart and life to the Lord Jesus Christ. If I had a thousand lives to live, I'd give Him every one of them. I really would.

I came to Jesus Christ as a teen. If I had understood sooner, I would have come sooner. I don't care how young you are or how old you are—if you are reading this, you can be saved. I don't care how good you are or how bad you are, there is no one so good that he doesn't need to be saved, and no one so bad that he can't be saved.

The Bible says, "Believe on the Lord Jesus Christ." That doesn't mean mere intellectual belief or just accepting some facts about Him. It means *trust*. You can believe an airplane can fly...you don't trust it until you get on it. Come to Jesus, and I promise you—on the authority of the Word of God—He will save you instantly. He will be with you continually. He will keep you eternally.

Billy Graham once said, "The greatest fears are those fears of death, judgment, and eternity." And thank God, through the gospel of our Lord and Savior Jesus Christ, these fears are removed. I wonder if you can say today, "Brother Rogers, I have believed in Christ. I have committed my all to Him, and He has taken from me the fears of death, judgment, and eternity. And I know that I'm saved. I know that I know that I'm a child of God. And if I should die today, I'd go to be with the Lord Jesus Christ."

ACTION POINT Commit your life to Jesus. Believe on Him. Trust Him, and a transformation will take place. He will save you. He will satisfy you. He will secure you if you trust Him.

3

So we may boldly say: "The LORD is my helper;
I will not fear. What can man do to me?"
HEBREWS 13:6

If you're going to face this year with steadfast resolve, you must find your contentment, companionship, and confidence in Christ. Then, you will find your comfort in Christ. Then you may boldly say, "The LORD is my helper; I will not fear. What can man do to me?"

I'm not telling you that life's going to be all honey and no bees. The Christians to whom the book of Hebrews was written faced heartaches, trials, mockery, brutality, and opposition from family, friends, and foes alike. Yet they could boldly say, "The Lord is my helper."

Worry is a form of atheism—acting like God doesn't exist. David Livingstone, a missionary to Africa, journaled on January 14th, 1856, that he was surrounded by hostile people in the heart of darkest Africa. Livingstone wrote, "Felt much turmoil of spirit in prospect of having all of my plans for the welfare of this great region and this teeming population knocked on the head by savages tomorrow....but I read that Jesus said, 'All authority has been given to Me in heaven and on earth. Go therefore and make disciples of all the nations...; and lo, I am with you always, even to the end of the age.' This is the word of a gentleman of the most strict and sacred honor."

Friend, this coming year may be difficult for you. But you can stand upon the promises of the Word of God.

ACTION POINT We don't know what the coming year will bring in the way of sickness, heartache or trouble. But I do know you can boldly say, "The Lord will be my helper. I will not fear. What can man do to me?" Find your contentment, your companionship, and your confidence in Jesus. In Him, you will find your comfort and your courage.

4

Therefore we must give the more earnest heed to
the things we have heard, lest we drift away.

HEBREWS 2:1

Life is like an ocean...a trackless ocean with winds, currents, and waves. We will meet ships we never knew were on that ocean, and we will have all kinds of opportunities, heartaches, tears and fears as we sail into a new year on an uncharted sea.

Scholars tell us that Hebrews 2:1 refers to the sea—the writer is using a nautical term. He must have spent time at sea because the phrase "giving more earnest heed" and the word *slip* refer to bringing a ship into the harbor, a difficult and sometimes dangerous task. A ship never just drifts into the harbor. The most skillful part of being a sea pilot is bringing the ship into the harbor. *Let them slip* literally means "drift away." You have to be careful when you enter the harbor that you don't end up on the rocks or drift past the harbor.

The worst thing that could happen to us this year is that we just drift through it, living an aimless life—letting this year *happen to us* rather than charting a course and getting into God's appointed harbor. The winds of worldliness, the tides of circumstance, and the currents of the old nature are determined to cause you to drift.

ACTION POINT You will drift unless you decide *not* to drift. You must have an anchor. You need a fixed direction. This is important, because drifting is one of the easiest things in the world to do.

5

> Not that I speak in regard to need, for I have learned in whatever state I am, to be content: I know how to be abased, and I know how to abound. Everywhere and in all things I have learned both to be full and to be hungry, both to abound and to suffer need.
>
> **PHILIPPIANS 4:11-12**

When Paul wrote this, he was in prison. But he said, "I've learned, in whatever state I am, to be content. All I need is in the Lord Jesus Christ. I don't have to go outside of Him for contentment."

The word *content* literally means "self-contained." Back when the stock market crashed, there were men who jumped out of skyscrapers, committing suicide. Why? Because they lost the things they were trying to satisfy their hearts with. That was where their security was. Friend, you had better have your security, sufficiency, and satisfaction in something that can't be tampered with. God is going to take care of you. He will never leave you nor forsake you.

We are afraid of being forsaken. Our friends will leave us. Our compatriots may forsake us. A lack of love causes depression, and that brings fear. Psychiatrists say that the greatest need we have on this earth is not a material need, but rather the ability to love and to be loved. And the Lord has said, "I will never leave you."

ACTION POINT Paul continues in verse 13, "I can do all things through Christ who strengthens me." That literally means "I can do all things through Christ who is pouring His life into me." Learn a life of contentment. Have the contentment of His provision—Christ Himself. The deepest need of your heart can be met in the Lord Jesus Christ.

January 6

I know how to be abased, and I know how to abound.
Everywhere and in all things I have learned both to be full
and to be hungry, both to abound and to suffer need.

PHILIPPIANS 4:12

As we face the coming year, what we have in Jesus Christ—eternal security, salvation, a relationship with the King of kings—is worth multiplied billions and more.

Today some of you find that you're abased, saying, "I can hardly make it till the next paycheck." Some of you are abounding. You have more than you ever thought or dreamed. If you have that, I'm happy for you. It is the Lord who gives you the ability to get wealth. Thank God for it. Don't be ashamed of it.

From his prison cell Paul says, "I know how to be abased, and I know how to abound." Would you say, "Lord, make me content with your provision. If I have food and clothing, I have enough. Forgive me, Lord, if I have the spirit of covetousness." And then thank Him for the companionship of His presence. Know that you would not trade that for all of the wealth of the world. Thank Him for the confidence that you have in His promise in Hebrews 13:5. "Let your conduct be without covetousness; be content with such things as you have. For He Himself has said, 'I will never leave you nor forsake you.'" And then take comfort in His protection and say, "God, no matter what happens, I will not fear what man shall do to me."

ACTION POINT Remember, whatever your situation is right now, God sees and knows. Nothing about you escapes His attention. Look to Him. If you have Jesus, friend, you have something wonderful. Thank Him, for in Him you have the riches of Christ, regardless of what you may or may not have in the bank.

7

Let your conduct be without covetousness; be content with such things as you have. For He Himself has said, "I will never leave you nor forsake you."

HEBREWS 13:5

If you want to face a new year without fear, know the contentment of His provision. Discontent is a disease that breeds fear. The secret of contentment isn't not wanting what we don't have, but being grateful for what we do have. I wouldn't sell the contentment I have in Jesus Christ for any price you could name. I am content in the Lord Jesus. That doesn't mean I'm satisfied with myself, but that along with the Apostle Paul I can say it gladly and surely: "I can do all things through Christ who is pouring His life into me," and "I have learned in whatsoever state I am, therewith to be content" (Philippians 4:11).

Hebrews 10:34 says to the Hebrew Christians, "For you...joyfully accepted the plundering of your goods, knowing that you have a better and an enduring possession for yourselves in heaven." Suppose today soldiers were to come into your house and carry out all of your material possessions. Could you still praise the Lord? If you were delighted in the Lord, you could. Psalm 37:4 says "Delight yourself also in the Lord, and He shall give you the desires of your heart." That doesn't mean you'll have every whim, every lust of your flesh satisfied. It means when you find all in Jesus Christ, when you delight yourself in the Lord, then what your heart has really been seeking for, it will find. What your heart really yearns for is God.

ACTION POINT If you want the source of your satisfaction, your sufficiency, and your security to be steadfast, then you must find it in the Lord Jesus Christ. As the hymn says, "All other ground is sinking sand."*

*"My Hope is Built on Nothing Less" — Edward Mote, 1834

8

Do you not know that those who run in a race all run, but one receives the prize? Run in such a way that you may obtain it.

1 CORINTHIANS 9:24

Are you drifting? Sometimes we don't realize what's happening to us. The things we allow in our lives have a pull—the entertainment we watch, the society we are in—and drifting is a determined thing, drifting is a deceptive thing, and drifting is always a dangerous thing. Most people do not plan to fail...they simply do not plan anything. You need to have a goal. What is it that ruins us? Not overt dissipation—simply neglect.

"For both He who sanctifies and those who are being sanctified are all of one, for which reason He is not ashamed to call them brethren" (Hebrews 2:11). That means we are partakers of the Divine nature. Have you become ho-hum about your salvation? Neglect your salvation this year, and you are going to end up on the rocks. You must determine your direction and firm up your discipline, or you're going to drift. You cannot neglect so great a salvation.

Many years ago, a Yale University study found that 3% of the students had written down specific goals. Twenty-two years later, a follow-up with those students revealed that the goal-writing 3% had achieved more than the other 97% put together. They were not drifters. They had goals in their lives. Sociologists find that 95% of people never have any written goals, but of the 5% that do have written goals, 95% of that 5% have reached their goals.

ACTION POINT Write down today some goals for yourself in the coming year. We are body, soul, and spirit, so make three divisions: On one page write "Spiritual Goals." On the second write "Physical Goals." And on the third write "Personal Goals." Do you have a goal? Do you have a vision? Be one of the 5%; not the 95%.

9

> Then I went down to the potter's house, and there he was, making something at the wheel. And the vessel that he made of clay was marred in the hand of the potter; so he made it again into another vessel, as it seemed good to the potter to make.
>
> **JEREMIAH 18:3-4**

The making of pottery is one of the oldest arts known to men. A potter takes clay and chops it and crushes it and molds it and squeezes it until it is soft and pliable. It is a beautiful thing to watch: a vessel of beauty, or a vessel of service, or both, emerge from that ugly clay.

There are three ingredients in the making of pottery: the Potter, the clay, and the wheel. God is the Potter. We are His workmanship. God is the Master Workman, working on us. Think of yourself as the clay and see what God can do with you, for He is at work in your life. The wheel is the circumstances of life. Don't think the incidences in your life are meaningless. God wants to make something beautiful out of you.

ACTION POINT Do you feel like a marred vessel today? Though you may not understand it now, every turn of the Potter's wheel has been a part of God's plan. If God does not rule, He overrules. He's going to turn every Calvary to an Easter, every midnight to a sunrise. He is going to turn every tear to a pearl and make a diadem (a jeweled crown) for you. The last turn of the wheel hasn't happened yet. Cease looking around. Instead, look up. Look to Jesus Christ. In faith, call out to Him.

10

Then the word of the LORD came to me, saying: "O house of Israel, can I not do with you as this potter?" says the LORD. "Look, as the clay is in the potter's hand, so are you in My hand, O house of Israel!"

JEREMIAH 18:5-6

God the Potter has the clay upon His wheel—but something happens. It's marred. It's ruined. Did God make a mistake? The problem is not in the hands of the Potter. The problem is in the clay.

Now, what could be the problem in the clay? First, there might be some rock, some hidden impurity keeping the vessel from becoming what it ought to be. There may be some hidden impurity in your life, marring what God wants to do. Or it may just be that the clay is not broken enough. The clay is too stiff. The clay does not yield to the hand of the Potter. What is clay to do in the hand of the potter? We are to yield.

ACTION POINT Are you yielded? Can God form and shape you and make out of you what He wants? We must be willing to say, "Lord, You are the Potter, I'm the clay; mold me, make me after Thy will."* Have you said, "Lord, here I am. Make of me what You wish. Do with me what You will"? Most of us dare not dream what we could be if we would allow God to have His way in our lives.

*"Have Thine Own Way, Lord" — lyrics by Adelaide Pollard, 1907

11

> The instant I speak concerning a nation and concerning a kingdom, to pluck up, to pull down, and to destroy it, if that nation against whom I have spoken turns from its evil, I will relent of the disaster that I thought to bring upon it.
>
> **JEREMIAH 18:7-8**

God is saying here, "If you will repent of your sin, I will repent of the judgment I had planned." That is a promise to every one of us today. Just because you may have failed in the past doesn't mean that God is finished with you. Are you ready for some good news on the threshold of a new year? You can have a brand new start! There is hope for you.

Our God is the God of the second chance. Your life may be marred. Your life may have gotten off track because of some hidden sin or some stubbornness when you refused to yield to God. But He is saying, "I don't hold grudges. I am the God of the second chance."

God says, "I'm the Potter; you're the clay: unable, unlovely, but you're something in My hand. I want to make something beautiful out of you. Respond to Me." That is the potential of a life that responds. There is the problem of a life that resists—if there's an unyielded or hidden impurity, it'll mess it up. But there is the promise of a life that repents! Maybe you messed it up, but you're saved by trusting Jesus Christ. He shed His blood on the cross to pay your sin debt. And He can take you, a lump of clay, and make you a vessel of beauty and service.

ACTION POINT This condition holds true for a life that is still pliable and gives God all the pieces. If your life is broken, give Him all the pieces, but do it while it is still pliable, and He can make another vessel out of you. Are you willing to do that?

12

Thus says the LORD: "Go and get a potter's earthen flask, and take some of the elders of the people and some of the elders of the priests....Then you shall break the flask in the sight of the men who go with you, and say to them, 'Thus says the LORD of hosts: "Even so I will break this people and this city, as one breaks a potter's vessel, which cannot be made whole again; and they shall bury them in Tophet till there is no place to bury."...."Thus says the LORD of hosts, the God of Israel: 'Behold, I will bring on this city and on all her towns all the doom that I have pronounced against it, because they have stiffened their necks that they might not hear My words.'"

JEREMIAH 19:1, 10-11, 15

When you say, "I'm not going to yield to God," you are the clay God is describing here in the book of Jeremiah. Clay that was once soft and pliable has now dried and hardened. It cannot be reshaped. It can only be thrown away without being broken and turned into clay again.

There is genuine peril in a life that rebels against God. Some people, when they realize their hidden impurities and stubborn resistance to God, are willing to be broken. They say, "Here I am, Lord. I yield myself to you. I repent. Take me, make me, mold me. Give me a new start." And God will.

On the other hand, you can say, "It's my life. I'm going to live it the way I want to. I'm not going to yield." That's your privilege. But if you do that, you'll be hardened in that position, and once the clay is hardened, the Potter cannot remold it. He cannot remake it.

ACTION POINT God offers a second chance. When you read the Bible, you find it's full of people to whom God gave a second chance. But always, always, they were pliable. They were willing to yield to Him. Search your heart...are you pliable?

13

Search me, O God, and know my heart; Try me, and know my anxieties; And see if there is any wicked way in me, And lead me in the way everlasting.

PSALM 139:23-24

F.B. Meyer was one of the greatest Christian authors of all time. As a pastor, Meyer was successful, but not as he ought to have been. He had friends, Charles Studd and Hudson Taylor, great men in the history of the church. They seemed to have victory day by day—joy and power in their lives. Meyer watched them. One day, he went to Studd and said, "You have joy in your life that I don't." Studd said, "There's nothing I have that you can't. Have you given everything to God?"

In his heart, Meyer knew there was something he didn't want to yield to God. He went back to his room that night and prayed. It seemed like a small thing, but it was standing between him and victory. He wrestled with God until, finally, he came to the place where he had to do something.

Meyer told what happened. "I took a bunch of keys out of my pocket and said, 'Lord, here. This key ring represents my life. I give it over to you.' It seemed as if the Lord said to me, 'Are all the keys there?' 'Yes Lord, they're all there except one small key, a key to a little cupboard. But it's just one little key.' The Lord handed the keys back and started to walk out the door. I said, 'Wait, Lord. Don't go. Here's that key. I don't believe I can give it to you, but I will hold it out. Please take it.' The Lord took those keys, every one of them, and went into that cupboard and began to do a work, and my life was transformed."

ACTION POINT Is there some little key like that in your life? Some little cupboard where you say, "Lord, You can be Lord of all—except this?" Have you yielded?

14

> And Jesus came and spoke to them, saying, "All authority has been given to Me in heaven and on earth. Go therefore and make disciples of all the nations, baptizing them in the name of the Father and of the Son and of the Holy Spirit, teaching them to observe all things that I have commanded you; and lo, I am with you always, even to the end of the age." Amen.
>
> **MATTHEW 28:18-20**

Do you know what worry is? Worry is a mild form of atheism. It's acting like God doesn't exist. It's like saying, "God, You have forsaken me. You're not able to see me through this thing."

I was born and raised in West Palm Beach, Florida. And every so often a hurricane would blow through. And we would get ready for the hurricane. They'd tell us when it's coming. And so we'd board up the windows. And we'd get some rope, go out in the yard and tie things down. What kept things safe was not the rope, but the mooring. And if the mooring doesn't hold, it doesn't matter what the rope is like.

Friend, Jesus is your mooring. You don't have to worry because Jesus will never move. When I'm discouraged, His presence sees me through. When I'm lonely, His presence cheers me up. When I'm worried, His presence calms me down. And when I'm tempted. His presence helps me out.

ACTION POINT Be ready for the hurricane. Anchor yourself to the Lord Jesus and practice the presence of the Lord this coming year. You're going to be tempted. You're going to go through trials. Know that Jesus Christ never leaves us, never forsakes us. When the devil comes and knocks at your heart's door, simply say, "Jesus, please go answer the door."

15

> But it has happened to them according to the true proverb: "A dog returns to his own vomit," and, "a sow, having washed, to her wallowing in the mire."
>
> **2 PETER 2:22**

An unsaved person can sit in church, sing in the choir, and sound holy and righteous. But as soon as he's back in the world, he'll return to the sordid sin he enjoyed before.

Peter likens the unsaved person who is religious on the outside to a dog and a pig. You can scrub him clean, brush his teeth, and dress him in a pink ribbon, but he will go right back into the mire. A scrubbing on the outside doesn't change his inner nature. The dog may feel better, and the pig may look better, but neither has been changed.

But a person who comes to know Jesus Christ as his personal Savior is changed. He doesn't want the same things anymore. He doesn't live the same way anymore. He's been born again into a new life. Those who live by truth get more and more freedom; those who live by lies experience more and more bondage. Reformation without transformation leads to greater degradation and final condemnation.

Jesus said of Judas, "It would have been better for him that he'd never been born." Judas heard the truth and was a disciple of the Lord Jesus. He escaped the pollution of the world for awhile, but he was not transformed. Sinful desires do not disappear by reformation. They only hibernate and wake up stronger. Salvation gives you a new nature.

ACTION POINT What has changed in your life since you came to know the Lord Jesus Christ? Are you different? The Bible says when we are "in Christ," we become new creatures—for the old has passed away, and all things have become new. Have you experienced that? Then thank Him today!

16

> Moreover, when you fast, do not be like the hypocrites, with a sad countenance. For they disfigure their faces that they may appear to men to be fasting. Assuredly, I say to you, they have their reward. But you, when you fast, anoint your head and wash your face, so that you do not appear to men to be fasting, but to your Father who is in the secret place; and your Father who sees in secret will reward you openly.
>
> **MATTHEW 6:16-18**

Someone has called fasting "the weeping of the soul." Fasting is a lost art in most of our churches, but it is one of the clearest taught doctrines in the Word of God, especially in a time of crisis.

When Ezra and his people were in a predicament, he "proclaimed a fast there at the river of Ahava..." (Ezra 8:21). Nehemiah said, "So it was, when I heard these words, that I sat down and wept, and mourned for many days; I was fasting and praying before the God of heaven" (Nehemiah 1:4). Jehoshaphat "feared, and set himself to seek the LORD, and proclaimed a fast throughout all Judah" (2 Chronicles 20:3). Joel said, "Blow the trumpet in Zion, Consecrate a fast; call a sacred assembly" (Joel 2:15). The Lord Jesus said, "Moreover, when you fast..." (Matthew 6:16-17).

Most of us have never practiced fasting with consistency. Fasting is not just going hungry, and it's not a way to lose weight. Fasting is the affliction of the soul for discipline and determination to humble ourselves before God and seek His face.

ACTION POINT When was the last time you "set your face" to seek the Lord? Is there a situation in your life, in your home, at your job or in your church, that merits serious, sustained prayer? If so, perhaps it is time to seek the Lord in fasting and prayer.

17

> In the first year of his reign I, Daniel, understood by the books the number of the years specified by the word of the Lord through Jeremiah the prophet, that He would accomplish seventy years in the desolations of Jerusalem.
>
> **DANIEL 9:2**

What caused Daniel to seek the Lord? It was reading the Old Testament prophets. As Daniel studied Jeremiah, God showed him that He had prophesied a seventy-year captivity for His people in Babylon (Jeremiah 25:11-12), and the seventy years were almost up. Through Jeremiah's prophecies, God said to Daniel, "I'm going to judge Babylon."

In reading the Word, Daniel saw God's blueprint and knew he was living at the end of an age. He sought God for wisdom. Bible study and prayer rise and fall together. Your study life will not be greater than your prayer life, and vice versa. There is no way you can separate Bible study from prayer.

A wise man learns to turn prophecy into prayer. For example, in Matthew 6:10 our Lord taught us to pray, "Thy kingdom come. Thy will be done." God said to Daniel, "I'm going to do this in seventy years," and yet Daniel prayed about it. Why, if I know that God's kingdom is going to come, should I pray for it to come? There are certain things God has prophesied He's going to do, and yet still God wants us to pray about those things. We know, for example, that Jesus is going to come, and the apostle John prayed in Revelation 22:20, "Amen, even so come, Lord Jesus."

ACTION POINT When you read the Bible, the Bible impels you to pray. And when you pray, your prayer life will urge you to read the Bible. Prayer and Bible reading go hand in hand. When you read the Word of God, God is speaking to you. Prayer is you talking back to God. Don't let it be a one-sided conversation from either side.

18

For all the promises of God in Him are Yes, and in Him Amen, to the glory of God through us.

2 CORINTHIANS 1:20

Another way of saying it is: "For no matter how many promises God has made, they are 'Yes' in Christ. And so through Him, the 'Amen' is spoken by us to the glory of God." God had already prophesied that He was going to do something for Israel (Daniel 9:2), but still Daniel prayed.

Daniel could have just leaned back, put his feet up, and said, "Well, God, since You prophesied You're going to do it, there's no need for me to pray about it." But he didn't.

It's a strange thing—the Bible teaches us to pray about what God has already promised He would do.

- Revelation 11:15 says, "...The kingdoms of this world have become the kingdoms of our Lord, and of His Christ; and He shall reign forever and ever!" Yet Jesus taught us to pray "Thy kingdom come and Thy will be done..."
- The Bible teaches there's going to be peace in Jerusalem, yet Psalm 122:6 tells us to "pray for the peace of Jerusalem."
- Jesus Christ is going to come again. In Revelation 22:20, John prays, "Even so, come, Lord Jesus!" It is prophesied, yet we're told to pray it will happen.

ACTION POINT Even when God says He's going to do something, He does it through the prayers of His people. God wants you and me to take part in bringing about His will on earth through prayer. So you and I need to pray! Be a part of what God is doing and will do through your prayers.

19

> And I prayed to the LORD my God, and made confession, and said, "O LORD, great and awesome God, who keeps His covenant and mercy with those who love Him, and with those who keep His commandments, we have sinned and committed iniquity, we have done wickedly and rebelled, even by departing from Your precepts and Your judgments."
>
> **DANIEL 9:4-5**

Daniel's prayer here is not the kind of prayer that makes God angry. Some people think "If we just pray, God will hear our prayer." My dear friend, it is not so. Prayers of a wicked people anger God. They make the matter worse. They are an affront to God.

The Bible says, "If I regard iniquity in my heart, the Lord will not hear me" (Psalm 66:18). "The LORD is far from the wicked: but He hears the prayer of the righteous" (Proverbs 15:29). Again, God says, "One that turns away his ear from hearing the law, Even his prayer is an abomination" (Proverbs 28:9).

Can you imagine—prayer could actually become an abomination to God. The psalmist said in Psalm 80:4, "...How long will You be angry against the prayer of Your people?"

ACTION POINT Have you ever thought that a prayer of yours, rather than enlisting God's mercy, might stir up God's anger? Nothing angers God more than for a people stuffed full of sin and self to be imploring God to do something good for them when they stand in need of judgment. If you are aware of sin, if you harbor it, even cherish it, the Lord will not listen to you (Psalm 66:18). Confess your sin. It will be forgiven, but it must be confessed.

20

> Then I set my face toward the Lord God to make request by prayer and supplications, with fasting, sackcloth, and ashes.
>
> **DANIEL 9:3**

So often, our prayer is casual prayer...prayer that comes with a take-it-or-leave-it attitude. Many of us can't even remember what we prayed for this morning or last night. We rattle off little "Now I lay me down to sleep" prayers. The truth is, more often than not, we're flabby, undisciplined, and exhibit no determination. Is it any wonder that we sow without reaping and have so little power in our lives?

Pray with serious concentration, steadfast confidence, and sincere confession—Daniel confessed both personal and national sins. Avoid exhibitionism, legalism, ritualism, asceticism, and egotism. Pray with spiritual concern. Read Daniel 9:17-19—what was Daniel's concern? Daniel was not merely trying to get out of difficulty, trying to get everything healed so he and the people could go back to their careless, selfish lives.

Is our prayer as Jesus taught us to pray? "Our Father in heaven, Hallowed be Your name. Your kingdom come. Your will be done on earth as it is in heaven." It's not that God is not concerned about our personal needs: we can pray for our daily bread, about our trespasses. But first of all, we pray for the glory of God.

It's not about how many prayers you pray, nor how eloquent or beautiful they may be. It's not about how long your prayer is. It's not about the emotion of your prayer, the logic of your prayer, or the argument of your prayer. It is the faith and the fervency of your prayer that gets to God.

ACTION POINT Have you ever set your face to prayer, and desperately sought the Lord? If you want to see God move in your life, devote yourself to prayer. Friend, God does business with those who mean business.

21

And I prayed to the LORD my God, and made confession, and said, "O LORD, great and awesome God, who keeps His covenant and mercy with those who love Him, and with those who keep His commandments....Therefore the LORD has kept the disaster in mind, and brought it upon us; for the LORD our God is righteous in all the works which He does, though we have not obeyed His voice.

DANIEL 9:4, 7, 9, 14

When you pray, is it with a clear picture in mind of the might, the power, and the holiness of the One you are addressing?

This passage reveals the character of God: His greatness, His awe, His power, His righteousness, and His mercy. We must see this about the great heart of our God: God is a God of righteousness, judgment, and justice, but God would rather show mercy than send judgment.

We don't have to come to God with our hands filled with the brass of our emotions or the pewter of our worth, but with the gold of His glory and the incense of His mighty name. Oh, the confidence that we have when we pray! What a mighty God we have!

"Confess your trespasses to one another, and pray for one another, that you may be healed. The effective, fervent prayer of a righteous man avails much" (James 5:16).

ACTION POINT It is impossible to see who our great God is in a time of crisis and not want to pray. See the character and nature of God. When you do, you can hardly keep from praying! God says, "The instant I speak concerning a nation and concerning a kingdom, to pluck up, to pull down, and to destroy it, if that nation against whom I have spoken turns from its evil, I will relent of the disaster that I thought to bring upon it" (Jeremiah 18:7-8). Pray today as never before. We need earnest prayer.

22

O LORD, according to all Your righteousness, I pray, let Your anger and Your fury be turned away from Your city Jerusalem, Your holy mountain. Because for our sins, and for the iniquities of our fathers, Jerusalem and Your people are a reproach to all those around us.

DANIEL 9:16

The sins of God's people were great. Daniel prayed, "Our sins have risen up in Your face. And O God, we're praying. Turn Your anger and Your fury away." God will judge any nation that continues to print pornography, abort babies, applaud sodomy, and sings, "God bless us" at the same time. God's fury is turned against that nation. But Daniel is standing in the gap saying, "O God, remove our guilt," then, "and for the Lord's sake cause Your face to shine on Your sanctuary, which is desolate" (Daniel 9:17).

Daniel's motivation is not for America's sake, not for Israel's sake, not for a denomination's sake, not for his sake, but for God's sake. "For Your city and Your people are called by Your name" (Daniel 9:19).

What a great man Daniel was. Most of us ask God to get us out of the mess we're in so we can drive new cars and not see the stock market tumble. How many are consumed for the glory of God? Very few. Daniel was. Daniel says, "God, for Your sake, for Your name, do it!"

ACTION POINT Do you have a burning in your heart for the name of our God to be exalted throughout this earth? His name has been stepped on, blasphemed, and ridiculed. Make the focus of your prayers and the goal of your prayers the glory of God.

23

> Now while I was speaking, praying, and confessing my sin and the sin of my people Israel, and presenting my supplication before the LORD my God for the holy mountain of my God, yes, while I was speaking in prayer, the man Gabriel, whom I had seen in the vision at the beginning, being caused to fly swiftly, reached me about the time of the evening offering.
>
> **DANIEL 9:20-21**

What is the "evening offering" Daniel is referring to? Daniel is living in Babylon. There was no temple or altar in Babylon. No sacrifices were being offered. Those had ended almost seventy years ago. And yet, Daniel says, "I was praying at the time of the evening sacrifice." That is, "I was praying on the basis of a sacrifice made a long time ago. I'm linking my prayer with that sacrifice."

In God's temple, back home in Jerusalem, evening sacrifice time was between 3 and 4 in the afternoon. That was when the animals were slain. It was also called "the ninth hour." Jesus died exactly the same hour of the day! "And about the ninth hour Jesus cried with a loud voice, saying, '*Eli, Eli, lama sabachthani*?' that is, 'My God, my God, why have you forsaken Me?'" (Matthew 27:46). Daniel was praying before the fact of Jesus' death, and after the time of those animal sacrifices.

ACTION POINT Daniel's prayer, like any prayer ever offered, will only get to heaven on the basis of a blood sacrifice. Whether that sacrifice was made seventy years ago, as in Daniel's case, or two thousand years ago as in our case, whenever we pray, we must link our prayer with Calvary. Real intercession is the Holy Spirit of God taking a desire in the heart of the Father and putting that desire into one's heart, and then sending it back to heaven in the power of a blood sacrifice.

24

Now godliness with contentment is great gain.

1 TIMOTHY 6:6

Many times we think we need something...when we really don't. At times, we want things that we don't need. We get our luxuries and necessities confused.

Discontentment is a disease that takes away your joy and peace. And what is contentment? It's not getting what you want, but wanting what you already have. Contentment will make a poor man rich. Discontentment makes a rich man poor. No matter how much you have, if you are discontented, you are really poor.

Sometimes it is God's grace that we don't receive what we think we want. Once upon a time, two tears met up along the river of life. One tear said to the other, "Where did you come from?" "Oh," the second tear said, "I'm the tear of a girl who loved a man and lost him. And where do you come from?" The first tear answered, "I'm the tear of the girl who found him and married him."

ACTION POINT You are rich today if you know the Lord and are content. Paul goes on to say, "For we brought nothing into this world, and it is certain we can carry nothing out. And having food and clothing with these we shall be content" (1 Timothy 6:7-8). If you have clothes to wear, food to eat, and Jesus Christ in your heart, my dear friend, you're blessed. Thank God today for what you have. Thank Him for food, clothing, shelter, and above all, thank Him for Jesus Christ, who with His blood paid the penalty for your sins.

25

> He who loves silver will not be satisfied with silver; nor he who loves abundance, with increase. This also is vanity.
>
> **ECCLESIASTES 5:10**

We live in a day that confuses luxuries and necessities. Material things can never bring contentment, for they can never satisfy the deepest need of your heart. Either you can't get enough of them, or, when you get them, you find out they don't meet your need.

Do you know the story of the little boy who loved pancakes? One day his mother thought she would satisfy him, so she decided she would cook all the pancakes he wanted. He ate the first ones with relish and the second plate—if not with relish, at least with delight. He ate more, and then some more, and she just kept cooking them. Finally she asked, "Johnny, do you want another pancake?" He said, "No ma'am. I don't even want the ones I've already had."

That's the way it is with money. "He that loveth silver shall never be satisfied with silver." When you get it all, it doesn't satisfy, and you want more.

ACTION POINT This round world will never fit into your three-cornered heart. There's nothing wrong with material things; the problem is they just can't satisfy the deepest longing of your heart. You'll never be satisfied with material things—only the living God can do that. Be content with such things as you have. Learn a life of contentment. The Lord Jesus Christ can meet the deepest need of your heart.

26

Delight yourself also in the LORD, and He shall give you the desires of your heart.

PSALM 37:4

This verse doesn't mean you'll have every whim fulfilled—you can have an island paradise somewhere, a luxury car, or a handful of diamonds. It means when you delight yourself in the LORD, what your heart has really been seeking for, it will find. What your heart really yearns for is God. Only Jesus can meet the deepest needs of your heart.

It is not that the world is too big for us; we are too big for the world. God made us with something different. "Delight yourself also in the LORD, and He shall give you the desires of your heart." Does that mean that if you love God, you can have whatever material thing you may want? No. Listen to it: "Delight yourself also in the LORD..." What is the desire of your heart? The Lord. I don't know how much of God you have, but you have all you want! Delight yourself in Him, and God will fill that void in your heart.

Do you know why we so often live in fear? We think our needs aren't going to be met, or that the things we believe are meeting our needs will be taken away from us. But 1 Timothy 6:5 speaks of "useless wranglings of men of corrupt minds and destitute of the truth, who suppose that godliness is a means of gain. From such withdraw yourself." On the other hand, "godliness with contentment is great gain. For we brought nothing into this world, and it is certain we can carry nothing out" (1 Timothy 6:5-7). We have something that can't be tampered with.

ACTION POINT Suppose someone were to go into your house and carry out all your material possessions. Could you still praise the Lord? Delight yourself in the Lord—then you could!

27

Fear not, for I am with you; Be not dismayed, for I am your God. I will strengthen you. Yes, I will help you, I will uphold you with my righteous right hand.

ISAIAH 41:10

I was raised in South Florida, in what you might call hurricane alley. When we knew a hurricane was coming, my dad would say, "Boys, go out in the back yard and tie things down."Sometimes, we would go out after a hurricane, and the thing we tied down was gone and the thing we tied it to was gone!

Friend, you better be tied to Jesus. He won't blow away. Where is your hope? Where is your security? I hope the solid rock, the Lord Jesus Christ, "So we may boldly say: 'The Lord is my helper; I will not fear. What can man do to me?'" (Hebrews 13:6) Friend, God has said He will never leave you. He will not forsake you. And you must not fear what man shall do to you. The sum of all this is security. It is courage that comes from knowing that God is present.

ACTION POINT A little boy being picked on by a bully may be frightened to walk to school, but if his big brother or his daddy is walking alongside him, then that fear is gone. Your Father is there. Your big brother is there. What God is saying is, "I am with you. You don't have to fear what man shall do." There is one fear that removes all other fears, and that is the fear of God. It was said of one great Christian, John Laird Mair Lawrence, that "he feared man so little, because he feared God so much."

28

> The LORD has appeared of old to me, saying: "Yes, I have loved you with an everlasting love. Therefore, with lovingkindness I have drawn you."
>
> **JEREMIAH 31:3**

George Matheson, a student at the University of Scotland in the 1880's, was taken with an eye disease. A beloved professor came to him and said, "George, the doctors told me to tell you that in three days you will be blind. If there is any face you want to look upon, do it now." George wrote to his beloved fiancée and asked, "Would you come to my side? I want to look into your face before I go blind." She wrote back, "If you are going blind, I don't want to be married to you," and broke the engagement.

George was crushed, but out of that pain, he wrote one of the most beautiful hymns ever written: "O Love that wilt not let me go, I rest my weary soul in thee; I give thee back the life I owe, that in thine ocean depths its flow may richer, fuller be....O Joy that seekest me through pain, I cannot close my heart to thee; I trace the rainbow thro' the rain, and feel the promise is not vain that morn shall tearless be."

Though blind, George Matheson became a mighty minister of the Gospel of Christ. This crushing experience allowed him to touch the world.

ACTION POINT We all experience painful losses in our lives—how we choose to handle them is key to what happens next. Take today's Scripture and apply it to your heart personally. None of us knows what tomorrow is going to bring. Choose to live with contentment, confidence, and courage, because Jesus has promised never to leave us nor forsake us (Hebrews 13:5).

29

> Let your conduct be without covetousness; be content with such things as you have. For He Himself has said, "I will never leave you nor forsake you."
> **HEBREWS 13:5**

This is one of the most encouraging verses in all the Bible. Greek scholars tell us this sentence actually has five negatives in it. Now we say a double negative is bad English, but evidently it wasn't bad Greek. It is like saying: "I will never, no not ever, no never leave you nor forsake you." Now friend, that will take the fear out of the future. Nothing can separate you from the love of God.

A preacher was visiting a grandmother in his church, trying to comfort her in her old age. I believe she knew the Lord better than he did, however, because when he took out his Greek New Testament and was reading this verse to her, explaining there were five negatives there, the grandma said, "Well, God may have to say it five times for you Greek boys, but once is enough for me."

We fear because we're afraid we're going to have to face something we don't understand, and that we'll have to face it alone. God wants us to walk in faith, not fear, because He is always with us—He dwells within us!

ACTION POINT Do you fear being forsaken, lonely? Most of us do. Yet we have the companionship of His presence. We fear our friends will leave us. Psychiatrists say the greatest need we have on earth is not material, but the need to love and be loved. The Lord has said, "I will never leave you." Do you believe that promise? God is speaking to you. Are you listening? It would be a good idea to commit Hebrews 13:5 to memory this week.

January 30

> Your Word is a lamp to my feet and a light to my path.
>
> **PSALM 119:105**

Most of us just kind of go window-shopping through the Bible. "Oh, isn't that a precious promise?" "Hmm, what a sweet promise." "Oh, that's a wonderful promise." We take verses, memorize them, and even put them on our refrigerator doors, but we never lay hold on them. Do we believe them?

Let your conduct be without covetousness; be content with such things as you have. For He Himself has said, 'I will never leave you nor forsake you'" (Hebrews 13:5). Now, "He Himself has said" is emphatic. It means He Himself has said. This is the Word of God. His promise cannot fail. It is God who makes this promise, not Adrian Rogers. His Omnipotence is the answer when you don't have strength. His Omnipresence is the answer when you are lonely. His Omniscience is the answer when you don't know what to do. This is God's Word!

Leonard Ravenhill said, "One of these days somebody is going to pick up this book, read it, and believe it, and the rest of us are going to be ashamed of ourselves." Promises are wonderful, but the Word of God was never meant to be just a grab bag of promises. It is a lamp to our feet, and the light for our path.

ACTION POINT Don't wait another day to commit to making this a year of being devoted to reading the Bible and to prayer. Plan to read through the Bible this year, cover to cover.

31

> The LORD is my Shepherd; I shall not want.
>
> **PSALM 23:1**

The Lord Jesus Christ is described as a Shepherd three times in the New Testament. He is called the Good Shepherd in John 10:11: "I am the Good Shepherd. The Good Shepherd gives His life for the sheep." That's the past—Mount Calvary.

He is called the Chief Shepherd in 1 Peter 5:4: "And when the Chief Shepherd appears, you will receive a crown of glory that does not fade away." In the future, He will return.

Finally, He is called the Great Shepherd in Hebrews 13:20-21: "...that great Shepherd of the sheep, through the blood of the everlasting covenant, make you complete in every good work to do His will, working in you what is well-pleasing in His sight, through Jesus Christ, to whom be glory forever and ever, Amen." That is the present. He makes us complete.

In Psalm 23, David begins by talking about His shepherd: "He makes me to lie down in green pastures; He leads me beside the still waters. He restores my soul; He leads me in the paths of righteousness for His name's sake. Yea, though I walk through the valley of the shadow of death, I will fear no evil; For You are with me..." (Psalm 23:2-4). But now that he's in the valley, David is talking to Him. There's nothing that will bring you face to face with God more than the dark valleys of life. But when you get into the valleys, you'll know what Jesus meant when He said, "Lo, I am with you always, even to the end of the age" (Matthew 28:20). The ultimate is my intimate. The Light is there. The Shepherd is there.

ACTION POINT The Good Shepherd cares for you, past, present, and future. Praise Him today. Thank Him for making provision for you—before you were even born.

If you have a Bible that's falling apart, you'll have a life that's not.

ADRIAN ROGERS

february

1

> But we are all like an unclean thing, and all our righteousnesses are like filthy rags. We all fade as a leaf, and our iniquities, like the wind, have taken us away.
>
> **ISAIAH 64:6**

What a beautiful, wonderful life Adam and Eve lived in the Garden of Eden. But when they disobeyed the Lord, they were immediately stricken with guilt. They hid themselves from His presence when God came walking through the Garden. They tried to cover their guilt by making clothes of fig leaves. But what looked good to them as a suitable covering could not stand under the gaze of a holy God. He knew they required something else, so He shed innocent blood to make them coats of skin (Genesis 3:7-8). For the first time in His perfect Creation, innocent blood was shed. Their covering is a picture of the covering of righteousness we receive in the Lord Jesus Christ who died for us.

So many of us have tried to dress ourselves in the rags of our own self-righteousness. We are helpless to cover our sin. We need the blood of Jesus.

ACTION POINT Examine your heart. What fruitless efforts are you making to sew a fig leaf covering for yourself? What is the only thing that will wash away sin and bring you purity, cleansing and righteousness? Apply that to your heart today. Ask Jesus to cleanse you.

2

Yea, though I walk through the valley of the shadow
of death, I will fear no evil; For You are with me;
Your rod and Your staff, they comfort me.

PSALM 23:4

In Psalm 23, David speaks of walking in the valley. But there can be no valley without mountains—is that not true? Psalm 23 is the valley psalm flanked by two great mountain psalms on both sides: Psalm 22 and Psalm 24. Psalm 22 tells of the crucifixion of the Messiah. Psalm 24 presents the coronation of the Messiah and His glorious Second Coming. So in the valley of Psalm 23, on one side of us we have the blood-drenched slopes of Mount Calvary. On the other side are the sunlit peaks of Mount Zion, where God reigns forever.

Remember that the Lord Jesus Christ is described as a shepherd in three ways in the New Testament. For example, the Lord Jesus is called the Good Shepherd. "I am the good shepherd. The good shepherd gives His life for the sheep" (John 10:11). The Lord Jesus is called the Chief Shepherd. "And when the Chief Shepherd appears, you will receive the crown of glory that does not fade away" (1 Peter 5:4). The Lord Jesus is called the Great Shepherd. "Now may the God of peace who brought up our Lord Jesus from the dead, that great Shepherd of the sheep..." (Hebrews 13:20a). The Good Shepherd died for me. The Chief Shepherd is coming for me. The Great Shepherd lives for me. In the valley of the shadow of death, He was raised from the dead. My friend, learn that there can be no valley without mountains. Are you down in the valley? Then look to the mountains!

ACTION POINT Praise Him for dying for you and rejoice in the hope of His coming again! Thank God we can say with David, "I will lift up mine eyes unto the hills" (Psalm 121:1, KJV).

3

Yea, though I walk through the valley of the shadow
of death, I will fear no evil; For You are with me;
Your rod and Your staff, they comfort me.

PSALM 23:4

In the much-loved, familiar 23rd Psalm, David starts out only talking about the Lord: "The LORD is my Shepherd...He makes me to lie down...He leads me...He restores my soul." But then in verse 4, there's a change. Now David is in the valley. Now he's no longer talking about the Lord. It switches here, and now David is speaking to Him: "You are with me; Your rod and Your staff, they comfort me." David is one-on-one with God in conversation.

Nothing will bring you face to face with God more than the dark valleys of life. But when you get in the dark valleys, you're going to find out what Jesus meant when He says to you, "I will never leave you or forsake you" (Hebrews 13:5), and, "I am with you always, even to the end of the age" (Matthew 28:20).

ACTION POINT Is the Lord your Shepherd? Here's how to find out. Ask yourself: "Is the Shepherd my Lord?" You see, the only way you can say "The LORD is my Shepherd" is to be able to say, "The Shepherd is my Lord." Not everyone can recite Psalm 23 and claim it for their own. It belongs to those who've found a personal relationship with the Lord—a personal, permanent, protected relationship that will endure for all eternity.

4

Do not lay up for yourselves treasures on earth, where moth and rust destroy and where thieves break in and steal; but lay up for yourselves treasures in heaven, where neither moth nor rust destroys and where thieves do not break in and steal.

MATTHEW 6:19-20

Years ago, I read about a man who had a rather ingenious way of getting rid of his garbage. He would gift-wrap it, put it out on the curb in front of his house, and invariably someone driving by would see that wrapped box, stop, and pick it up. And the man would be behind the curtains, watching those people drive away with their gift-wrapped garbage! So many times that's what the devil does—he takes the things of this world and wraps them up so beautifully. But what we get isn't treasure...it turns out to be trash.

The Bible doesn't say that it's wrong to have material things. "Command those who are rich in this present age not to be haughty, nor to trust in uncertain riches but in the living God, who gives us richly all things to enjoy" (1 Timothy 6:17). God doesn't mind you enjoying your wealth; only, don't let it make you proud, and don't put your trust in your possessions. And "Do not lay up for yourselves treasures on earth" doesn't mean that you're not to work. "Go to the ant, you sluggard! Consider her ways and be wise, which, having no captain, overseer or ruler, provides her supplies in the summer, and gathers her food in the harvest" (Proverbs 6:6-8).

What does this mean then, when Christ says, "Do not lay up for yourselves treasures on earth"? Don't let the devil cheat you—don't cling to the worthless things of this world, but use your resources and energy wisely to invest in souls and store up eternal treasures in Heaven!

ACTION POINT Add up everything you have that money can't buy and death can't take away. The sum will reveal to you how rich you really are.

5

And when Saul had come to Jerusalem, he tried to join the disciples; but they were all afraid of him, and did not believe that he was a disciple. But Barnabas took him and brought him to the apostles. And he declared to them how he had seen the Lord on the road, and that He had spoken to him, and how he had preached boldly at Damascus in the name of Jesus.

ACTS 9:26-27

I've heard that in the first year, it's virtually impossible to spoil a baby. You can't give that little one too much love.

Now, you can spoil kids, and we've all seen the results of that, but it's virtually impossible to spoil a newborn. All the love, the attention, the hugging, the kissing and coddling you want to do—just do it.

And I want to say, correspondingly, that it s virtually impossible to spoil a newborn Christian. He needs to be loved. Barnabas took the new-born-again convert, Saul, to the apostles and told them how Saul had seen the Lord. While the apostles were scared of Saul, Barnabas introduced him, made him feel as if he were part of them, and encouraged him in his new way of life. Thank God for Barnabas!

ACTION POINT Some of us have known firsthand what it's like to have a Barnabas in our lives. Others, new believers, may be wishing they had one—or not even realize how much they need one. Keep your eyes and ears open. Let the Holy Spirit show you if there is someone you can befriend and help to grow, as Barnabas did for Saul.

6

> The Lord is not slack concerning His promise, as some count slackness, but is longsuffering toward us, not willing that any should perish but that all should come to repentance.
>
> **2 PETER 3:9**

Did you know Methuselah lived to be 969 years old? Before the Flood, people lived much longer lives than now. Scholars have speculated that their longevity was in part due to the protective canopy surrounding the earth's atmosphere, giving it almost a greenhouse effect.

But apart from that, God had a very good reason for extending Methuselah's life. His name means "When he is gone, it will come." The "it" refers to The Flood. And according to the Word of God, The Flood began the very day Methuselah died. God kept letting him live and live because He didn't want anyone to perish in that flood. God kept giving one more opportunity and one more chance. As it says, He is "not willing that any should perish but that all should come to repentance."

ACTION POINT Reflect upon your life—are there times you can name when God intervened with mercy when He might have sent judgment instead? Perhaps there were times when He spared you from something, and later you look back upon that time and say, "God was so merciful." Remember His mercy today and thank Him specifically for how He has covered your life with His garment of mercy.

7

> Therefore He is also able to save to the uttermost those who come to God through Him, since He always lives to make intercession for them.
>
> **HEBREWS 7:25**

Do you want a blessed thought? You are on Jesus' prayer list. There is nothing more comforting to me than for someone to tell me they pray for me. I once met a man who said, "Adrian, I prayed for you this morning. I pray for you every day." That moved me greatly. There are billions of people on this earth—some have never been prayed for even one time. If you are on anybody's prayer list, you are blessed.

I can tell you that you are on Jesus' prayer list! The Lord Jesus knows you by name. The finished work of Jesus is Calvary. The unfinished work of Jesus is His prayer ministry.

I am governed by His providence. I am growing by His plan. I am graced by His prayers. He prayed for His disciples in the midst of their storm. Do you have any reason to doubt that He is praying for you in the midst of your storm? How would you feel if you knew that while you're in your bedroom, Jesus is on His knees in your living room, praying for you? Is it any less real that you're in the boat and He's on the shore? Or that you're here on this earth and He's in glory, praying for you? He ever lives to make intercession for you.

ACTION POINT Thank Him today for the truth that "He always lives to make intercession" for you.

8

Forever, O LORD, Your Word is settled in heaven.
PSALM 119:89

Is that not a beautiful verse? You know, the Bible is not the book of the year—it is the book of the ages. It is settled in Heaven and on Earth. We can depend upon the Word of God. It's not up for a vote—but it does have its enemies.

The liberal will try to water it down, the atheist will deny it, and the cultist will twist it. There are those who despise it, distort it, and dissect it. They're ever learning, but are never able to come to the knowledge of the truth. There are those who disregard the Word, who say, "It's not really relevant. We live in the 21st century—forget all of that religious hocus pocus." They spend all their energy creating a better place to go to Hell from.

But I believe the greatest enemies of the Bible today are the Christians who do not love it, memorize it, practice it, and obey it. They give lip service to the fact that the Bible is the inspired, inerrant, infallible, authentic Word of God. But they don't study it, know it, or live by it. They don't assimilate it. They don't stand on it. Dust on the Bible, drought in the heart.

It is absolutely imperative that you are certain about the Bible as the Word of God. You'll never get much of anything else settled until you get that settled. Your salvation, sanctification, usefulness, and assurance depend upon it.

ACTION POINT If you want your life to be an exclamation point rather than a question mark, then you need to be certain the Bible is the Word of God—especially in these days, when everything that's not nailed down is coming loose...and the devil is pulling nails as fast as he can. But here are things that he will not be able to disturb you on—if you stand on the Word of God.

9

He who is faithful in what is least is faithful also in much;
and he who is unjust in what is least is unjust also in much.

LUKE 16:10

Have you ever thought about how the vast ocean is really made up of single drops of water, built from tiny molecules, which are made of microscopic atoms? Even in our lives, it is the small things that really do make the difference. All big things are made of little things. Big things are made of little choices, little acts, little words, and little thoughts.

Exercise integrity in the small things. Wilbur Chapman, who was mightily used by God, said this: "The rule that governs my life is this: Anything that dims my vision, or takes away my taste for Bible study, or cramps my prayer life, or makes Christian work difficult, is wrong for me, and I must, as a Christian, turn away from it."

This is so important for us to realize because every day we impact others by the little things we say or do. But if we are faithful in the little things, it follows that we will be faithful in that which is much. In other words, if we get the little things right, the big issues will take care of themselves.

ACTION POINT "Little drops of water, little grains of sand..." goes the children's rhyme. Be on guard for those little things that may slip in unnoticed, but which undermine God's greater purpose in your life.

10

> He who has My commandments and keeps them, it is he who loves Me. And he who loves Me will be loved by My Father, and I will love him and manifest Myself to him.
>
> **JOHN 14:21**

In frustration, many people say, "Well, there's so much in the Bible I don't understand." Do you feel that way? But Mark Twain was once reported to have said, "It's not that part of the Bible I don't understand that gives me so much trouble; it's the part I do understand." I'm afraid that's true of many of us. We must learn to practice the Word of God.

There may be mysteries you don't understand, but you can understand when the Bible says "love one another," can't you? If you want to learn more about the Word of God, first you must obey the part you do know. You see, when it comes to obedience, the rich will get richer. It's not enough to recite the promises without obeying the commandments. The more you obey, the more you will learn and understand.

ACTION POINT Keep the Word of God. That's a simple principle, but how important it is. Jesus said, "He who has My commandments and keeps them, it is he who loves Me. And he who loves Me will be loved by My Father, and I will love him and manifest Myself to him." Do you want Him to be real to you? Then obey His Word.

11

For what will it profit a man if he gains the whole world, and loses his own soul?

MARK 8:36

Some years ago, I went to visit the ruins of the ancient city of Pompeii. When the volcano Vesuvius erupted centuries ago, volcanic ash fell on everything and preserved the city just as it was. In fact, in the ruins there's a very interesting skeleton of a man. Evidently, when the ash began to fall, this man ran back to his home for his bag of gold. The gold spilled on the floor, and he reached out for it, just as the fumes overcame him. In seeking to gain that gold, he lost his life.

Now, he is embalmed for all time, grasping that gold. What profit was his gold? Friend, the wisest thing that anybody can do is give his heart to Jesus Christ. That's the only way to save your soul! God does not need you—you need God.

ACTION POINT What are you grasping for today? Position? Power? Possessions? Prestige? Whatever it is, if you desire it more than you desire to know Him, it will turn to ash in your hand. Or else the Lord may have to gently pry it loose from your hand. Instead, say with Paul, "Yet indeed I also count all things loss for the excellence of the knowledge of Christ Jesus my Lord, for whom I have suffered the loss of all things, and count them as rubbish, that I may gain Christ....that I may know Him" (Philippians 3:8,10a)!

12

Then Jesus spoke to them again, saying, "I am the light of the world. He who follows Me shall not walk in darkness, but have the light of life."

JOHN 8:12

If you wanted to get rid of darkness in a room, how would you do it? Would you curse the darkness? Would you take a broomstick and try to beat the darkness out? Would you grab a shovel and shovel it out? Or take a vacuum cleaner and suck it out? How are you going to get the darkness out of a room?

There is no way, except one: turn on the light. Just turn on the light! The darkness cannot stand the light. When Jesus comes, darkness is going to go. It has to go! And when it goes, everything that loves it will go with it. What a day it will be when Jesus comes and all the wicked, vile, filthy things in the spiritual world flee His light!

When we are faithful, when we live as Christians ought to, everywhere we go, as we let the light shine, we are making evident the deeds of darkness.

ACTION POINT Do not have any fellowship with the unfruitful works of darkness! We are to walk in the light. There is to be godly fruit, godly fellowship, and godly faithfulness in us. "But if we walk in the light as He is in the light, we have fellowship with one another, and the blood of Jesus Christ His Son cleanses us from all sin" (1 John 1:7).

13

> He will sit as a refiner and a purifier of silver; He will purify the sons of Levi, and purge them as gold and silver, that they may offer to the LORD an offering in righteousness.
>
> **MALACHI 3:3**

Do you know that God is not as interested in making you happy as He is in making you holy? His goal is to purge and purify you. The moment you were saved, God began His work to make you pure and holy. He wants to burn out the dross and impurities in your life and present you as pure gold.

You see, He is not as interested in your possessions as you are. He is not as interested in your job as you are. He is not as interested in your health as you are. But He cares for you so much that He wants to make you pure. And God will touch all of those things, if necessary, to make you holy.

ACTION POINT How much do you want to be made pure and holy before the Lord? If that is your desire, ask Him to begin to burn out the dross and impurities. There may be something in your life right now that you recognize as being dross. If so, start a "closet-clean-out" in your heart today. He will help you bag it and take it to the curb!

February 14

> Abide in Me, and I in you. As the branch cannot bear fruit of itself, unless it abides in the vine, neither can you, unless you abide in Me.
>
> **JOHN 15:4**

Galatians 5:22-23 says, "But the fruit of the Spirit is love, joy, peace, longsuffering, kindness, goodness, faithfulness, gentleness, self-control." Have you ever seen a fruit factory? No. You might have seen a shirt factory, but you will not see a fruit factory. You will only find a fruit orchard.

You see, there is no fruit without life. You cannot manufacture patience. The same Bible that says "But the fruit of the Spirit is love" says, a few verses later, " If we live in the Spirit, let us also walk in the Spirit" (Galatians 5:25). The only way that fruit is going to ripen and grow is in the right climate. You can't grow bananas in Alaska, and friend, you're not going to grow the fruit of the Spirit unless you're walking in the Spirit. And even then, you don't produce that fruit; you bear it. Jesus said, "Abide in Me, and I in you." Then, you will be fruitful.

ACTION POINT Are you abiding? Are you being fruitful? Ask God to show you where you need to make changes so that you are walking in the Spirit.

15

> Create in me a clean heart, O God, and renew a steadfast spirit within me. Do not cast me away from Your presence, and do not take Your Holy Spirit from me. Restore to me the joy of Your salvation, and uphold me by Your generous Spirit. Then I will teach transgressors Your ways, and sinners shall be converted to You.
>
> **PSALM 51:10-13**

The most miserable person on Earth is not an unsaved person, but someone who knows God, who has experienced salvation and what it means to have a relationship with Him, yet is out of fellowship with God. Stop and think about that—it is absolutely true.

If you are truly a child of God and are out of fellowship with Him, I can state that you are carrying a big burden. Now, if you're not saved, you're not carrying this burden at all. But if you are truly saved and are out of fellowship with God, that's a different story completely.

When David got out of fellowship with God, he came to the point that he cried out to the Lord, "Restore unto me the joy of Your salvation." He didn't say, "Lord, restore unto me Your salvation," but "restore unto me the joy of Your salvation." He was miserable when he was running from God.

ACTION POINT Are you running from God? Or perhaps you know someone who is. Pray for restoration. Today's passage is a good one to pray for them. Insert the person's name—or yours, if you are running—into the verse. Ask God to restore and renew the individual.

16

> Now when evening came, the boat was in the middle of the sea; and He was alone on the land. Then He saw them straining at rowing, for the wind was against them. Now about the fourth watch of the night He came to them, walking on the sea, and would have passed them by.
>
> **MARK 6:47-48**

A miracle occurred that day, and more than 5,000 people witnessed it. With no more than five small loaves of bread and two fish, Jesus prayed over the food and instructed His disciples to begin dividing it among the crowd. Not only did everyone have enough to eat, but the Bible also records the leftovers amounted to twelve baskets full. What a day—to have seen that!

As the day drew to an end, Jesus sent His disciples on ahead in the boat while He withdrew to spend time alone with His Father in prayer. The disciples were way out in the Sea of Galilee. But He saw them toiling and rowing in the midst of a storm. He was never unaware of where they were or what they were experiencing.

Are you in the midst of a storm? Do you know He sees you right now? You say, "He doesn't know where I am. He doesn't know this difficulty. Why is He so far away? Why am I in the storm, and He is on the shore?" Friend, He is there, and He's praying for you. He sees right through the dark. You can't see Him, but He sees you.

ACTION POINT My advice for you in the midst of your storm is to see Jesus, the great I AM, and see Him walking on the water. That situation that looks like it's going to be over your head is already under His feet. You're seated in the heavenlies with Him. And you can't drown with your head above water. He is the great I AM. You can put it down: you are guarded by His power.

17

Now when evening came, His disciples went down to the sea,
got into the boat, and went over the sea toward Capernaum.
And it was already dark, and Jesus had not come to them.
Then the sea arose because a great wind was blowing.

JOHN 6:16-18

In my journeys to Israel, one of the most delightful times for me is to sit at twilight on the shores of Galilee. The tranquility is like a dream. You're almost intoxicated by beauty as the sun sets over the Sea of Galilee. The Golan Heights across the sea from Tiberius turn a rosy color. You can hear birds nesting in the trees. I believe the Sea of Galilee is one of the most beautiful bodies of water on Earth. The old rabbis used to say that God created all the other seas, then He created Galilee just for Himself.

It had been a wonderful day after the feeding of the 5,000. The disciples were full of success and self-confidence when they climbed into their boat that evening. Then it happened. The wind began to rise. Clouds darkened the moon. An angry wind beat the sea with its fists, and the water rose up, striking the disciples in the face. Galilee, quiet as a millpond, now had become dangerous. Seasoned sailors, filled with fear, then saw Jesus, walking on the water, saying, "Don't be afraid." In another gospel it records Him saying, "Be of good cheer. It is I."

ACTION POINT Are you in a storm? You say, "No, Pastor, I'm not." Well I'm glad for you. Enjoy this season. We're fools if we don't enjoy the good times of life. But just wait awhile. Sooner or later, you're going to find yourself in a storm. It may be that God has engineered your storm; if not, He has certainly allowed it, because our God is over everything. The first thing you can say when difficulty comes is that God's providence is over it all. You can say, "I am governed by His providence."

18

> So when they had rowed about three or four miles, they saw Jesus walking on the sea and drawing near the boat; and they were afraid.
> **JOHN 6:19**

In the Bible there are correcting storms and there are perfecting storms. Jonah, who spent the night on a foam blubber mattress, was inside a whale because he was out of the will of God. He was running from God. And God sent a correcting storm.

But there are also perfecting storms. Jesus' disciples weren't out of the will of God. Why were they in a storm? Because—don't miss this—they were in the will of God. It was Jesus, Matthew tells us, who directed them to get into the boat and sail ahead, across the Sea of Galilee. They were in this storm because they were obeying Jesus. Why would Jesus want them to be in a storm? Because He wanted them to grow.

ACTION POINT I've often shared these words, written by Robert Browning Hamilton: "I walked a mile with pleasure, she chatted all the way. But left me none the wiser, for all she had to say. I walked a mile with sorrow, not a word said she. But oh, the things I learned from sorrow, when sorrow walked with me." Is that not true? Someone said that faith is like film. It's developed in the dark. Learn to trust the Lord even in dark days.

19

Those who go down to the sea in ships, who do business on great waters, they see the works of the LORD, and His wonders in the deep. For He commands and raises the stormy wind, which lifts up the waves of the sea....Their soul melts because of trouble....Then they cry out to the LORD in their trouble, and He brings them out of their distresses. He calms the storm, so that its waves are still....So He guides them to their desired haven.

PSALM 107:23-30

God is the master of the winds and the waves. He is able to cause storms to come or to calm them.

A very shallow theology says if we're in the will of God, we'll always sail smoothly on the sea of life. We'll have no sickness, no sorrow and no disappointment. We'll know no separation. There'll be no problems in our families. The "joy boys" get on television and say, "You just believe God and send me an offering, and you'll never be sick, never know loss, everything'll be fine." That's the gospel of Cash and Cadillacs. Friend, there's a Greek word for that—*baloney*.

No, we're going to have difficulty. When it comes, you can say, "I'm governed by His providence, but I'm also growing by His plan." God's plan is not to indulge you; God's plan is to enlarge you. "Thou hast enlarged me when I was in distress" (Psalm 4:1).

ACTION POINT Those of you who've been on the trail for a while, who have walked a long time with the Lord, when did you grow the most? When everything was fine? When there was smooth sailing? Or when the storm came? Did you not grow more in the storm, in distress, when you were crowded to Christ, and when you had to call upon Him? Based on what you already know, trust that you are growing by His plan.

20

But He said unto them, "It is I; don't be afraid."

JOHN 6:20

God tells us one way or another some 365 times in the Bible, "Don't be afraid." That's one for every day in the year. Do you think God knows our tendency is to continually resort to fear? The devil is the sinister minister of fear, but our Lord is the opposite.

The disciples, some of whom are seasoned sailors, are filled with fear, bending their backs to the boat's oars. They fear they may drown. On top of all of this, where's Jesus? Why hasn't He come to them? Why has He forsaken them?

Then they see Him—walking on the water. That doesn't bring them joy. Now their fear turns to raw terror. Who? What is that walking on the water? Is it a phantom? A ghost? And then they recognize—it's Jesus.

We all have storms, if not now, then later. We are usually either going into a storm, in the middle of a storm, or coming out of a storm. Lengthy times of peace are rare. Peace in your life is not the subtraction of problems; it's the addition of power to meet those problems. That's God's peace.

ACTION POINT This week, commit John 14:27 to memory: "Peace I leave with you, My peace I give to you; not as the world gives do I give to you. Let not your heart be troubled, neither let it be afraid."

21

They will put you out of the synagogues; yes, the time is coming that whoever kills you will think that he offers God service....These things I have spoken to you, that in Me you may have peace. In the world you will have tribulation; but be of good cheer, I have overcome the world.

JOHN 16:2, 33

Andrew Murray said, "God is willing to assume full responsibility for the life totally yielded to Him." In this world we are going to encounter tribulation. Are you aware it's growing more, not less, intense? Where is Jesus? Jesus has overcome the world. That's what He's telling you and me.

The spiritual barometer is falling, and all of us who can read the signs of the times know a storm is gathering. The Bible tells us that. But soon our Lord, who has been on the mountain of His glory praying for us, is going to rise from His throne. And then, walking on the water will be child's play. He'll come stepping on the clouds! He will come in His glory. And those of us who are here on the sea of time will be on the shores of eternity in an instant when He comes. Won't that be a day?

ACTION POINT The storm ceased when they received Him into the boat. Receive Him. Trust Him today and He will either calm the storm or calm you in the midst of the storm.

22

> Only do not rebel against the LORD, nor fear the people of the land, for they are our bread; their protection has departed from them, and the LORD is with us. Do not fear them.
>
> **NUMBERS 14:9**

When the Israelites were headed into the Promised Land, some demon-possessed giants, who were called Anakim, already lived there. When the twelve Israelite spies went to scope out the land, ten came back saying, "Oh, it's a good land—a land full of milk and honey, corn and wine, oil and pomegranates, figs and grapes. But, hey, we can't take this land—there are giants in it!"

But two of the spies, Joshua and Caleb, had an entirely different perspective. They said, "Don't fear the people of the land, for they are bread for us. Their defense is departed, and the Lord is with us; fear them not." In other words, "Look, these people are a piece of cake. They're toast!"

Why do you eat bread? For strength. Bread gives energy. Bread is the stuff of life. What was God saying? "These things that look like problems? They are your food. Anakim—the breakfast of champions."

ACTION POINT It's when you feed on problems that you grow. Our Lord isn't looking for softies as disciples. Remember, you're governed by His providence when you're in a storm. He rules over all. And you are growing by His plan. In the storm, allow Him to grow you and shape you to become more and more like the Lord Jesus Christ.

23

> Then to Adam He said, "Because you have heeded the voice of your wife, and have eaten from the tree of which I commanded you, saying, 'You shall not eat of it': cursed is the ground for your sake; in toil you shall eat of it all the days of your life."
>
> **GENESIS 3:17**

When God created mankind, He put him in a garden. In the Garden of Eden, there were no thorns. A curse came upon Adam and Eve because they disobeyed God. What does a crown of thorns speak of? The thorn symbolizes the curse upon humanity—on you, on me, on all of us—because of sin.

Jesus wore a crown of thorns because He bore that curse. He took upon Himself our curse and bore it for our sakes. The thorns on His head speak of the hardship, sorrow, and death that came with sin.

Do you have a heartache? Sorrow? Sickness? Can I tell you the thorny pathway we walk is because of sin? The bed of briars we sleep on is because of sin.

When in sorrow and trials you praise and glorify the Lord, saying with Job, "Though He slay me, yet will I trust Him," the world will know there's a quality of life about you that is different. Paul learned that and was able to say, "Your grace is sufficient for me."

ACTION POINT Memorize Isaiah 41:10 today: "Fear not, for I am with you; be not dismayed, for I am your God. I will strengthen you, Yes, I will help you, I will uphold you with My righteous right hand."

24

> Your father Abraham rejoiced to see My day: and he saw it, and was glad.
>
> **JOHN 8:56**

In His answer to His critics, the religious leaders of His day, Jesus made this shocking statement, bringing up one of the most dramatic scenes in the Old Testament. Isaac, the long-promised son of Abraham, was stretched out on an altar. His father lifted a gleaming knife into the sky, prepared to plunge it into the heart of his son. But then he heard a voice intervening, "Abraham, Abraham, don't harm the lad. I have provided a substitute."

Abraham looked—and there was a ram caught in a thicket. The Hebrew word used here actually means "a thicket of thorns." His head was caught in the thorns. God said, "Take the ram I have provided, Abraham, and sacrifice him instead."

That ram caught in a thicket, crowned with thorns, became the sacrifice that day in the place of the one who would have died. No wonder Jesus said, "Abraham saw My day and was glad." God preached the gospel to Abraham long ago.

ACTION POINT Abraham's willingness to sacrifice his son, Isaac, has always portrayed for us the Father's willingness to sacrifice His only Son, the Lord Jesus. Thank Him again today for that holy sacrifice. Jesus paid it all so that we might have it all—eternal life, eternal joy—through Him.

25

> Therefore humble yourselves under the mighty hand of God, that He may exalt you in due time, casting all your care upon Him, for He cares for you.
>
> **1 PETER 5:6-7**

I read about a man whose dog was swimming. The man called to the dog because it was time to go home. The dog was having such a great time, he wouldn't come. So the man picked up a stick and threw it in the water. When the dog saw the stick, he instinctively swam to the stick, put it in his mouth, came back, and laid it at his master's feet.

There are three kinds of burdens that we bear: the burdens that we willingly take up, the burdens that we faithfully stay under, and the burdens that we wisely lay down. "Cast your burden on the LORD, and He shall sustain you; He shall never permit the righteous to be moved" (Psalm 55:22).

I wonder if the burden you have has been given to you by God to cause you to come to His feet. Maybe He's called you other ways, but you wouldn't come. Maybe the burden is what God is using to bring you to your Master's feet. But thank God we can cast all our cares upon Him, for He cares for us.

ACTION POINT What burden weighs on your heart today? Did you know we have a high priest, the Lord Jesus, who, the Bible says, is not high and mighty and aloof, but one who can relate to our sufferings and understand them? For He Himself knew the greatest pain, suffering, and loss. Read Hebrews 4:15-16, then cast your cares upon Him today.

26

> Brethren, if a man is overtaken in any trespass, you who are spiritual restore such a one in a spirit of gentleness, considering yourself lest you also be tempted.
>
> **GALATIANS 6:1**

I read that each morning in Africa, a gazelle wakes up and says to himself, "If I cannot outrun the fastest lion on these plains today, I will be devoured." And somewhere that same morning, a lion wakes up and says, "If I cannot outrun the slowest gazelle today, I will starve." So they run. Every morning you and I need to wake up running because we are running from sin, and Satan is running after us. Do you know the difference between my life before I was saved and my life after? Before I got saved, I was running to sin, but now I am running from sin. But sometimes we are overtaken by sin, and the Bible tells us to "restore one another."

Our Scripture today is hope for that person who has been overtaken by sin. If you're that kind of a person, who is away from God, yet, in your heart of hearts, you've been saved, then this message is a word of hope for you. And if you have not been overtaken in sin, thank God for it! But this message is a word of warning for you. And it's a call to action for all of us. A brother can be restored, and that's good news. Our God is a God of a second chance. The Bible tells about men who got away from God and then came back to God, because the Bible does not mistake the moment for the man.

ACTION POINT Do you know a brother or sister in Christ who's been running toward sin and has walked away from the faith? Ask the Lord how He might use you and other believers to "restore such a one." We who are Christians are to be in the restoration and reclamation business!

27

> Yet man is born to trouble, as the sparks fly upward.
>
> **JOB 5:7**

It starts almost the day we're born. We come in crying, and from there it just goes on. We have burdens. If you don't have burdens, the problem is probably really that you're not a thinking person. But I want to tell you today what to do with your burdens.

There are the burdens that we willingly take up, where we bear somebody else's burden. Are you willing to do that? "Bear one another's burdens, and so fulfill the law of Christ" (Galatians 6:2). What is the law of Christ? "For all the law is fulfilled in one word, even in this: 'You shall love your neighbor as yourself'" (Galatians 5:14). That is the law of Christ: it's love! Genuine, Christ-like love. Loving our neighbors as we love ourselves. Look at that person who is burdened and understand that you're to love him as you'd want somebody to love you if you were in the same situation.

And there are the burdens we are to faithfully endure. David wrote, "Cast your burden on the LORD, and He shall sustain you. He shall never permit the righteous to be moved" (Psalm 55:22). David was a king. He was wealthy and powerful. What do we learn from this? That burdens come to the high as well as to the low. They come to saints as well as to sinners. They come to the old as well as to the young.

What do we do with our burdens? We have to cast them upon the Lord.

ACTION POINT Do you have a broken heart? Has one of your children ripped your heart out? Is there a husband who has forsaken you? Is there a physical malady gnawing away at your body? Is there a problem perplexing you? The Bible says you are to "Cast your burden on the LORD, and He shall sustain you."

28

> Therefore, if anyone is in Christ, he is a new creation; old things have passed away; behold, all things have become new.
>
> **2 CORINTHIANS 5:17**

Some people want to get everything in their lives straightened out before they come to Christ. But you'll wake up in Hell and still not have it straightened out. Don't try to grow up before you get born. First the inside, then the outside.

Man says, "First the outside...perhaps it will change the inside." But he needs a birth from above, not merely a boost from below. What Jesus said to the Pharisees is that man needs a divine change, an inner change, an inner cleansing.

It's like trees that don't lose their leaves in the fall: the leaves wither and turn brown, but they hold on until the spring. But when the new leaf comes, it pushes the old leaf off. That's exactly what happens to your old habits, your old life, when you find the Lord Jesus. The new life pushes your old life off. It's not a matter of plucking off this leaf and knocking off that one. You'll never do it that way. Let the new life within you do its work.

ACTION POINT Have you come to grips yet with the fact that your "old nature" is dead and you are a new creature in Christ? You can't "kill" the "old nature" on your own. You have to "reckon" him as dead and allow the "new nature"—the new creature you are in Christ—to come alive and to be fed and nurtured by the Holy Spirit.

29

But from there you will seek the LORD your God, and you will find Him if you seek Him with all your heart and with all your soul.

DEUTERONOMY 4:29

The scourge of the 21st century is half-hearted Christianity. Half-hearted Christianity will not do. It never could, but it surely won't in these times. "And you will seek Me and find Me, when you search for Me with all your heart" (Jeremiah 29:13).

Are you seeking for Christ with all your heart? James 1:8 says, "He is a double-minded man, unstable in all his ways." The word for double-minded literally means "two souls." Here's a person trying to face both ways at the same time. Trying to live with one foot in the church and one in the world. Such people have just enough of the world in them that they can't be happy in church and just enough Christ in them they can't be happy in the world. They've become spiritual schizophrenics, two-soul persons. We are to love the Lord with all our hearts.

ACTION POINT Is there anything in your life you love more than the Lord Jesus Christ? If so, then my friend, that thing—whatever or whoever it is—has become an idol in your life. Realizing that, what steps can you take today to remove the idol from the throne and put Christ back in His proper place in your life?

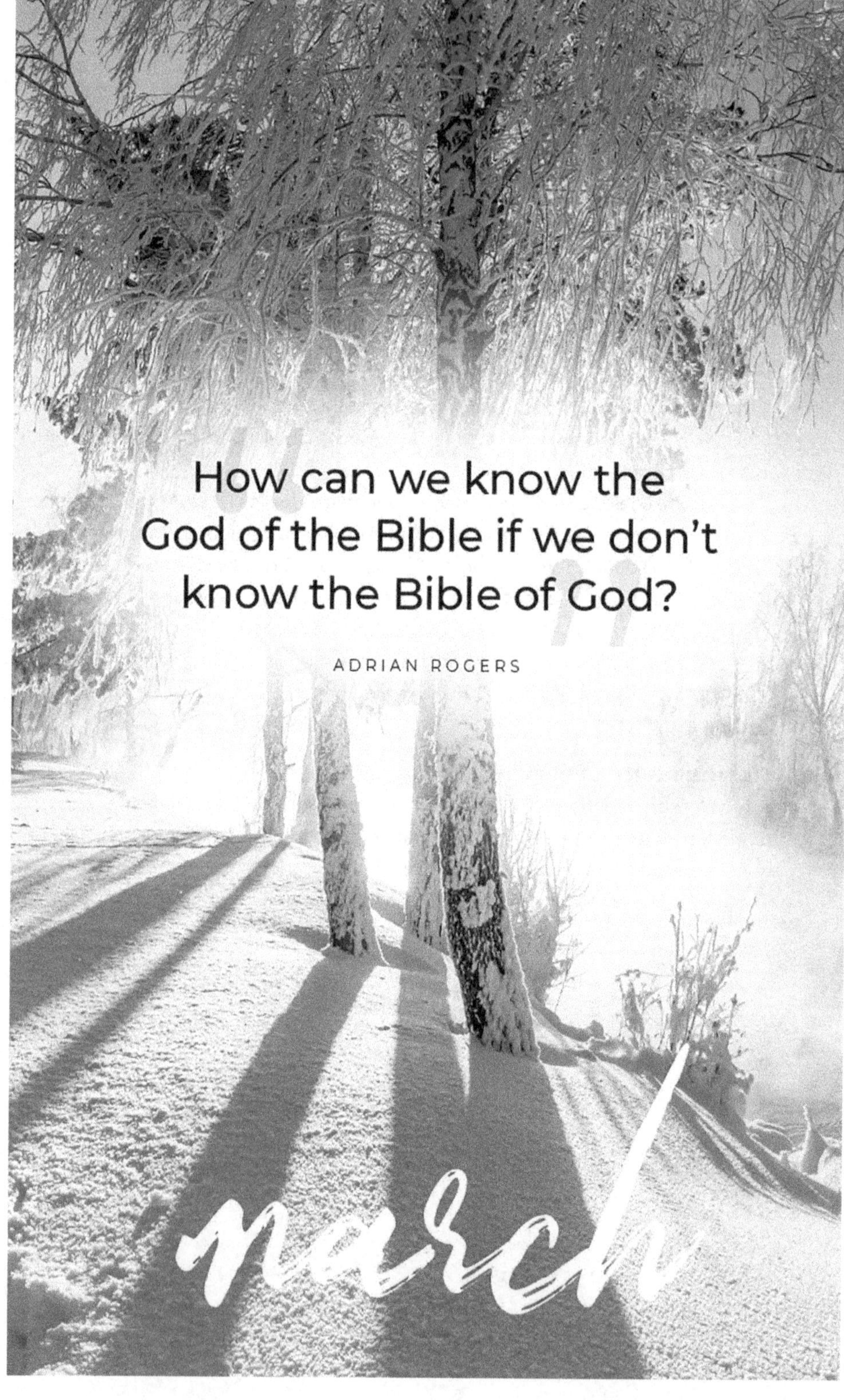
How can we know the God of the Bible if we don't know the Bible of God?
ADRIAN ROGERS
march

1

Now the just shall live by faith; but if anyone draws back, My soul has no pleasure in him.

HEBREWS 10:38

This great statement, so abundantly true, was actually first stated in the book of Habakkuk. The writer of Hebrews is quoting the prophet Habakkuk.

When Habakkuk wrote this, he was perplexed. He lived in a day of violence, degradation, apostasy, and danger. So he bombarded Heaven, asking God to answer, to explain things so that he could make sense of it all. But God said, "Habakkuk, you couldn't understand it anyway if I told you what I'm up to. Do you think I'm not working? I am working, and Habakkuk, here is your responsibility in this day: you must live in this uncertain age by faith. Do you want me to tell you how to live? Don't live by explanations. Live by faith."

Now, that's not just smoke and mirrors. That has spiritual steel and concrete in it—"the just shall live by faith." Are you lonely? You are never alone when you have genuine faith, because faith brings God so near. Some people are burdened with guilt...why? Faith understands that the precious blood of the Lord Jesus Christ has atoned for that sin. You can believe that intellectually, hear about it theologically, but faith lays hold of it.

Faith is my acceptance of God's acceptance of me. God receives us—not because of our own goodness—but when we come to Him in faith. "Therefore, having been justified by faith, we have peace with God through our Lord Jesus Christ, through whom also we have access by faith into this grace in which we stand, and rejoice in hope of the glory of God" (Romans 5:1-2).

ACTION POINT "By faith" is the only way to live. This passage from Habakkuk is quoted three times in the Word of God...I wonder if God is trying to tell us something. The challenge for us today—and every day—is to live by faith.

2

> For You have delivered my soul from death,
> my eyes from tears, and my feet from falling.
> **PSALM 116:8**

A minister spends a lot of time visiting hospitals and going to funerals. I've been with those who are dying and those who are facing heartaches. I've watched those who know the Lord Jesus Christ, and I've seen a difference in those who know Christ and those who don't.

I spent some time in the hospital with a man who in just a few hours would step over on the other side. I held his hand. We prayed. I asked, "Is everything right between you and the Lord?" He said, "Pastor, everything is right. I'm ready. For me to live is Christ and for me to die is gain." He had the assurance of one who knew that God would not forsake him.

"Let your conduct be without covetousness; be content with such things as you have. For He Himself has said, 'I will never leave you nor forsake you.' So we may boldly say: 'The LORD is my helper; I will not fear. What can man do to me?'" (Hebrews 13:5-6). What that literally means is, "I will not leave you a helpless orphan." He will not forsake you. You will not be forsaken.

ACTION POINT What would it take for you to have that assurance? Do you have it now? Then thank God for it. If you don't, have you given your heart fully to the Lord Jesus Christ? "F-A-I-T-H" means Forsaking All, I Trust Him. Trust Him fully today, and He will come to dwell within.

3

For the Word of God is living and powerful, and sharper than any two-edged sword, piercing even to the division of soul and spirit, and of joints and marrow, and is a discerner of the thoughts and intents of the heart.

HEBREWS 4:12

The Word of God is all-powerful. Satan fears the Word of God. He knows its overcoming power. Jesus defeated him by that Word. We must learn to use it against the devil and his minions.

It's an offensive weapon. Like any weapon—especially spiritual ones—you have to be trained to use it. Many of us study the Bible, but it's not enough just to study it, we must learn to employ it. The Word of God is a sword, and it is meant to be used. But you must be in His Word, studying it, to know how to implement it.

Our Lord Jesus Christ, tempted by Satan in the wilderness, took the Word of God—that sharp two-edged sword—and time after time plunged it through Satan. Jesus said, "It is written...It is written...It is written..." For that, Satan had no comeback. We can rely on the Word of God. We must!

ACTION POINT When God speaks, everything else is irrelevant. Sharpen your Sword today by reading the Scripture. Spend time in His Word. Meditate on it. Stay in the Word daily. Memorize the Word. Begin today. If you only memorize one verse per week, by this time next year you'll have committed to memory 52 verses! How many will you have memorized if you don't? "Your Word I have hidden in my heart..." (Psalm 119:11).

4

> And Elijah came to all the people, and said, "How long will you falter between two opinions? If the LORD is God, follow Him; but if Baal, follow him." But the people answered him not a word.
>
> **1 KINGS 18:21**

Jim Elliot, martyred missionary to the Auca Indians, wrote: "He is no fool who gives what he cannot keep to gain what he cannot lose." He's talking about giving his life for Christ and the Gospel. The most dangerous choice you could make is to play it safe. You're safer out on the waves with Jesus than in the boat without Him.

What if the Gospel isn't true? Let's suppose what I believe is wrong, the Bible is fiction, there's no God, and Christ never died for our sins. You come and put your faith in a fictitious Christ. You and I are going to die anyway, so we're no worse off.

But suppose I'm right: there is a God, the Bible is His word, and Jesus is His Son. By coming to Jesus, you've got everything to gain and nothing to lose. If I'm right but you reject Him, you've lost everything.

Now, it takes more than just my reasoning with you to come to the Lord Jesus, because the Holy Spirit must open your eyes to know the Gospel is true. Anything I can talk you into, somebody else could talk you out of.

ACTION POINT Dear friend, God the Holy Spirit is telling you about your eternal destination. I want you to be convinced. He will convict and convince you, but the devil will do all he can do to keep you from it. Don't yield to him. Instead ask God to reveal Himself to you. He will.

5

When they [the council] heard this, they were furious
and plotted to kill them [Peter and the apostles].
ACTS 5:33

Suppose you're on the battlefield and someone's coming at you. You warn him, "Don't come any further! I'll shoot!" He answers, "I don't believe in your gun. As a matter of fact, I don't believe in guns at all." That's not going to change anything, is it?

Likewise, the Bible is the sword of the Spirit. Someone may say, "Well, I don't believe the Bible." But it will cut him anyway! The apostles preached the Scripture, and when the people heard it, they were cut to the heart. The Word cuts even an unbeliever. It's a two-edged sword. It cuts to heal, or it cuts to judge. But it will cut—believe it or not.

Before going into battle, soldiers are dedicated to training in the use of their weapons. How foolish to go into battle without training. How familiar are you with your sword?

ACTION POINT God has given you a weapon for spiritual battles—"the sword of the Spirit, which is the Word of God" (Ephesians 6:17). In the armor of God, it is the only offensive weapon—the rest are defensive. To have the victory God wants for you, recognize your Bible as a sharp sword for attacking the enemy's strongholds. Every soldier spends a lot of time getting familiar with his weapon. Get trained in the Bible. Study it. Practice it. Use it daily.

6

> Stand therefore, having girded your waist with truth, having put on the breastplate of righteousness, and having shod your feet with the preparation of the gospel of peace; above all, taking the shield of faith with which you will be able to quench all the fiery darts of the wicked one. And take the helmet of salvation, and the sword of the Spirit, which is the Word of God.
>
> **EPHESIANS 6:14-17**

Do you have integrity? Is your life a life of truth? Do you have purity, or is there some unconfessed sin in your life? Do you have tranquility? Is the peace of God ruling in your heart? Do you have certainty? Do you have the shield of faith?

Did you know that this armor we're talking about, the armor of God, is really Jesus Christ? The belt of truth—Christ is the Truth (John 14:6). The breastplate of righteousness—Christ is our Righteousness (1 Corinthians 1:30). The shoes of peace—Christ is our Peace (Romans 5:1). The shield of faith—we have the faith of God (Romans 3:3). The helmet of salvation—Christ is our Salvation (1 Thessalonians 5:9). You see, all we need, He supplies. To put on the armor is just to put on Jesus.

ACTION POINT As you begin each day, "put on" the armor of God. Consciously say, "Lord, I'm putting on the helmet of the hope of my salvation and the breastplate of righteousness"—take on each piece, all the way down to your feet. Take up the sword of the Spirit and the shield of faith. Pray this protection also for your family members: "God, clothe us with Your armor." Call them by name. "Put on us the belt of truth, the breastplate of righteousness, etc." Don't go into your day defenseless!

7

For whatever is born of God overcomes the world. And this is the victory that has overcome the world—our faith.

1 JOHN 5:4

Are you uncertain about some things? Are you walking on eggshells and Jell-O theologically? Don't do it! Get a bulldog grip on the truth and stand by it. Learn to feed your faith and starve your doubts.

If you don't consistently, regularly, join with fellow believers to experience worship and the teaching of the Word, daily reading your Bible and praying, then you have no shield of faith! Sometimes at the university, college students who aren't deeply grounded in the Word will let some ungodly, unbelieving professor make fun of their faith. They'll fall apart like a house of cards. That's because they don't have a strong, rock-ribbed faith in God.

Faith will be like a shield to you to protect you: "Above all, taking the shield of faith with which you will be able to quench all the fiery darts of the wicked one" (Ephesians 6:16). Faith will give you certainty. Feed your faith. How do you do that? "So then faith comes by hearing, and hearing by the Word of God" (Romans 10:17).

ACTION POINT Put on the armor of God. Every day. Don't go into your day defenseless. Actively make the conscious choice to dress yourself in His armor. Commit to reading His Word, studying His Word, meditating on His Word. Learn how to wield your sword.

8

> Therefore take up the whole armor of God, that you may be able to withstand in the evil day, and having done all, to stand. Stand therefore, having girded your waist with truth, having put on the breastplate of righteousness, and having shod your feet with the preparation of the gospel of peace.
>
> **EPHESIANS 6:13-15**

A Roman soldier had to have sandals with hobnails to give him firm standing, very much like a golfer's spikes. He had to be able to stand his ground. And because the devil would love to trip us up, God tells us, as we're putting on our armor, to put on our shoes—and not just any shoes, but shoes of the gospel of peace.

You see, your enemy, the devil, can defeat some people through error. They embrace error because they don't have sound doctrine, the belt of truth. Others the devil can defeat through sin because they don't have on the breastplate of righteousness.

But some, the devil will get through discouragement; they'll lose their peace. He'll plant thorns, briars, and set up stumbling blocks. If we don't have our shoes on, our spiritual feet will be bruised and bleeding. Rather than leaping, we'll be limping because we don't have peace.

ACTION POINT Every morning as you start your day, ask the Lord: "Clothe me with Your armor. Put on my feet the shoes of the preparation of the gospel of peace, peace with You, O Lord." The peace of God dwelling in your heart enables you to fight Satan. Do you have this peace? If not, ask God to show you how to have it.

9

Keep your heart with all diligence; for out of it spring the issues of life.

PROVERBS 4:23

The Bible warns, "Keep your heart with all diligence." You must have the breastplate of righteousness covering your heart. We're told not to provide room for the devil or give him an opportunity (Ephesians 4:27). He's watching—searching—waiting for any crack in our armor.

Wouldn't it be awful to be dressed head to foot with all of the armor except for one little crack where the devil slips the knife in? Satan can get some people through error—they don't have on the belt of truth. Other people he gets through sin—they don't have on the breastplate of righteousness. Some of you he'll get through discouragement, for your feet are not shod with the preparation of the gospel of peace. (Ephesians 6:10-19)

A little poem I heard says it this way:

"Who is it knocks so loud?"
"A lonely little sin."
"Slip through," I answered.
And soon all hell was in.

ACTION POINT "A lonely little sin." Check your attitudes and your actions. Examine your ambitions and motives. Are there any that aren't absolutely pure? Cleanse them and get them right. If you don't, you are a sitting duck for Satan.

10

> You are of God, little children, and have overcome them, because He who is in you is greater than he who is in the world.
>
> **1 JOHN 4:4**

Praise God, Satan is a defeated foe! Satan's back has already been broken at the cross. When Jesus Christ prepared to go to that cross in anticipation, He said, "Now is the judgment of this world; now the ruler of this world will be cast out" (John 12:31).

"Cast out." Satan has already been defeated. We as Christians need to learn that! The devil hopes you never fully grasp that "He who is in you is greater than he who is in the world." He hopes you never find out that his power has been stripped away from him by Jesus, King of Kings, who conquered death and Hell (Revelation 1:18). Charles Haddon Spurgeon offers this reassuring word:

> *Hell and death, terrible powers as they are, are not left to riot without government. Death is a land of darkness, without any order, yet a sovereign eye surveys it, and a master hand holds its key. Hell trembles at the presence of the Lord, and there is a throne higher than the throne of evil. Let us rejoice that nothing in heaven, or Earth, or in places under the Earth, is left to itself to engender anarchy. Everywhere, serene above the floods, the Lord sits King for ever and ever. No province of the universe is free from the divine rule. Things do not come by chance. Nowhere do chance and chaos reign.*

Jesus said, "I give you authority...over all of the power of the enemy..." (Luke 10:19).

ACTION POINT Satan is a defeated foe. Do you live like you believe that? Get off the defensive. When you pray, don't beg God for victory. Instead, pray from the victory Jesus has already won.

11

And behold, I am coming quickly, and My reward is with Me, to give to every one according to his work.
REVELATION 22:12

We ought to be living as though Jesus died yesterday, rose this morning, and is coming back tonight. "Little children, it is the last hour; and as you have heard that the Antichrist is coming, even now many antichrists have come, by which we know that it is the last hour" (1 John 2:18). The Old Testament is preparation for the coming of Christ—the cross of Christ. The New Testament is preparation for the second coming of Christ—the coronation of Christ. Everything leading up to the cross was "the former days." Everything after the cross is "the final days," "the last days," looking forward to the Second Coming. From the time that Christ went away, the Bible has taught that He could come back at any moment; therefore, all Christians are to be looking for Jesus to come at any moment.

No one can set a date, but I'm kind of like that old farmer who woke up in the middle of the night and heard the grandfather clock sounding the hour. "Bong!" One o'clock; "Bong!" Two. "Bong!" Three. "Bong!" Four. On it went. "Bong!" Ten..."Bong!" Eleven... "Bong!" Twelve... "Bong!" Thirteen... "Bong!" Fourteen. That frightened him. He turned over, shook his wife, and said, "Wake up!" She said, "Why? What time is it?" He said, "I don't know, but it's later than it's ever been before."

ACTION POINT I believe it's late in the age. It's certainly later than it's ever been before. The spirit of the age is on a rampage. The enemy of our souls has turned up the heat because he believes his time is short. Are you prepared for the coming of our Lord? Anything you hope to do before Jesus' return, do it now. Any souls you want to see saved—witness to them now. Time is short. Be prepared for His coming.

march

12

> And Adam lived one hundred and thirty years, and begot a son in his own likeness, after his image, and named him Seth.
>
> **GENESIS 5:3**

Did you know you have never really seen a man? Well, you have, but not the way man was originally created. Suppose you had never seen a railroad train, and I showed you a train that has been wrecked, with all the twisted metal on the tracks. Have you seen a train? Not really—you've seen a train wreck.

Likewise with people. We talk about being "made in the image of God," but after mankind fell in Genesis 3, we find we are made in the image of Adam. Adam was created in the image of God, but that image was wrecked and spoiled by the Fall. Adam brought forth a son in his image.

But, oh, what a change there's going to be someday when we become what our Lord made us to be!

ACTION POINT One of the most encouraging verses in the Bible says, "And as we have borne the image of the man of dust [Adam], we shall also bear the image of the heavenly Man [Jesus] (1 Corinthians 15:49). Take heart, friend. We're going to be like Jesus Christ. We've borne the image of the earthly long enough. Get ready for a transformation. Don't be discouraged. Be confident in this: you will bear the image of the heavenly. You will be like the Lord Himself.

13

> But the LORD said to Samuel, "Do not look at his appearance or at his physical stature, because I have refused him. For the LORD does not see as man sees; for man looks at the outward appearance, but the LORD looks at the heart."
>
> **1 SAMUEL 16:7**

David's older brother Eliab was a big, broad-shouldered, winsome man. If you had gone to look for a king, you would have said, "Surely there's a kingly man if I ever saw one." But God didn't have His eyes upon Eliab; He had his eyes on David.

Sometimes we see people and say, "Oh, they have it all. I wish I could be like that person, look like that person, sing like that person, serve like that person. I wish I had his ability. I wish I were this or that." It's so great to know that God doesn't see as man sees. Man looks on the outward appearance, but God looks on the heart.

At the judgment seat of Christ, there will be a day of revelation. When everything is revealed, the things that are highly esteemed by people today will look much different then.

Jesus said to those in His day who were self-righteous, "You are those who justify yourselves before men, but God knows your hearts. For what is highly esteemed among men is an abomination in the sight of God" (Luke 16:15).

ACTION POINT Aren't you glad, dear friend, for a day when everything will be revealed? When it does, the emphasis is not going to be on appearances but upon quality. God is more interested in quality than in quantity. Is this good news to you, or does it make you nervous? Start following Christ in word and deed and not just in appearance. Walk the walk.

14

In the beginning God...

GENESIS 1:1A

The Bible begins with this statement in Genesis 1:1. It doesn't argue for the fact of God's existence. It doesn't explain His nature and being. It just presents Him: "In the beginning, God...." No philosophy, no argument, no apology offered, and no explanation given; just, "In the beginning, God...."

The Bible writers never tried to prove God. They presented Him. They never tried to explain His existence. Nor should you. You are very foolish if you try to prove God.

Now, as you know, people always talk about "the proofs for God." There are none. Now, don't let that shock you! The finite can never prove the infinite, you see. The Bible writers never tried to prove God. The Bible writers presented God. God does not need any proof. You are incapable of proving God.

To try to prove God by looking through physical or material things would be like tearing apart a piano trying to find "The Hallelujah Chorus." The first four words of the written Word of God say all we need to know: In the beginning—God!

ACTION POINT You will never really comprehend anything else in the Bible unless you understand Genesis 1:1, "In the beginning, God created the heavens and the Earth." The key to the rest of the Bible is hung right here at the front door. Don't expect to understand the Bible unless you believe this foundational truth.

15

> The fool has said in his heart, "There is no God." They are corrupt, they have done abominable works, there is none who does good.
>
> **PSALM 14:1**

Can a person find God by reasoning? No. We are incapable of proving God. Sometimes an atheist will swagger up to a believer and say, "Prove there is a God!" That never threatens me. I just smile and say, "Prove there is no God!"

Sometimes this is leveled against Christians as though it's an accusation: "You just accept by faith that there is a God." That's right! And let me tell you what the unbeliever does: He accepts by faith that there is no God. He does not know there's no God; He has never proven there is no God. He accepts by faith that there is no God.

You see, all men are believers. I choose to believe in God. The atheist chooses not to believe in God. If a man doesn't believe in God, it's because he doesn't want to believe in God. He has chosen not to believe in God. But make no mistake, we're all believers.

Some of the finest minds this world has ever known have been given to the gospel of Christ. It's not a matter of intellect. It's not a matter of reason. It's beyond reason and above reason.

ACTION POINT You cannot prove or disprove the existence of God. The evidence is clear—it's all around you in His creation. Believe in God. He is the God who is presented, not proven.

16

> Or do you not know that your body is the temple of the Holy Spirit who is in you, whom you have from God, and you are not your own? For you were bought at a price; therefore glorify God in your body and in your spirit, which are God's.
>
> **1 CORINTHIANS 6:19-20**

There is a familiar story about a little fellow who lost a little red sailboat he had made. It sailed away from him across the pond. Later, he saw it in a second-hand store, and the proprietor made him buy it back. He bought it back, and as he carried the little sailboat out of that second-hand store, he hugged it to his chest and said, "Little sailboat, you're mine. You are twice mine—you're mine because I made you, and you're mine because I bought you back."

Not only did God create you, but He then redeemed you. God bought you with His blood. And God says, "Christian, you're mine. You are twice mine. You're mine because I created you, and you're mine because I redeemed you." If you believe Genesis 1:1, then you have to believe that we have a moral responsibility to God, and if we don't meet it we'll answer for it at the judgment. "Woe to him who strives with his Maker" (Isaiah 45:9a)! "Remember now your Creator in the days of your youth" (Ecclesiastes 12:1).

ACTION POINT We must live out this verse, today and every day: "You are not your own. You are bought with a price. Therefore, glorify God in your body and in your spirit, which are God's."

17

> The devil, who deceived them, was cast into the lake of fire and brimstone, where the beast and the false prophet are. And they will be tormented day and night forever and ever.
>
> **REVELATION 20:10**

The devil hates Genesis and Revelation! He has waged war against them. He would tell us that Genesis is myth and Revelation is mystery. In the book of Genesis, you see sin as it begins and brings death and a curse. In the book of Revelation, sin is gone. There is no more death and no more curse.

In the book of Genesis, Satan appears for the first time. In the book of Revelation, he appears for the last time. There's a special blessing in both Genesis and Revelation:

- In Genesis is the seedbed of all theology.
- In Revelation is the culmination of all theology.
- In Genesis, the devil's doom is pronounced (Genesis 3:14-15).
- In Revelation, it is carried out (Revelation 20:10).

What we see begin in the book of Genesis, we see in completion and fulfillment in the book of the Revelation.

ACTION POINT See these books as they are. Compare and contrast them, and you will see that what God began years ago at the first creation, He ultimately completes in His new creation.

Then he [one of the thieves crucified with Jesus] said to Jesus, "Lord, remember me when You come into Your kingdom." And Jesus said to him, "Assuredly, I say to you, today you will be with Me in Paradise."

LUKE 23:42-43

The Polish astronomer Copernicus, through his writings and education, changed the concepts of what men think about the Universe and how the Universe runs. He was a brilliant man. But when Copernicus came to die, he did not see himself as an astronomer, but as a sinner in need of forgiveness. He asked that this epitaph be inscribed on his gravestone:

"Lord, I do not ask the kindness Thou didst show to Peter. I do not dare ask the grace Thou didst grant to Paul; but, Lord, the mercy Thou didst show to the dying robber, that mercy show to me. That earnestly I pray."

Copernicus was a brilliant man, but he didn't let fame or brilliance get in the way of his salvation.

ACTION POINT Do you want that today? Do you want the mercy that God showed to the dying thief? Ask Him, and He will show it to you and save you today. "Surely goodness and mercy shall follow me all the days of my life; and I will dwell in the house of the LORD forever" (Psalm 23:6).

19

Which of you by worrying can add one cubit unto his stature?
MATTHEW 6:27

The best thing you can say about worry is: it does no good. The worst thing is: it does much harm. I'm reminded of the little lady who said, "Don't tell me worry doesn't do any good. Most of the things I worry about never happen."

But worse than that, it's an expression of unbelief. Of lack of faith in God. It reveals that we are not trusting Him at that moment for the thing we are worried about.

Worry is absolutely useless. It doesn't cure any problems. It doesn't lift any burdens. It doesn't wipe away any tears. It never has; it never can; it never will! Worry can't make you any taller, shorter, fatter, or thinner. It is so senseless, and it is therefore useless. But even worse, it is faithless. Worry is just the opposite of faith.

God has lovingly told us: "Be anxious for nothing, but in everything by prayer and supplication, with thanksgiving, let your requests be made known to God; and the peace of God, which surpasses all understanding, will guard your hearts and minds through Christ Jesus" (Philippians 4:6-7).

ACTION POINT When we worry, we make God out to be a liar when God has said He will take care of us. See what God has said in Philippians 4:6-7. Memorize this passage today and get it in your heart: "Be anxious for nothing, but in everything by prayer and supplication, with thanksgiving, let your requests be made known to God; and the peace of God, which surpasses all understanding, will guard your hearts and minds through Christ Jesus."

20

His mother said to the servants, "Whatever He says to you, do it."

JOHN 2:5

We must obey whether we can understand or not. When Jesus was at the wedding in Cana, the servants had no way of knowing what Jesus was going to do. It must have seemed silly to be filling pots with water. But Jesus' mother gave them some very wise advice we would do well to heed: "Whatever He says to you, do it." That is a practical lesson concerning service. Whatever He says to you, if you are His servant, do it. Why? There are three reasons: for your good, for their gladness, and for His glory. When the servants obeyed the Lord, everybody else got blessed. Let me tell you something. Did you know that when I obey God, I'll be a blessing to you? When you obey God, you'll be a blessing to me. You cannot obey God without your obedience spilling out in a blessing to all those round about you.

It wasn't a matter of whether they understood it or not, just that He told them to do it. The same Jesus who turned water into wine can transform your home, can transform your life, can transform your family, can transform your future. That same Jesus is still in the miracle-working business. His business is the business of transformation.

Someone has well said that nature forms us, sin deforms us, the penitentiary reforms us, education informs us, the world conforms us, but only Jesus transforms us.

ACTION POINT Many times, your mind is going to say, "Well, that's old-fashioned," or "That doesn't make sense." Never come to the Bible that way. Never parade the Bible across the judgment bar of your reason. Whatever He says to you, do it.

21

> When Jesus saw him lying there, and knew that he already had been in that condition a long time, He said to him, "Do you want to be made well?"
>
> **JOHN 5:6**

"Do you want to be made well?" That sounds like a silly question. It really does sound foolish to ask a man who is sick if he wants to be made whole. But Jesus respected this man's will just as He respects your will and every human will.

If God were to transgress your will, if He were to force you to do something you did not want to do, you would no longer be a free human being with your own will. You would become a machine. So God gave you a will; and because you have a will, you must decide if you want to be made whole by accepting Him as your Savior.

You see, you don't have the strength to be godly, and that's the strength you need. "For when we were still without strength, in due time Christ died for the ungodly" (Romans 5:6). Why did He? Because we ought to be godly. The unsaved man is able to do what he wants, but he's not able to do what he ought. Christ gives us the power to do what we ought. This crippled man in John 5—the source of his disability was his sin. It drained him of his strength. And therefore he is a picture of every man who is apart from the Lord Jesus Christ.

The offer made available to you today is whosoever will may come (Revelation 22:17). Do you want to be made well?

ACTION POINT Ask the Lord to give you the kind of faith it takes to have your life transformed. Ask for the faith that can see the invisible, believe the incredible, and receive the impossible. Doubt dreads to take a step; faith soars on high. Doubt questions "Who believes?" Faith answers, "I do!"

22

These things I have spoken to you, that My joy may remain in you, and that your joy may be full.

JOHN 15:11

Joy is the birthmark of the child of God. Every Christian ought to have conscious joy. And if you're not living a life of joy, you're living beneath your privileges.

It's so important that you have joy shining from your life in order to win the lost. If you want people to believe in your Savior, the mark of the authenticity of Christ in your life is the joy of the Lord Jesus Christ.

He says "My joy"—not "joy like His." Jesus wants to take the joy that He has and place that joy in you. Perhaps you've thought of Jesus only as a man of sorrows, and you've never thought of Jesus as the Jesus of joy. But John 15:11 speaks of His joy! And the Bible says that we are to "Rejoice in the Lord always. Again I will say, rejoice" (Phillipians 4:4)! And, concerning the Lord Jesus, that God "has anointed You with the oil of gladness more than Your companions" (Hebrews 1:9b). And do you know what the word gladness means? The original word means "to leap, to jump!"

People are not all that interested in your creed or your doctrines—they want to know if it's working for you. And there is nothing more attractive in winning the lost to the Lord Jesus Christ than the joy of the Lord that is evident in your life.

ACTION POINT Don't try to carry the burdens of this life without the joy of the Lord to put a spring in your step, a beat in your heart, and a smile on your face. Thank God for real joy because "...The joy of the LORD is your strength" (Nehemiah 8:10).

23

> Your word I have hidden in my heart,
> that I might not sin against You.
> **PSALM 119:11**

Your home is a good place for the Bible—your hand is a better place. Your heart is an even better place. We must learn to hide God's Word in our hearts. And in order for it to get in our hearts, we have to read it. We have to study over it.

How much time are you spending with the Word of God? Do you wonder why you can't live a pure life? Or live in victory? Why you cave in when temptation comes? Why you can't be an overcomer? How much time are you spending daily with the Word of God? Many spend far more time watching TV or on their phones than with the Word of God. And then they wonder why they fail. This is the book God has given to help you to live victoriously.

Many of you are just playing at Bible study. You never really get into it. You say, "Oh, the Bible is a wonderful book." What good is that going to do you? What good are the promises in God's Word unless you appropriate them into your life?

ACTION POINT Set a time, a quiet time when you get alone with God each morning. Get up every day and first saturate your soul with the Word of God. Bathe your soul in the presence of Jesus.

Blessed are You, O LORD! Teach me Your statutes.

PSALM 119:12

Did you know you could read and even memorize the Bible, but if that's all that happens, it won't change your life? You're not changed by the words of the Bible but by the Holy Spirit of God, who takes the words and applies them to your heart.

You see, you'll never learn this book unless God teaches it to you. And it is not enough just simply to read it. You must come to God saying, "Lord, I want to have a controlled, disciplined mind. I want You to teach me."

David goes on to say in verse 18 of this Psalm, "Open my eyes that I may see wondrous things from Your law."

You cannot separate the God of love from the God of the word. Many read the Bible like a math book rather than a love story. They get the words, but they don't get the music. But you'll never learn the Bible unless God teaches it to you. Not only must the Word of God get into you, but the Spirit of God must come into you.

ACTION POINT Make this your prayer today: "Open my eyes that I may see wondrous things from Your law. Teach me Your statutes. Come, Holy Spirit, control my thoughts and guide me into Your truth. And Lord, as I get my heart cleansed, committed and conditioned, let my life be completely controlled by You."

25

I am a stranger in the earth; do not hide
Your commandments from me.
PSALM 119:19

One man loved to study the Bible, but every time he came to something he couldn't understand, he thought of his friend Charlie, a great student of the Bible. The man would ask, "Charlie what does this verse mean?" Or, "Charlie, tell me about this." One day in his Bible study, the Holy Spirit said to him, "Why don't you ask Me? I'm the One who taught Charlie!"

Pray and say, "'Open my eyes, that I may see Wondrous things from Your law' (Psalm 119:18). 'Teach me Your statutes' (Psalm 119:12)." As you study the Bible, ask yourself these questions:

- Is there a promise to claim?
- Is there a lesson to learn?
- Is there a blessing to enjoy?
- Is there a command to obey?
- Is there a sin to avoid?
- Is there a new thought to carry with me?

I thank God for Bible students and Bible scholars and people who can teach, but the same God who teaches them is the God who wants to teach you.

ACTION POINT The Word of God will be dynamite in your life. But to make that happen, you need to verbalize it. Start speaking the Word of God. Speak it clearly. Speak it courageously. You'll discover that as you share, quote, and sing it—as what is in your heart finds its way to your lips—it will mold your mind in a way you never knew before. It will become vital in your heart and in your life.

26

> "Because your heart was tender, and you humbled yourself before God when you heard His words against this place and against its inhabitants, and you humbled yourself before Me, and you tore your clothes and wept before Me, I also have heard you," says the LORD.
>
> **2 CHRONICLES 34:27**

How many truly victorious Christians do you know? How many genuinely victorious churches are you aware of? Do you know what the problem is with many of us? We are failing, but we don't weep over it. We are not living in victory, but it doesn't seem to bother us. We know very little about victory, and we seem to be quite content to live day after day without it. We seem to think that victory is for others, but not for us.

Today's verse occurred at a time of utter devastation in Israel. Young Josiah—a mere boy—became king. He wanted to get things right with God. He humbled himself. Our Bible passage today is God's answer. Read it again!

ACTION POINT This is a beautiful chapter—one you should read today. Do you think you were behind the door when victory was passed out, and it's not your fault you live in defeat? Could it be that it is your fault that you're not victorious? You ought to be weeping over your shame and over your sin. Follow Josiah's example in this chapter and humble yourself before our great God.

27

And He said to me, "My grace is sufficient for you, for My strength is made perfect in weakness." Therefore most gladly I will rather boast in my infirmities, that the power of Christ may rest upon me....For when I am weak, then I am strong.

2 CORINTHIANS 12:9-10B

The reason many people aren't overcoming the devil is that they're using spiritual weapons, but trying to wield those weapons in their own strength.

You say, "I'm just too weak to win the battle." You're right. But you may not be weak enough yet. God identifies Himself with our obedient weakness. Your problem may be that you're still trying rather than trusting. The battle is not yours; it's the Lord's!

Your weakness is not a liability; it's an asset. Your strength is not an asset; it's a liability. If we could only learn that God does not need our strength! He calls for our obedience! God has the strength! The battle is the Lord's.

God has given us mighty weapons.

- The precious blood of Jesus that covers us, for example. "And they overcame him [the devil] by the blood of the Lamb and by the word of their testimony" (Revelation 12:11).
- The Word of God is another. This Bible, "sharper than any two-edged sword" (Hebrews 4:12), is to be our battle-axe, our sword, our bow, our arrow, as we go against the enemy.
- Prayer is another. "For the weapons of our warfare are not carnal [of the flesh] but mighty in God for pulling down strongholds" (2 Corinthians 10:4).

ACTION POINT You have a spiritual enemy. Only spiritual weapons will be successful in defeating him! Take up the weapons God Himself has placed in our hands.

28

And He said to me, "My grace is sufficient for you, for My strength is made perfect in weakness." Therefore most gladly I will rather boast in my infirmities, that the power of Christ may rest upon me.

2 CORINTHIANS 12:9

When Paul wrote that he would rather boast in his infirmities, he didn't mean he was bragging about his sickness. Have you ever met anyone who brags about his sickness? You don't dare ask how he feels, or he'll give you an organ recital.

It is not God's plan that we escape all trouble. Nor is it God's plan that we merely "endure." Rather, God wants to enlist your sickness. Your infirmity can be used to reveal His glory. It can be used for Christ's sake.

It wasn't that Paul enjoyed poor health. But Paul learned his weakness could become a strength. God had a higher plan. How do you enlist your suffering? Receive the gift of God, rely upon the grace of God, and reflect the glory of God.

ACTION POINT There's nothing wrong with praying, "Lord, I want to escape this suffering." Paul did—three times. Our Lord Himself in the Garden of Gethsemane asked the Father, "If it be possible, let this cup pass from Me." But the Lord had a higher plan. So the first thing we ought to do when we hurt is pray, "Lord, take it away, please." If He doesn't, ask Him again and continue to ask Him until He tells you that He has a better or a higher plan.

29

> For what will it profit a man if he gains the whole world, and loses his own soul?
>
> **MARK 8:36**

Do you know what a lemming is? It's a little animal who somehow gets in his mind a weird compulsion. And then all of the lemmings get it. They go headlong on a journey toward the sea. Over the mountains they go. Across the rivers they go. Through the woods they go. Over the marshes and the moors they go—on and on until they get to the sea. Then they jump in and drown. They're doing everything to get there—then that's it.

There are a lot of lemmings these days. They're working, striving, and building, but all to end in a Christless existence. Jesus Christ did not come to save you from Hell—He does save you from Hell, but that's a byproduct. The angel Gabriel said, "And she will bring forth a Son, and you shall call His name Jesus, for He will save His people from their sins" (Matthew 1:21). He didn't come to save you for Heaven. You will go to Heaven, but that's a byproduct, a fringe benefit. He came, dear friend, to make you *holy*. That is the purpose of your redemption. You have been redeemed to be a holy person.

ACTION POINT Jesus Christ did not bathe this planet with His blood to have you serve the world, the flesh, and the devil. The chief religion in America is the cult of conformity. The theme is "everybody's doing it." But God saved you out of that—for a purpose! "You are not your own. For you were bought at a price; therefore glorify God in your body and in your spirit, which are God's" (1 Corinthians 19b-20). He redeemed you from meaninglessness. Know for certain—you have a purpose in life!

30

> For by grace you have been saved through faith, and that not of yourselves; it is the gift of God, not of works, lest anyone should boast.
>
> **EPHESIANS 2:8-9**

Some Christians believe you can lose your salvation. Whether or not you can lose it depends on how you got it.

If you "got it" by works, then I could understand how you could lose it by works, right? I mean, if you had to work in order to be saved, then if your works fail, you're no longer saved.

If sin could cause you to lose your salvation, one half of one sin would do it, because God demands perfection. Don't think "God will tolerate a little, but He won't tolerate a lot." He won't tolerate any! You would have to be completely sinless (an impossibility).

But if you're saved by grace (and we are), then you are kept by grace. You keep it the same way you got it—by His grace alone through faith alone.

When you believe in the Lord Jesus Christ, God counts your faith for righteousness. God says to the believer, "You are righteous." You don't deserve it, you didn't earn it, you don't merit it, but when God sees you, He sees the righteousness of the Lord Jesus Christ.

The Bible tells us we are clothed in His righteousness. And one part of the armor of God, which we are to put on each day, is the breastplate of righteousness. It's available every day, not by our own merit, but because we've been clothed with His righteousness—the righteousness Jesus purchased for us on the cross.

ACTION POINT Thank Him today for His incredible grace in saving you, and read Ephesians 6:10-18. As you do, take on yourself the whole armor of God.

31

Do not cast me away from Your presence, and do not take Your Holy Spirit from me. Restore to me the joy of Your salvation, and uphold me by Your generous Spirit.

PSALM 51:11-12

Sometimes when you go out and witness, you knock on a door and a man comes out and says, "Yeah, I used to go down to that church. I guess you could call me an old backslider, ha, ha, ha."

He is not a backslider. He is as lost as a goat. No backslider says, "I'm just an old backslider." If you know God and you've been saved, His Spirit has come into you. And the Holy Spirit in you is grieved when you sin. You don't laugh about it and make jokes about it. I tell you, the most miserable person on Earth is not a lost person—it's a saved one who is out of fellowship with God.

"For whom the LORD loves He corrects, Just as a father the son in whom he delights" (Proverbs 3:12). "But if you are without chastening, of which all have become partakers, then you are illegitimate and not sons" (Hebrews 12:8). No child of God can live any old way he wants just because of eternal security. With an eternal security comes an eternal responsibility. But there's a difference between God's chastisement and God's judgment. If God were to impute that sin to me rather than chastise me for it, if God were to put that on my account, then I'd be eternally lost.

ACTION POINT If you are truly saved, God will carry you to the woodshed when you sin! You can know for sure that you truly belong to God if your sin bothers you. Look inward. Does sin grieve you? If you are saved, it does. Better said, it grieves the Holy Spirit residing in you.

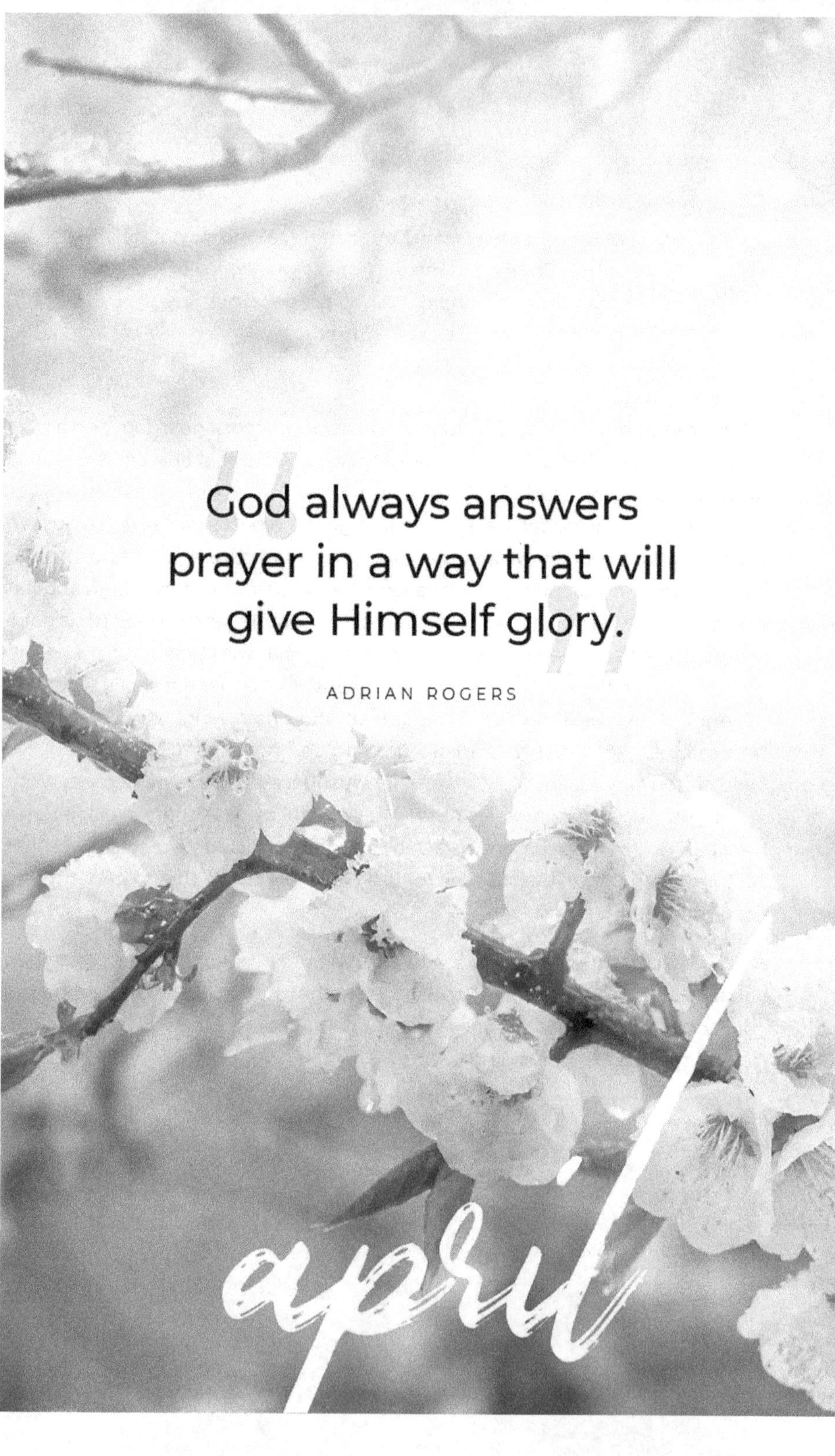
God always answers prayer in a way that will give Himself glory.
ADRIAN ROGERS
april

1

> So the great dragon was cast out, that serpent of old, called the Devil and Satan, who deceives the whole world; he was cast to the earth, and his angels were cast out with him.
>
> **REVELATION 12:9**

Sometimes people ask, "Is the Bible to be interpreted literally or figuratively?" I answer, "Yes!" It is to be interpreted both figuratively and literally, all at the same time.

The Bible is full of symbolism. But you must find out what the symbol stands for, and then you literally believe it. For example, in the book of Revelation, the devil is symbolized as a huge dragon. Don't say, "Oh, that's just symbolism, there is no devil." When you see those golden arches, the symbol of McDonalds, you don't say, "Oh, that's just a symbol. There is no McDonald's restaurant. There's no such thing as a hamburger." You wouldn't say that. No, the dragon is a symbol, but when you know what the symbol stands for, you can apply it literally.

ACTION POINT When you open the Word of God, first pray over it. Then ponder it. Ask these six questions:

- Is there a promise to claim?
- Is there a lesson to learn?
- Is there a blessing to enjoy?
- Is there a command to obey?
- Is there a sin to avoid?
- Is there a new thought to carry with me?

Pray, "Oh God, open my eyes. Move upon my heart. Give me understanding." Then with a pen close by, write these things down. Read it through, think it clear, write it down, pray it in, live it out, and pass it on.

2

> As newborn babes, desire the pure milk of the word, that you may grow thereby.
>
> **1 PETER 2:2**

Can you imagine a conversation that goes like this?

"I'm just so weak! I can hardly get out of bed. I just don't want to go to work, I'm so weak."

"Well what's the matter? Have you been to the doctor?"

"No."

"Do you have a disease?"

"I don't think so."

"What are you eating?"

"Well, I have this restaurant I go to just on Sundays—sometimes—if it's not raining, and I get a meal there. That's all I eat."

"You mean that's all you eat?"

"Yeah, and I'm just so weak."

Friend, organized worship is just to whet your appetite. If you don't learn how to feed yourself upon the Word of God during the week, you will never grow. You'll be sick and weak spiritually.

ACTION POINT Dig in to the abundant nourishment of God's Word. It will be a source of victory, a source of strength, and a source of joy.

3

He [Abraham] did not waver at the promise of God through unbelief, but was strengthened in faith, giving glory to God, and being fully convinced that what He had promised He was also able to perform.

ROMANS 4:20-21

Adoniram Judson was a great missionary. He went to Burma and labored long there. He prayed, fasted, and witnessed. But rather than seeing souls come to Jesus, Adoniram Judson was arrested. He was tortured and cast into a vile, filthy, vermin-infested prison. Later, when he was home on furlough, he was asked if the prospects were bright for the conversion of the world. His famous reply was, "As bright, Sirs, as the promises of God!"

Hebrews 11:6 says, "But without faith it is impossible to please Him, for he who comes to God must believe that He is, and that He is a rewarder of those who diligently seek Him." If you please God, it doesn't matter whom else you displease; if you displease God, it doesn't matter whom else you please. And there is no way to please God without faith. Christians were called "Believers" before they were called Christians. It is our chief duty to believe God.

You must guard your heart. The devil will war against your faith. God had given Abraham and Sarah a promise (Genesis 17-18). Friend, God will test your faith. A faith that cannot be tested cannot be trusted. And then, "By faith Sarah herself also received strength to conceive seed, and she bore a child when she was past the age, because she judged Him faithful who had promised" (Hebrews 11:11).

ACTION POINT Without faith, it is impossible to please God. You will never succeed in your Christian life without believing. If you know the Lord Jesus Christ, then you are an heir of the kingdom of God, and you can say, "My future is as bright as the promises of God!"

April 4

> When Jesus heard that, He said, "This sickness is not unto death, but for the glory of God, that the Son of God may be glorified through it."
>
> **JOHN 11:4**

The devil's charge against Job was that Job didn't really love God—that the only reason he served God was that God had bribed him. So God said, "To prove He loves me, Satan, you can take anything from him except his life."

Even after Satan did his worst, however, Job continued to serve the Lord and said, "Though He slay me, yet will I trust in Him..." (Job 13:15). Isn't that great?

God often gets the glory through our trials. There are servants of God today, special people who've been chosen of God to shut the devil's mouth by saying, "Though I do not have physical health or a lot of this world's goods, I love God. Jesus Christ is real to me, and Jesus Christ is enough for me."

Sometimes sickness may glorify God. Andrew Murray, a dear old saint, wrote:

> *In times of trouble, the trusting child of God may say, "First, He brought me here. It is by His will that I'm in this great place. Next, He will keep me here in His love and give me grace in this trial to behave as His child. Then He will make the trial a blessing, teaching me the lessons He intends for me to learn and working in the grace He means to bestow. And in His good time He can bring me out again. How and when—He knows."*

ACTION POINT So many people have an "if" faith: "Lord, if you do this..." But what you need is a "though" faith. "Though He slay me, yet will I trust in Him." And that shuts the mouth of the devil!

5

> The next day a great multitude that had come to the feast, when they heard that Jesus was coming to Jerusalem, took branches of palm trees and went out to meet Him, and cried out: "Hosanna! Blessed is He who comes in the name of the LORD! The King of Israel!"
>
> **JOHN 12:12-13**

Lambs specifically designated for Passover sacrifice were bred and cared for in the fields of Boaz outside of Bethlehem. It's not without significance that Jesus was born in Bethlehem, or by coincidence that so close to Jerusalem, about five miles away, those lambs would be raised and cared for.

On a specified day, the shepherds would bring the lambs into the city through the Sheep Gate to be sacrificed. Did you know—the day they were brought in was the day we now call "Palm Sunday"? Christians around the world celebrate Palm Sunday, the day our Lord came triumphantly into Jerusalem, riding a white Syrian colt. The day the lambs were coming in, the Lamb of God came in.

They cut down palm branches and put them under His feet. The crowd waved at Him shouting, "Hail Him, Hail Him." Five days later, on Passover, they would be shouting, "Nail Him, Nail Him." Jesus, God's Passover Lamb, died in our place so we can be reconciled to God.

ACTION POINT If you've never received Him, never bowed the knee, made Him your Lord, or allowed Him to become your sacrifice for sin, one day you will experience a Calvary of your own. The Savior is waiting to enter your heart. What is your answer to Him?

6

> How much more shall the blood of Christ, who through the eternal Spirit offered Himself without spot to God, cleanse your conscience from dead works to serve the living God?
>
> **HEBREWS 9:14**

Do you realize that Jesus never corrected, withdrew, or amended any statement He ever made? Jesus Christ never apologized for anything He ever did or said. He never sought advice from anyone or had to ask for forgiveness. Jesus Christ doesn't have any strong points. For Him to have strong points, He would have to have weak points.

Robert Clark has rightly given this assessment of the character of Jesus:

There was meekness without weakness, tenderness without feebleness, firmness without coarseness, love without sentimentality, holiness without sanctimoniousness, lowliness without lowness, truth without error, enthusiasm without fanaticism, passion without prejudice, heavenly mindedness without forgetfulness, carefreeness without carelessness, service without servility, self exaltation without egotism, judgment without harshness, seriousness without somberness, mercy without softness.

What can you do with Jesus? If you do not accept Him, you reject Him. Either you crown Him or you crucify Him. You cannot be neutral. You either confess Him or you deny Him. You are free to choose, but you are not free to not choose—and you are not free to escape the consequences of your choice.

ACTION POINT The greatest question that could be asked was recorded in Matthew 27:22. Pontius Pilate asked: "What shall I do with Jesus?" Receive Him, and though your sins are like scarlet, they shall be white as snow (Isaiah 1:18). Reject Him, and no matter how much good you think you do, you will spend eternity forever separated from Him.

7

Inasmuch then as the children have partaken of flesh and blood, He Himself likewise shared in the same, that through death He might destroy him who had the power of death, that is, the devil.

HEBREWS 2:14

When Hebrews 2:14 says, "Inasmuch then as the children have partaken of flesh and blood," it's talking about you and me—for we are flesh and blood children of Adam. "He Himself likewise shared in the same" says that Jesus took upon Himself flesh and blood. Why did He do that? Why did He step out of glory? Why did the Word (Jesus) become flesh (see John 1:1-3)? Why His virgin birth?

So that He might die.

Now, understand—God is Spirit, and God in Spirit cannot die. But not so for mankind, the crown of His creation. For us, "the wages of sin is death" (Romans 6:23), "The soul who sins shall die" (Ezekiel 18:20) and "Without the shedding of blood there is no remission [of sins]" (Hebrews 9:22).

You see, because every single one of us has sinned, we were headed not only for death but also eternal separation from God. Jesus had to become a flesh and blood human being so He might become the sinless sacrifice upon the cross of Calvary.

Doing that, He not only provided eternal salvation, but also brought Satan's kingdom crashing down!

ACTION POINT When you say "Jesus Christ is Lord" over your life, you have awesome power within you. To confess "Jesus is Lord" subdues Satan. Listen to Revelation 12:1, "And they overcame him [Satan] by the blood of the Lamb and by the word of their testimony." What is "the word of your testimony?" That Jesus Christ is Lord. The Lord of glory destroyed the power of Satan's kingdom. Now you belong to Him and He belongs to you.

8

> Then to Adam He said, "Because you have heeded the voice of your wife, and have eaten from the tree of which I commanded you, saying, 'You shall not eat of it:' Cursed is the ground for your sake. In toil you shall eat of it all the days of your life. Both thorns and thistles it shall bring forth for you, and you shall eat the herb of the field."
>
> **GENESIS 3:17-18**

Before His crucifixion, Roman soldiers crowned the Lord Jesus with a circlet made of long, sharp thorns. It was a sick form of torture, a cruel mockery, a wicked act of hatred and rebellion. Unwittingly, they were part of a drama that had been written before the world was swung into space. It was not accidental. Though done by wicked men, it was part of God's magnificent plan.

In the Garden of Eden, there had been no thorns, thistles or brambles. The first rose bloomed without thorns. The crown of thorns symbolized the curse that fell upon all humanity—you, me, all of us—because of sin.

Jesus wore the thorns because He bore the curse resulting from our rebellion. No matter your occupation or station in life, you'll be among thorns. Your body, like the apostle Paul, will have a thorn in the flesh. The thorns on Jesus' head spoke of the sickness and suffering we all experience because sin marred creation (Romans 8:22). Death always accompanies sin.

ACTION POINT The thorny pathway we walk, the curse that's on everything, is because of sin. Look at every hospital, mental institution, jail, every sick or crippled body and say "Sin did this." Look at heartache, pain, and anguish. Write over it one word: SIN. Thorns are the symbol. Who is taking care of your sin today? Who is paying the price for it? Is it under the blood? Are you trusting Christ alone?

9

> For Christ also suffered once for sins, the just for the unjust, that He might bring us to God, being put to death in the flesh but made alive by the Spirit.
>
> **1 PETER 3:18**

Imagine this scene: A Roman soldier and a prison guard walk down a narrow corridor in a Roman prison. The soldier holds up a torch. Back in the shadows, a man crouches in terror. The guard with his key opens the door. "Barabbas, get up and come with me."

Barabbas begins to plead, "No! No, wait! Don't take me! Have mercy!" The soldier says, "You're not going to die. Come, look over on that hill. That's the cross we made for you. But there's somebody else on it. He's taking your place."

I'm not implying that Barabbas was saved, but that God arranged a perfect picture of substitution.

When the Lord Jesus Christ died, He fulfilled yet another Old Testament symbolism. The high priest would take a goat called "the scapegoat," lay his hand upon its head, and confess the sins of the people. Their sins were symbolically transferred to the goat, which would then be led outside the city walls, where the goat would be killed and his blood shed. Jesus was led outside Jerusalem's walls where His blood was shed and He died. Jesus was our scapegoat. Our sins were laid upon Him. He carried them to the cross where in agony and blood He died.

ACTION POINT The sole purpose for the cross of Calvary was substitution. God forgave our sin through Jesus' suffering in our place. Just and sinless, Jesus died for the unjust—Barabbas, you, me, everyone—that He might bring us to Himself. Salvation, eternity in fellowship with God—it's all there for the taking. Receive God's offered gift today. All you must do is receive Him and make Him Lord.

10

> Surely He has borne our griefs, and carried our sorrows; yet we esteemed Him stricken, smitten by God, and afflicted. But He was wounded for our transgressions, He was bruised for our iniquities; the chastisement for our peace was upon Him; and by His stripes we are healed. All we like sheep have gone astray; we have turned, every one, to his own way; and the LORD has laid on Him the iniquity of us all.
>
> **ISAIAH 53:4-6**

Jesus Christ did not die as a helpless victim. He said, "Therefore My Father loves Me, because I lay down My life that I may take it again. No one takes it from Me, but I lay it down of Myself. I have power to lay it down, and I have power to take it again. This command I have received from My Father" (John 10:17-18).

The cross was not an accident or an afterthought; it was in the heart and mind of God before the world was framed. Jesus was born in the shadow of the cross. John the Baptist announced, "Behold! The Lamb of God who takes away the sin of the world" (John 1:29)! More than 2,000 years before this, as a foreshadowing of Jesus' death, Abraham had told his son Isaac, "God will provide Himself a lamb, my son" (Genesis 22). Jesus said, "Your father Abraham rejoiced to see My day, and he saw it and was glad" (John 8:56).

Jesus, the Lamb of God, died on the same day, at the same time, that the Passover lambs were being slain on Mount Moriah. To the priests, Jesus Christ could say, "Put away your knives. Your work is over. We need no more Passover lambs, no more sacrifices. The Lamb has died and has paid in full."

ACTION POINT Don't let this go quickly past you. Meditate today upon the price paid for your salvation. Read Matthew 26-27. Hallelujah, God of Abraham, God of Isaac, God of Israel: thank You for the Lamb!

11

> And according to the law, almost all things are purified with blood, and without shedding of blood there is no remission.
>
> **HEBREWS 9:22**

We must come to grips with this: the Bible is a bloody book. Cut the Bible anywhere, and it will bleed. But it's not a gory story—it's a glory story, for "the blood of Jesus Christ, His Son, cleanses us from all sin" (1 John 1:7b).

The theme of the Bible is Jesus Christ and His blood redemption. A thread runs all the way through from Genesis to Revelation: the scarlet thread of redemption.

The night before the Israelites came out of Egypt, God told them to take the blood of a lamb and apply it to the top and sides of the doorframes of their houses. Then when the angel of death came through the land, he would pass over and spare them. Years later when Joshua and Caleb came to Jericho, they told Rahab, "Tie a scarlet cord in your window. When the instruments of God's justice come through, we will pass over your house. You'll be safe if you're in there."

On it goes throughout the Bible, the red thread of redemption.

God put Calvary, with its blood-stained cross and its blood-drenched slopes, across the path of every hell-bound, hell-deserving sinner. And just as Rahab was delivered so long ago, so you can be too. The blood of Passover lambs pointed to "the Lamb of God who takes away the sin of the world." Christ our Passover Lamb is sacrificed for us.

ACTION POINT God doesn't want you to go to Hell. He put a roadblock in your path: the Cross. If you're on that path today, Calvary stands in your way. And if you do go to Hell, you'll have to climb over Calvary to get there. What will you do with Jesus?

12

And if Christ is not risen, then our preaching is empty and your faith is also empty. Yes, and we are found false witnesses of God, because we have testified of God that He raised up Christ, whom He did not raise up—if in fact the dead do not rise. For if the dead do not rise, then Christ is not risen. And if Christ is not risen, your faith is futile; you are still in your sins!

1 CORINTHIANS 15:14-17

It is an unthinkable question: What if there had been no Easter?

Suppose Jesus had not risen from the dead? Our faith would be futile, death would have dominion, sin would be sovereign, and the future would be fearful. His death without His resurrection cannot save anybody. Our faith is worthless if He is still in the grave. Confucius died. Buddha died. Muhammad died. Jesus Christ is alive! We don't put our faith in a dead Messiah.

How do we know that Jesus Christ was not just a religious fanatic, someone with a martyr complex who happened to get crucified? How do we know He is the Son of God, God incarnate? Romans 1:4 says He is "declared to be the Son of God...by the resurrection from the dead." How do we know God accepted His sacrifice at Calvary? By the resurrection.

The Bible says He was delivered for our offenses and raised again for our justification. No resurrection, no Savior. No Savior, no forgiveness. But Jesus went into the tomb and three days later walked out like a butterfly bursting from a cocoon—He is a risen Savior!

ACTION POINT Celebrate the risen Savior! Read 1 Corinthians 15 carefully. Ask the Lord to reveal to you all it means for your salvation.

13

> And if Christ is not risen, then our preaching is empty and your faith is also empty. Yes, and we are found false witnesses of God, because we have testified of God that He raised up Christ, whom He did not raise up—if in fact the dead do not rise. For if the dead do not rise, then Christ is not risen.
>
> **1 CORINTHIANS 15:14-16**

Paul isn't saying, "If Jesus is still in the grave, then we are mistaken." He's saying, "If Jesus is still in the grave, we're all liars."

It is one thing to be mistaken; it's another to be a false witness. Were the disciples liars when they said Christ was risen? If so, why would they lie? If Jesus was still in the grave, what did they have to gain?

Among the twelve disciples, all but the Apostle John died as martyrs. They were tortured, persecuted, stoned, crushed, humiliated, burned at the stake. They reddened the mouths of lions. Hypocrites and martyrs are not made of the same stuff. People tell lies to get out of trouble, not to get into trouble. A man may live for a lie, but few if any will willingly die for a lie.

The disciples said, "Listen! We have seen Him! We have touched Him!" Are you going to tell me that Simon Peter, whom tradition says was crucified upside down, was a con man? That John the apostle was a crook? That the Apostle Paul, who wrote most of the New Testament, was a known perjurer, deceiver, and false witness? That these men would die for a lie?

Of course not. Jesus Christ has indeed risen, as they said!

ACTION POINT If someone were to ask you, "What proof do you have that Jesus Christ really rose from the dead?"—what would you answer them? Are you prepared with a well-thought-out, logical answer?

april

14

> But be doers of the word, and not hearers only, deceiving yourselves. For if anyone is a hearer of the word and not a doer, he is like a man observing his natural face in a mirror; for he observes himself, goes away, and immediately forgets what kind of man he was. But he who looks into the perfect law of liberty and continues in it, and is not a forgetful hearer but a doer of the work, this one will be blessed in what he does.
>
> **JAMES 1:22-25**

James gives this description of a person who hears the Word but doesn't practice it: he says they are like someone who wakes up in the morning and sees his beard grown out, his hair tousled, bags under his eyes, and soup still on his mustache from last night. He glances in the mirror, sees that he needs to put everything in shape, but he just goes on his way, off to work! He forgets what he saw in the mirror. There is no change—no shower, no shaving, no combing. He is just like he was. He glanced in the mirror, saw it, and forgot it.

Notice James uses two contrasting words here.

- He says one person "observes"—and soon forgets.
- The other "looks into" and continues—he obeys the Word of God.

"Beholding" or "observing" means a casual glance. "Looking into" means a careful gaze. It's the same word used when the disciples raced to the empty tomb, and bending over, they looked into—they peered intently into the darkness, eyes set, searching, trying to see everything, looking steadfastly.

ACTION POINT That is the way you're to look into the Word of God: not just a casual glance, but a steadfast looking into the Word and a careful examination of the Word. Pick it up, read it, study it, scrutinize it.

15

Trust in the LORD with all your heart, and lean not on your own understanding; In all your ways acknowledge Him, and He shall direct your paths.

PROVERBS 3:5-6

A fine expositor of the Word of God, A.C. Dickson, once said:

When we depend upon organization, we get what organization can do. When we depend upon education, we get what education can do. When we depend on money, we get what money can do. When we depend on singing and preaching, we get what singing and preaching can do. But when we depend upon prayer, we get what God can do.

Oh, what this world needs is what God can do! What our cities need is what God can do! What your home needs is what God can do! What our churches need is what God can do! You don't have a need in your life that earnest, persistent, believing prayer could not supply. There is not a sin in your life that effectual, fervent prayer would not have prevented.

"Then He spoke a parable to them, that men always ought to pray and not lose heart" (Luke 18:1). "And let us not grow weary while doing good, for in due season we shall reap if we do not lose heart" (Galatians 6:9). "Continue earnestly in prayer, being vigilant in it with thanksgiving" (Colossians 4:2).

Sometimes, because God has a gracious purpose, God delays. "Therefore the LORD will wait, that He may be gracious to you; and therefore He will be exalted, that He may have mercy on you. For the LORD is a God of justice; blessed are all those who wait for Him" (Isaiah 30:18). God's delays are not denials.

ACTION POINT Are you depending on what God can do? Are you depending on prayer? May God enable you to find a holy purpose and continue with God in prayer until that purpose is realized.

16

> Confess your trespasses to one another, and pray for one another, that you may be healed. The effective, fervent prayer of a righteous man avails much.
>
> **JAMES 5:16**

Most of us are not very good at confessing our faults. We're pretty good at criticizing our friends, and we are very good at castigating our foes; but we're also very good about concealing our faults, right?

To err is human, and to cover it up is, too. We don't want anybody to know we have any faults. But let me tell you something: if you study the history of revival, you will find out that great revivals are not necessarily marked with great singing or great preaching, but with great confession of sin—not only to God, but also to one another. Where God's people are broken, God seems to move. Think of the things that can take place when we confess our faults.

When we go to our brother and say, "I have sinned against God and I have sinned against you, and I want to make that right," don't you know, dear friend, that heaven begins to rejoice? The angels begin to sing, because there is fellowship and reconciliation.

ACTION POINT Is there something God is bringing to your mind right now that you need to confess to Him? Is there a confession you need to make to someone else? When a wrong has been done, there is no reconciliation until there is confession.

17

> You lust and do not have. You murder and covet and cannot obtain. You fight and war. Yet you do not have because you do not ask.
>
> **JAMES 4:2**

A little girl once heard the choir singing that song "God Is Still on the Throne." She didn't understand it quite correctly and told someone the choir was singing "God is still on the phone." Well, He is! Thankfully, we have a heavenly hotline. The one who scooped out the seas, heaped up the mountains, and flung out the stars, the omnipotent God, has invited us to talk with Him.

More things are wrought by prayer than this world dreams of. Prayer, dear friend, is not just getting ready for Christian service—prayer is Christian service. And you are serving God when you pray. I serve God more when I pray than when I preach. You can do more than pray after you pray, but you can do no more than pray until you pray...that is, in order to be effective for Almighty God. This is what God is saying.

Prayer—the ability for you and I to talk with God—is the greatest Christian privilege. The omnipotent God has invited us to talk with Him, and He answers our prayers. There is no possible way I could overstate the importance of prayer.

ACTION POINT Prayer is our greatest privilege and our greatest power. But it's also the Christian's greatest failure. We do not have because we do not ask! May God forgive us! I pray that you will never underestimate the importance of prayer.

april 18

> Brethren, if a man is overtaken in any trespass, you who are spiritual restore such a one in a spirit of gentleness, considering yourself, lest you also be tempted.
>
> **GALATIANS 6:1**

Have you ever noticed that sometimes when a new convert comes down the aisle, especially if he's been a notorious sinner, everybody watches him like a hawk? Well, the first thing you know, if he slips back into his old world, so many of the Christians say, "Uh huh, just as I thought. Look at him—look how he failed." And rather than helping him, it seems as though they put their collective heel on his head and push him down further into the mud.

The Church's fellowship should not be frozen together by formalism, nor wired together by organization, nor rusted together by tradition. We should be melted together by prayer—praying for one another. I want your home blessed by prayer. I want your estranged children brought back by prayer. I want your weak will made strong by prayer. I want your needs met by prayer. I want you to have victory over the world, the flesh, and the devil by prayer. And James says that we have not because we ask not. Your friends need your prayers—pray one for another. I need your prayers. You need my prayers. Oh, God grant that we might pray with fervency and frequency and fruitfulness!

ACTION POINT Someone has said that the Christian army is the only army in the world that shoots its wounded. God forgive us. We are not to criticize. We are to help, lift, and boost our fellow believers. "Confess your faults one to another and pray one for another" is the command we should obey. We must uphold one another in prayer.

19

> Confess your trespasses to one another, and pray for one another, that you may be healed. The effectual, fervent prayer of a righteous man availeth much.
>
> **JAMES 5:16 (KJV)**

These words, *effectual* and *fervent*, are a translation of one Greek word. We have two words in English, but one word in the Greek. And it literally means "stretched out." The idea is like a horse who is jumping over a barricade, and that horse is stretched out as it leaps over. Or it's like an athlete who is running for the goal—he bursts through the tape, and stretches himself out for the goal.

James says that is the way we are to pray. We are to be striving for the goal. We are to be eager, earnest, fervent, and impassioned in our prayers. God forgive our cold, lukewarm, good/evil, milquetoast, take-it-or-leave-it prayers! Our prayers are to be effectual; they are to be fervent. They are to be on fire, stretched out—and by stretched out I don't mean stretched out on your bed, half asleep. That is not what James is talking about at all. He's talking about prayer that is intense.

When we give without sacrifice, pray without fasting, and witness without tears, is it any wonder we sow without results?

ACTION POINT How God has convicted my heart as I've studied the book of James! I've had to bow my head, confess my sin and say, "God, forgive my cold, lukewarm, indifferent prayers. I want to learn how to pray effectively, fervently, as James taught us to pray." What does James mean when he talks about the conditions that we should meet? He's talking about the intensity of the asking. That's the kind of prayer that brings results.

20

Can a man take fire to his bosom, and his clothes not be burned?
PROVERBS 6:27

The walls of decency are decaying. Look what's happening to us: pornography stares you in the face as if a broken sewer line were overflowing in the media. Evolution is in, homosexuality is in, murderous abortion is in, and God is out. We have ceased to be shocked. What used to amaze us now simply amuses us. What was horrible yesterday is acceptable today, and has become a stepping stone for something worse tomorrow.

But when they come under fire for the content of what they produce, filmmakers and TV executives tell us that what kids watch in movies or TV doesn't affect them. Why would a corporation spend hundreds of thousands of dollars for one minute of television time to showcase a product if what is seen has no effect on the viewer? You can't tell me that people sitting and watching some sex-saturated show for one hour are not going to be affected. Of course they are! We are affected by what we see. As a matter of fact, what we see makes us what we are. Do not buy into this foolishness!

The walls have fallen, and it is time that we open our eyes and see. My dear friend, aren't you glad that, as God's children, we have His protection? Aren't you glad that He has given us His letter—His holy Word? Jesus said, "Behold, I give you the authority to trample on serpents and scorpions, and over all the power of the enemy, and nothing shall by any means hurt you" (Luke 10:19).

ACTION POINT There's an old saying: "The eyes are the window to the soul." Job vowed in Job 31:1, "I have made a covenant with my eyes." God has given you individual freedom. It is your responsibility to set a guard over your eyes and what they take in.

21

Now these are the ones sown among thorns; they are the ones who hear the word, and the cares of this world, the deceitfulness of riches, and the desires for other things entering in, choke the word, and it becomes unfruitful.

MARK 4:18-19

People have many misconceptions and illusions about money. Money can buy some things but not others. It can buy marriage, but it can't buy love. It can buy four years in college, but it can't buy an education. Money can hire a doctor, but it can't make you well. Money can take you almost anywhere except to Heaven. It can buy almost anything except happiness.

Some people think money means security. But there's no security in money. It fades away. Do you want to know how rich you really are? Add up everything you have that money cannot buy and that death cannot take away. Then you will know how rich you are.

"Let the lowly brother glory in his exaltation, but the rich in his humiliation, because as a flower of the field he will pass away" (James 1:9-10). James tells the rich man to rejoice that God has opened his eyes to a new perspective, to see new prosperity. He is rich, but this time he is truly rich. He discovers that he, like the poor man, is a spiritual millionaire in Christ.

"The rich and the poor have this in common, The LORD is the maker of them all" (Proverbs 22:2). Isn't it great that the ground around the cross is level? In Jesus, we are all one, all fabulously wealthy in the Lord Jesus Christ.

ACTION POINT The Bible speaks of "the deceitfulness of riches" because earthly treasures can be wiped away so easily. Are you putting your trust and hope in things of this world or in things of eternal value?

22

> Therefore, if anyone is in Christ, he is a new creation; old things have passed away; behold, all things have become new.
>
> **2 CORINTHIANS 5:17**

When I first got saved, I learned about Jesus in the Bible, and that was wonderful to me. And then as I began to live the Christian life, I would see what Jesus would do in the lives of other people. I saw Jesus in history and Jesus in action, and that was wonderful. Then as I studied more, I began to learn about Jesus in Heaven, seated at the right hand of God the Father, ruling and reigning from His throne, and that was wonderful.

Jesus is in the Bible, Jesus is in history, and Jesus is in Heaven, but—here's the great truth—Jesus Christ lives in me. "...the glory of this mystery...which is Christ in you, the hope of glory" (Colossians 1:27). He possesses me. I am His purchased possession, and therefore, I am under new management.

When we were saved, God put a mark on us. That mark is the Holy Spirit. After we have believed, we have been sealed with the Holy Spirit.

ACTION POINT If you have made Jesus your Lord and Savior, He lives within you. You can rejoice today with the apostle Paul who said in Colossians 1:27, "To them God willed to make known what are the riches of the glory of this mystery among the Gentiles: which is Christ in you, the hope of glory."

23

It is easier for a camel to go through the eye of a needle, than for a rich man to enter the kingdom of God.

MARK 10:25

Around the walls of Jerusalem and other Bible-era cities, there were small, low gates they called the "Eye of a Needle" to keep people from riding through at night. A person could get through, but camels could not easily go through. The camel would have to get down on his knees and have his entire load taken off his back.

The reason it is so difficult for a rich man to get to Heaven is that he, like the rest of us, has to get low—humble himself—like that camel and get that burden off his back. You can often tell a lot about a person by his attitude toward money. One marriage counselor estimates 80% of all divorces in America have money mismanagement, in some way or other, at the root.

Some people believe money can buy security. But the Bible speaks of the deceitfulness of riches, which can be wiped out in an instant. Jeremiah 9:23-24 says, "'Let not the wise man glory in his wisdom, let not the mighty man glory in his might, nor let the rich man glory in his riches; but let him who glories glory in this; that he understands and knows Me, that I am the LORD, exercising lovingkindness, judgment, and righteousness in the earth. For in these I delight,' says the LORD."

ACTION POINT It is not wrong to have money. You are not especially holy if you're poor, and you are not ungodly if you're rich. Both wealth and poverty can create stumbling blocks. Rich or poor, you must rely upon Christ alone.

24

How long, you simple ones, will you love simplicity? For scorners delight in their scorning, and fools hate knowledge.
PROVERBS 1:22

A Greek statesman and orator named Demosthenes was once addressing a bored and listless audience, so he told them a story:

Once there was a man struggling with a great load. Along came another man with a donkey and said, "Rent my donkey, and he'll carry your load." He did. Later, as they tried to find relief from the hot sun, they began to argue over who owned the donkey's shade.

At this point, Demosthenes walked off the stage. The audience became agitated, wanting to know how the argument was resolved. Demosthenes returned to the stage and said, "Earlier, I was talking about issues of life and death, and you were bored. But now you're all worked up about who owns the shade of a donkey!"

What are the marks of a simple person? He loves simplicity—a happy, easy-go-lucky lifestyle. No responsibilities, no problems. He has no real, serious thoughts. That means he lacks understanding, and he needs to come to God's Word to get understanding. He's not going to know the truths of God's Word. He is led easily. "The simple believes every word, but the prudent considers well his steps" (Proverbs 14:15). The Hebrew word for "simple" means "open." The simple person is what we would call *gullible*. Lastly, he's liable for judgment. He doesn't see that there's a death to die, a judgment to face, a God to honor.

ACTION POINT Demosthenes' audience was a simple-minded bunch. They tuned out issues of serious truth, but were entranced with the trivial. In an age in which we're covered by trivia in our media, what are you tuned into?

25

> How much better to get wisdom than gold! And to get understanding is to be chosen rather than silver.
>
> **PROVERBS 16:16**

I was interested in a story about several billion dollars being physically moved from one bank to another. And there to protect the money was an army of one hundred policemen and guards—all with guns, tear gas, and all forms of electronic communications—because, of course, everybody wants money, don't they? People would do anything to get their hands on that money.

If they had a truckload of wisdom going down the street, how many policemen do you think they would need to guard it? I wonder how many people would have said, "That's what I want more than silver, more than gold, more than rubies. I want wisdom."

"Then I said: 'Wisdom is better than strength. Nevertheless the poor man's wisdom is despised, and his words are not heard. Words of the wise, spoken quietly, should be heard rather than the shout of a ruler of fools. Wisdom is better than weapons of war; but one sinner destroys much good'" (Ecclesiastes 9:16-18).

The Lord came to King Solomon and said, "I'll give you anything you want, anything you ask for." Solomon asked for wisdom. "Then God said to Solomon: 'Because this was in your heart, and you have not asked riches or wealth or honor or the life of your enemies, nor have you asked long life—but have asked wisdom and knowledge for yourself, that you may judge My people over whom I have made you king—wisdom and knowledge are granted to you; and I will give you riches and wealth and honor, such as none of the kings have had who were before you, nor shall any after you have the like'" (2 Chronicles 1:11-12).

ACTION POINT Begin today to seek after wisdom with the same intensity and commitment as you would seek after money.

26

For the message of the cross is foolishness to those who are perishing, but to us who are being saved, it is the power of God.

1 CORINTHIANS 1:18

I once met a lawyer on an airplane. We began to talk about what we like to read. I said, "I read newspapers, books, journals, devotional studies, but primarily the Bible."

He said, "If you don't read any further than that, how do you know what to talk about when you speak to people?"

I said, "Sir, man has only three problems: sin, sorrow, and death."

He answered, "There are more than that."

I replied, "No, only three."

"Oh," he said, "there are other problems."

I said, "All right, tell me another."

He thought for a long time, came back, and said, "Man has only three problems."

That's true. And the cross of Jesus Christ is the only answer to those three problems. You could give me all of the wisdom of this world, but there is no other answer apart from the cross. The message of the cross is foolishness to human ego. But all that human pride calls "wisdom," God calls foolishness. And all that God calls wisdom, the world calls foolishness.

ACTION POINT The Jews look for a sign—it is the cross. The Greeks want wisdom—it is the cross. To this world it is foolishness, but to God it is not foolishness. Now, thank God for the message of the cross!

27

Behold, I stand at the door and knock. If anyone hears My voice and opens the door, I will come in to him and dine with him, and he with Me.

REVELATION 3:20

A man once told me, "Back in the Depression, we had three meals a day. We had oatmeal for breakfast, cornmeal for dinner, and no meal for supper."

You may feel like that. You may not feel as if you have much now. But I don't care what is set on your table today, friend, listen—when you become a Christian, whether or not you have a freezer full of filet mignon, it makes no difference. There's Someone else who prepares a table before you in the presence of your enemies, and He is the Lord Jesus Christ. As a Christian, you eat at the King's table.

We are joint heirs with Jesus—"heirs of God, and joint heirs with Christ" (Romans 8:17). "For you know the grace of our Lord Jesus Christ, that though He was rich, yet for your sakes He became poor, that you through His poverty might become rich" (2 Corinthians 8:9). "I thank my God always concerning you for the grace of God which was given to you by Christ Jesus, that you were enriched in everything by Him in all utterance and all knowledge" (1 Corinthians 1:4-5).

ACTION POINT If you have opened the door to Him, you feast in Him. You are in the Lord's fellowship. You sit at His table! And no matter how poor you are, you eat with the King! Open your heart's door to the Lord Jesus Christ.

April 28

> Will You not revive us again, That Your people may rejoice in You?
> **PSALM 85:6**

We must face the grim fact that America is in danger. Whether you like it or not, that is true. I believe that America has a general trend toward the likes of Sodom and Gomorrah. And I believe the wrath of God is in the imminent foreground for America unless we repent. We are losing our freedom in America by degrees every day that we live, and freedom is like help: you must lose it, sometimes, in order for it to be appreciated.

People say the decline of a nation occurs in a cycle of nine "from-to" steps. People go from:

- Bondage to spiritual faith
- Spiritual faith to courage
- Courage to liberty
- Liberty to abundance
- Abundance to selfishness
- Selfishness to complacency
- Complacency to apathy
- Apathy to dependence
- Dependence back again to bondage

And the only answer to militant godlessness is militant godliness. What we need in America is a sweeping revival of the Christian religion—I'm talking about the old-time religion that made America the great nation that she is.

ACTION POINT This cycle is being revealed in today's current status. But it is time that some of us took our place and prayed for God to send a mighty revival, and for us to return to Him. It is not too late with God!

29

> And do not grieve the Holy Spirit of God, by whom you were sealed for the day of redemption. Let all bitterness, wrath, anger, clamor, and evil speaking be put away from you, with all malice.
>
> **EPHESIANS 4:30-31**

Bitterness creates a climate for the devil. Did you know the devil is bitter? In Revelation 12:17, you find the devil, pictured as a dragon, pursuing the nation Israel. The devil has bitterness, a vendetta against God's holy people, and he is pursuing. He's trying any way he can to hurt them.

To be filled with the Spirit of God means that there's not one room in the temple of your life where He's out of bounds; there's not one closet He doesn't have a key to. You are filled with the Spirit in your sex life, in your business life, in your political life, in your church life, in your social life, in your money, in your exercise, in your sleep, in your eating, in your lying down, in your waking up. If there's room for Satan, the Spirit is grieved and you're not filled with the Spirit. Repentance, resistance ,and renewal. Don't try to repent until you're honest in facing your sin. Don't try to resist until you've repented. Don't try to be filled until you resist, until you choose against Satan and yield to God's blessed Holy Spirit.

I've seen some Christians with bitterness in their hearts. I don't know where they got it; evidently someone hurt them. But the real problem is, there's a root of bitterness down in their hearts. In this, they are like the devil.

ACTION POINT Are you bitter? If so, in that regard, you are like the devil. If you're not careful, before long you're going to be full of the devil. Don't let another day go by without bringing that bitterness to God and asking Him to help you release it.

30

> Now this is the confidence that we have in Him, that if we ask anything according to His will, He hears us.
>
> **1 JOHN 5:14**

Do you know why our prayers sometimes are not answered? We are saying, "Not Thy will, but mine be done." Let me tell you something: prayer is not some exercise where you talk God into doing what He doesn't want to do. You'll never do that. Prayer is not bending God's will to fit your will. Prayer is finding the will of God and getting in on it. Do you know where man got into trouble? In the Garden of Eden, when the first Adam said, "Not Thy will, but mine be done."

Our problem is that we are so unbroken, so haughty, and so arrogant. We come strutting into the presence of God. No wonder God doesn't answer our prayers! "Therefore submit to God. Resist the devil and he will flee from you" (James 4:7). Are you submitted to God? Is His will your will? Do you love, more than anything else today, to do the will of God? Prayer is not for rebels. James says, "You ask and do not receive, because you ask amiss, that you may spend it on your pleasures" (James 4:3). Therefore submit to God.

Oh, my dear friends, when we begin to take the Lordship of Jesus Christ seriously, then our prayers are going to be answered!

ACTION POINT Thank God for the second Adam, the Lord Jesus, who prayed in another garden, saying, "Father, if it is Your will, take this cup away from Me; nevertheless not My will, but Yours, be done" (Luke 22:42). Are you submitted to the will of God?

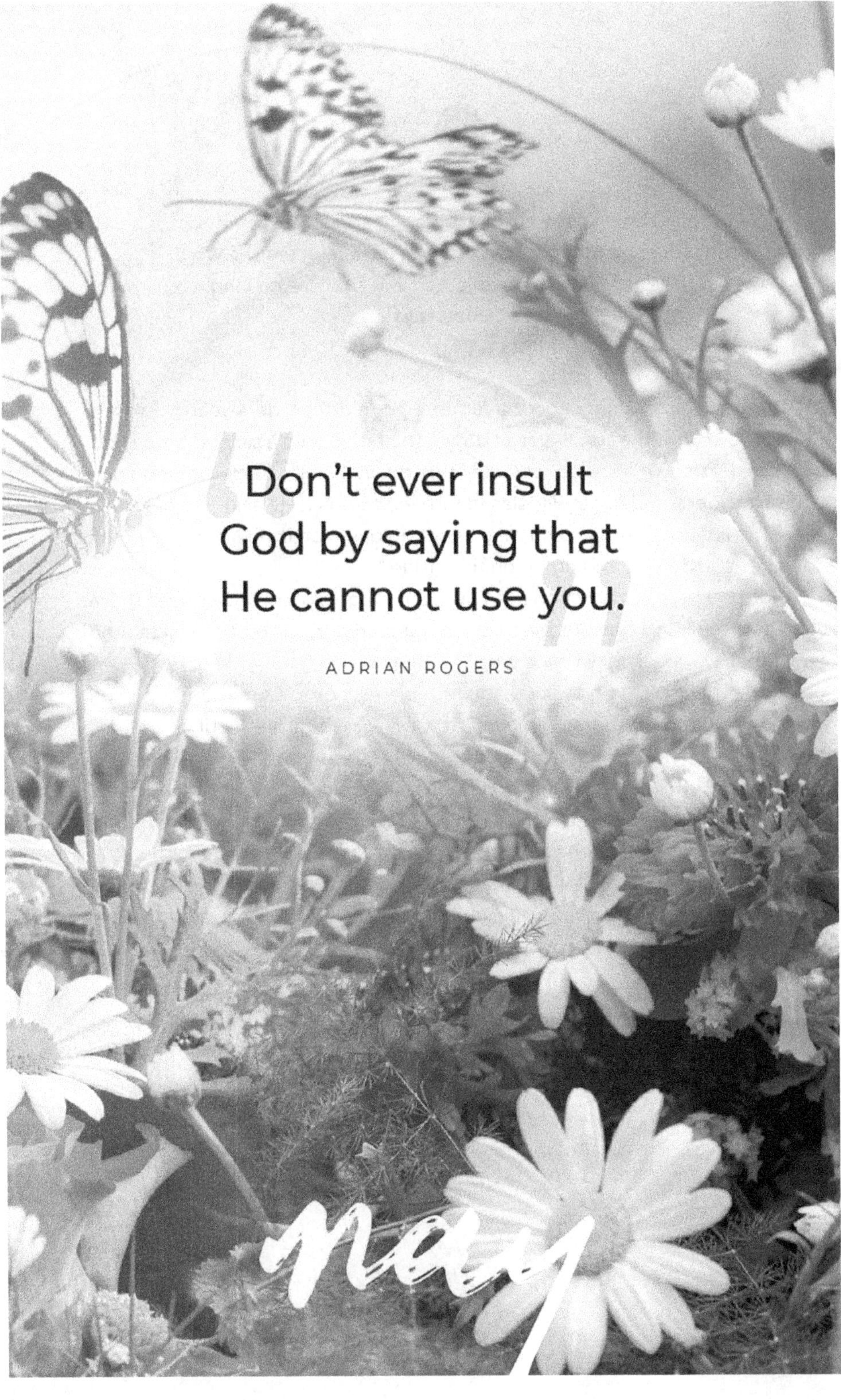
Don't ever insult
God by saying that
He cannot use you.
ADRIAN ROGERS
may

May 1

> For rebellion is as the sin of witchcraft, and stubbornness is as iniquity and idolatry. Because you have rejected the word of the Lord, He also has rejected you from being king.
>
> **1 SAMUEL 15:23**

There is a classic story about a father who told his little 4-year-old son to sit down, but the son didn't sit down. The father said a second time, "Son, I said sit down." The boy still didn't sit down. Finally, the father took him by the shoulders, and forcefully placed him in the chair. He said, "Now, son, sit there!" The little boy answered, "I may be sitting down on the outside, but—" he added defiantly, "I'm standing up on the inside!"

A lot of us are in that mode. While we may grudgingly get under those authorities that God has put over us, we are standing up on the inside. And many times we speak in ways we wish we hadn't.

A rebellious spirit is not always discernible except to God and the person who has it. Around the dinner table, when you begin to carp and criticize school principals, teachers, policemen, pastors, parents, presidents, or whatever it is you do, do you know what you are building in your children? A spirit of rebellion! It's going to come back on you. You're going to have a little rebel on your hands, and you'll say, "What happened? Why will not this person submit to authority?"

God wants His people to live with kingdom authority, but we will never be over those things that God has put under us until we are willing to get under those things that God has put over us.

ACTION POINT Is there some area in your life where you're "standing up on the inside"? If on the inside you still harbor a rebellious spirit, you are not really obeying.

May 2

Now therefore, I pray, if I have found grace in Your sight, show me now Your way, that I may know You and that I may find grace in Your sight. And consider that this nation is Your people.

EXODUS 33:13

There are two ways you can know God: casually or intimately. You can know about God, or you can know God. To know "about" God is to know His works. To know God intimately is to know His way. And how sad it will be in the resurrection to meet a God face to face, whom we have not known heart to heart.

Moses asked to know God intimately. But most people know God on the first level. All they know are the works of God. They know what God does, but they don't know the ways of God. Not everybody—even among those who claim to be saved—knows God intimately. They don't know who God is.

Now that brings a question: Does God have favorites? No, but He does have intimates. And even in the New Testament you will find there was that little trinity of disciples, Peter, James, and John, who were not the favorites of the Lord Jesus, but were His intimates. How would you like to be on intimate terms with God? How would you like for God to show you His ways? Knowing the ways of God will bring peace to your troubled soul and bring stability, victory, and tranquility into your life.

ACTION POINT As you go through your day, ask God to show you His ways and to reveal to you how they are in contrast to the way the world thinks. Align your thoughts with His ways—you learn His ways by reading His Word.

3

He made known His ways to Moses,
His acts to the children of Israel.

PSALM 103:7

Rest in the LORD, and wait patiently for Him; do not fret because of him who prospers in his way, because of the man who brings wicked schemes to pass.

PSALM 37:7

In the book of Acts, Peter and James were both put in prison for preaching the gospel. But James had his head cut off while Peter was miraculously delivered out of the same prison. Did God love Peter more than He loved James?

Peter preached on the Day of Pentecost. He stood up for the Lord Jesus Christ, and 3,000 souls were saved. (Acts 2) But Stephen preached, and he got 3,000 stones—they stoned him to death! (Acts 7:59)

If all you see are the works of God, you are going to be hopelessly confused. If you don't have a deeper insight into the ways of God, you're going to be pushing the panic button all the time. You will never be able to rest until you know God intimately. To know God intimately is the way of tranquility. There is nothing that will bring rest to your troubled soul like an intimate knowledge of God! If all you see is what God does in this world, you are going to be one nervous Christian—until you learn to know the ways of God.

ACTION POINT To know God intimately begins with two things: time in His Word and time in prayer. You know God intimately by directly dealing with God. You can't know anyone whom you don't spend time with. Commit today to spending time in His Word and in prayer.

4

"For My thoughts are not your thoughts,
nor are your ways My ways," says the LORD.
ISAIAH 55:8

Remember Psalm 103:7? "He made known His ways to Moses, His acts to the children of Israel." If all you see is what God does, and you don't know God intimately, then you will never have rest. You will have the spiritual heebie-jeebies all your life.

"And He said, 'My Presence will go with you, and I will give you rest'" (Exodus 33:14). You see, the children of Israel were doing fine as long as the works of God pleased them. As long as God was opening the Red Sea, giving them water out of a rock, and feeding them with manna from heaven, they were doing fine—as long as the works of God pleased them. But then when God didn't do things just the way they thought God ought to, they pushed the panic button.

There is an oft-repeated illustration about an old bookmark. On one side, it was beautifully embroidered and said, "God is Love." But on the other side, it was just a mass of tangled threads. In order to have it embroidered on one side, you must have all those threads on the other side.

Now, some people only look at it from the back side, and they see only the mess. They don't know the ways of God and that God is love. But you see, our ways and God's ways are so different. You'll never have peace—that deep peace—until you understand that the ways of God are often confusing by the standards of human wisdom. While we see events like a tangled tapestry, He sees far into the future.

ACTION POINT What issue in your life do you need to surrender to Him today? Confess: "I do not understand, Oh God, but I know you are faithful. You are trustworthy."

5

> Now godliness with contentment is great gain.
>
> **1TIMOTHY 6:6**

Dr. Vance Havner said, "I'm often amused and amazed at the way we equate Christianity with success, popularity, and prosperity. We may not admit it, but we use the same old gauge the world uses, except we employ religious language. It would appear that gain is godliness with us, in spite of Paul's formula that godliness plus contentment equals prosperity."

So often we say that money will not satisfy, but that all depends on what we're trying to satisfy. The problem is not that money doesn't satisfy. The greater danger is that it does—that you have and you are satisfied. If you are satisfied with the things of this world, that's a dangerous place to be spiritually.

Herbert Henry Farmer wrote: "To Jesus the terrible thing about having wrong values in life and pursuing wrong things, is not that you are doomed to bitter disappointment, but that you are not; not that you do not achieve what you want, but that you do." If you can be satisfied with the things of this world, if you can have Canaan without the presence, victories, and angels clearing the way, that is a very dangerous thing.

To know God intimately is tranquility, stability, and necessity. Don't you take prosperity, or victory, or a land flowing with milk and honey, or anything as a substitute for knowing God intimately.

ACTION POINT The Apostle Paul had one of the best pedigrees any person could have. Yet he wrote in Philippians 3:7-8, "But what things were gain to me, these I have counted loss for Christ. Yet indeed I also count all things loss for the excellence of the knowledge of Christ Jesus my Lord, for whom I have suffered the loss of all things, and count them as rubbish, that I may gain Christ."

6

"Go up to a land flowing with milk and honey; for I will not go up in your midst, lest I consume you on the way, for you are a stiff-necked people."....Then he [Moses] said to Him, "If Your presence does not go with us, do not bring us up from here."

EXODUS 33:3, 15

Moses is saying, "God, if You're not going, I'm not going."

St. Augustine once asked this hypothetical question, as if God were speaking to him: "I'll give you anything you want, every pleasure you desire. Nothing will be withheld. You will live forever. Every desire of your heart will be met. Nothing will be a sin to you. You can have whatever you want—with this one exception: you will never see My face." Would you take that proposition? St. Augustine said, "If a chill went over your soul when you heard that phrase, 'You will never see My face,' thank God for that chill. That is the most precious thing about you, because it means you have the pure love of God."

God offered to send the Israelites along their way with the protection of an angel. He promised them victory in the Promised Land. But Moses said: "I don't want Canaan without you. I don't want an angel to guide us. I don't want victory. I don't want milk and honey. I want You, God."

How do you know God intimately? You're not going to know God intimately by human reason. You know God intimately by direct dealing with God.

ACTION POINT Is there anything today you want more than God's presence? Think carefully. If so, then that thing—whatever or whoever it is—is an idol. Abandon it. Dismantle that idol's altar in your life.

And you, fathers, do not provoke your children to wrath, but bring them up in the training and admonition of the Lord.
EPHESIANS 6:4

Be the kinds of fathers and mothers that children can honor. Love them. Love is not giving your children what they want—it is giving them what they need. Love them by blessing them, comforting them, listening to them. Love them steadfastly and constantly. Love them by limiting them—your child needs limits! Love them with your prayers, and love them by lifting them. Wise encouragement is better than lavish praise.

Children need encouragement like a plant needs water. They need it over and over again. Catch them doing something right! Let them know through your encouragement that you believe in them. Let your speech affirm them. Be positive. Constantly encourage them.

Now there is nothing wrong with praise, but encouragement is twice as strong. Encouragement teaches your child, "I can earn approval. If I will do good, then they will approve of me. When my performance is good, the approval rate goes up. When my performance is bad, my approval rate goes down, and my self-image goes down with it."

Encouragement looks at a child and values that child—not primarily for what the child achieved, but for the child who is achieving it.

ACTION POINT I would like to be the kind of a dad, and I know you'd like to be the kind of parent that the Bible speaks of when it says, "Children, obey your parents in the Lord, for this is right" (Ephesians 6:1). I would like to make it a lot easier for my children to do just that...wouldn't you?

8

> Honor your father and your mother, that your days may be long upon the land which the LORD your God is giving you.
>
> **EXODUS 20:12**

When we observe Mother's Day or Father's Day, we are obeying this Scripture. You can honor your father and mother in three ways: obey them when you're young, care for them when they are old, and honor them at all times. How do you give them honor?

Show them respect. "Every one of you shall revere his mother and his father, and keep My Sabbaths: I am the LORD your God" (Leviticus 19:3). The word "fear" here is the same as we use for "the fear of God"—it means reverence. You're to revere your parents. Express gratefulness. Give them thanks. Learn to develop the attitude of gratitude. Have you thanked your parents for all that they've done? Listen to their counsel. "My son, hear the instruction of your father, and do not forsake the law of your mother; for they will be a graceful ornament on your head, and chains about your neck" (Proverbs 1:8-9). Show your parents love. Think of what you owe your parents. They gave you life! Their blood flows through your veins. I'm convinced that the closest thing to God's love is the love of a mother.

ACTION POINT Now would be a good time to call, text, or write a letter to your mother and father and tell them how grateful you are for them. I'll tell you one thing: they will read it over and over again. And when they die and you're going through their things, you'll find that letter tucked away in their most treasured possessions. Do it, rather than saying "I wish that I had." And if your parents are not living, give them honor and thank God for their memory.

9

> The father of the righteous will greatly rejoice, and he who begets a wise child will delight in him. Let your father and your mother be glad, and let her who bore you rejoice.
>
> **PROVERBS 23:24-25**

Children are extensions of their parents. When I see my children do something good, godly and worthy, that gives me such great joy. Third John 1:4 says, "I have no greater joy than to hear that my children walk in truth." Before my parents went to Heaven, one of the greatest joys of my life was to do something that would cause them to rejoice and say, "Adrian, we're proud of you." I am so grateful for that.

"Honor your father and your mother, that your days may be long upon the land which the Lord your God is giving you" (Exodus 20:12). This is the fifth of the Ten Commandments, and God puts the Ten Commandments into two categories: the first four deal with our relationship to God, then the last six deal with our relationship to one another. And God starts the last six with our relationship to our parents.

They are the first people we meet. If we can't honor our father and our mother, how can we honor strangers? In later commandments God tells us not to steal, kill, or commit adultery, but first He tells us to honor our father and mother.

ACTION POINT Reflect on your life today. Does your life honor God and give your parents joy? Does it gladden their hearts—and His? Live in such a way as to cause your parents to stick out their chests a little bit—not in a prideful way, but in saying, "Thank God for my children." Your mother will have no greater joy than to know you are walking in the truth.

May 10

Therefore, a man shall leave his father and mother and be joined to his wife, and they shall become one flesh.

GENESIS 2:24

I have a friend with a wonderful Christian wife and two fine, godly sons, but one time one of the boys was really rude to his mother. The dad took the son aside and said, "Son, I want to tell you something. When you talked like that to your mother, you sinned against God because God says you're to honor your mother, so you're going to have to answer to God for that. And you sinned against your mother. She went down into the valley of the shadow of death to bring you life. That is so ungrateful for you to speak to your mother like that, and you are going to have to answer to her. But not only is she your mother, she is my wife, and you're not going to talk that way to my wife. So now you've not only got God to deal with, and her to deal with, you've got me to deal with, because you disrespected my wife."

What a lesson for a kid! I think it's one of the greatest I've ever heard of, to see a husband come to the protection of his wife, even if he has to take sides with her against his own child.

ACTION POINT This is the kind of teaching and training you should be giving your children. If you are a father, show them that a husband will protect his wife like this. It will be one of the greatest lessons you can teach them.

11

But his delight is in the law of the LORD; and in
His law he meditates day and night.

PSALM 1:2

Ted Koppel, ABC's original Nightline host for decades, once addressed the 1987 graduating class at Duke University. He said a mouthful to those students:

"In the place of truth we have discovered facts; for moral absolutes we have substituted moral ambiguity. We now communicate with everyone and say absolutely nothing. We have reconstructed the Tower of Babel, and it is a television antenna—a thousand voices producing a daily parody of democracy in which everyone's opinion is afforded equal weight, regardless of substance or merit. Indeed, it can even be argued that opinions of real weight tend to sink with barely a trace in television's ocean of banalities. What Moses brought down from Mount Sinai were not 'The Ten Suggestions.' They are commandments—are, not were. The sheer brilliance of the Ten Commandments is that they codify in a handful of words acceptable human behavior, not just for then or now, but for all time."

Mr. Koppel got it just right!

ACTION POINT It is a tragedy that The Ten Commandments have been removed from the walls of many public schools. But more important than being on the wall at the local school is that The Ten Commandments are being taught in your home and written upon the walls of your hearts and your children's hearts. Are you intentional about doing this?

12

But know this, that in the last days perilous times will come: For men will be lovers of themselves, lovers of money, boasters, proud, blasphemers, disobedient to parents, unthankful, unholy, unloving, unforgiving, slanderers, without self-control, brutal, despisers of good, traitors, headstrong, haughty, lovers of pleasure rather than lovers of God, having a form of godliness but denying its power. And from such people turn away!

2 TIMOTHY 3:1-5

If you claim to be a Christian but you dishonor your parents, all that you've got is a form of godliness. You do not have the real thing. Faith begins at home. If you can live for Jesus at home, you can live for Jesus anywhere. If you can't live for Jesus at home, it doesn't really matter where else you try to live for Jesus.

God gave Ten Commandments, but the fifth is the one with a promise: "Honor your father and your mother, that your days may be long upon the land which the LORD your God is giving you" (Exodus 20:12). Before God tells us "don't steal, don't kill, don't commit adultery," etc., He tells us to honor our fathers and mothers.

ACTION POINT I believe the respect and obedience a child shows his parents is a strong indication of how that child will turn out. Dwight L. Moody said, "I've lived 60 years, and I've learned one thing if I've learned nothing else: No man or woman who dishonors father or mother ever prospers." Be faithful in teaching your children this truth of life. Help guard them against becoming like the men Paul warned Timothy about in the "perilous times" of the "last days."

13

"For this reason a man shall leave his father and mother and be joined to his wife, and the two shall become one flesh." This is a great mystery, but I speak concerning Christ and the church.

EPHESIANS 5:31-32

Now wait a minute. Is Paul talking about a man and his wife or about Jesus and the church? Paul is talking about both.

In the Bible, the Church of the Lord Jesus Christ is called, figuratively and symbolically, "the bride." The Church is also referred to as a building, a holy temple, and sometimes "the body of Christ." (1 Corinthians 12:27) But sometimes the Church is described as a bride—"Then I, John, saw the holy city, New Jerusalem, coming down out of heaven from God, prepared as a bride adorned for her husband" (Revelation 21:2). And there are some wonderful truths that we can learn by thinking of the Church as the bride of the Lord Jesus Christ.

When it is right, marriage is one of the sweetest and most sublime things we know here on Earth. Of course, when it is wrong, it's very wrong, but I am not talking about that kind of marriage. I'm talking about marriage as God intended it to be. Then, the physical relationship, the psychological, and the spiritual relationship between a husband and a wife are but an illustration of the greater spiritual relationship of Christ and the Church.

ACTION POINT When I gave my heart to Jesus Christ, that meant I belong to Jesus Christ and to Him alone, and I must be true to Him—and you must be true to Him, too. Seek the Lord today to know how you can be a better picture of Christ and the Church in your marriage.

14

> And if it seems evil to you to serve the LORD, choose for yourselves this day whom you will serve, whether the gods which your fathers served that were on the other side of the River, or the gods of the Amorites, in whose land you dwell. But as for me and my house, we will serve the LORD.
>
> **JOSHUA 24:15**

It has always amazed me when critics say, "These evangelical Christians are trying to cram their values down the throats of other people."

In response, I want to ask: Who is it that redefined when life begins? Who is it that has changed the way Americans think about premarital sex? Who is telling us what is decent and what is not? Who wants to dictate when and where you can pray and when you can't? Are they not the same ones that want to decide who lives and who dies?

Why did God give us families? One, for living together. Children need families. Two, for learning. The Ten Commandments were given to the home—not to the school, the industry, or the government. They apply there also, but they're given primarily to the home. Three, for lasting. When the home begins to decay, it follows, like night follows day, the nation begins to decay.

ACTION POINT We have people out there who are trying to remold and remake society in their own image. It is time that God's people said, "Enough is enough!" Make this a time of prayer, for we are in a spiritual battle for the hearts and minds of our nation, neighbors, and loved ones.

May 15

> Train up a child in the way he should go,
> and when he is old he will not depart from it.
> **PROVERBS 22:6**

Some parents have almost put themselves in an early grave because they have a wayward child. And they have prayed, and sacrificed, and loved, and taught, and that child has done wrong anyway, and someone has taken Proverbs 22:6 and beaten the parents over the head with it.

Friend, this verse is a proverb. If you read the book of Proverbs and try to turn proverbs into promises, you will lose your faith! A proverb is a proverb, and a promise is a promise. A precept is a precept. A parable is a parable. A prophecy is a prophecy. You have to be careful. When you understand the Bible correctly, it is a wonderful book, but you have to be careful to understand it correctly.

There are proverbs that tell you the way to be wealthy. Does that mean that everybody who follows one of these proverbs is automatically going to be wealthy? If so, why are there godly people who are not wealthy? A proverb is a general principle, generally applied, bringing a general result—even our normal, natural proverbs. A proverb is a short sentence based on long experience.

ACTION POINT Instead of grabbing Proverbs as promises, ask God for discernment to understand their purpose. He desires us to "rightly divide the word of truth," not to use it as a club to beat up fellow believers. "Be diligent to present yourself approved to God, a worker who does not need to be ashamed, rightly dividing the word of truth" (2 Timothy 2:15).

16

A merry heart makes a cheerful countenance,
but by sorrow of the heart the spirit is broken.
PROVERBS 15:13

There are three things that animals don't do that humans do: One, animals don't blush. Mark Twain once wryly observed, "Man is the only animal who can blush—or needs to." Two, animals don't cry. Three, animals don't laugh. This tells me that man, made in the image of God, reflects the character of God. And God is a God of joy.

I'm not talking about unwholesome, cheap, coarse, degrading humor; the Bible warns against that. "But fornication and all uncleanness or covetousness, let it not even be named among you, as is fitting for saints; neither filthiness, nor foolish talking, nor coarse jesting, which are not fitting, but rather giving of thanks" (Ephesians 5:3-4). Crude jokes have no place.

But laughter comes innately! And if you really have the joy of the Lord in your heart, it's going to show up on your face.

When Proverbs 15:13 says "the spirit is broken," that spirit is the wellspring of life. That's the true inner man, and when that spirit is broken, the zest, the enthusiasm, the spark, the thrill, the fight is gone out of life. Having a merry heart is wonderful medicine. A merry heart is the sign of happiness. Happiness and joy are not the same thing, but they are first cousins. Joy is that constant presence of God, no matter what happens, but a merry heart is the ability to capture and enjoy those wonderful times of life—even to turn them to laughter.

ACTION POINT Does your face today reflect the joy of the Lord, or something else? Nehemiah 8:10 says, "The joy of the Lord is your strength." Decide today that you're going to choose joy rather than fear or despair. Memorize Psalm 16:11: "You will show me the path of life; in Your presence is fullness of joy; at Your right hand are pleasures forevermore."

May 17

If anyone among you thinks he is religious, and does not bridle his tongue but deceives his own heart, this one's religion is useless.

JAMES 1:26

"So then, my beloved brethren, let every man be swift to hear, slow to speak, slow to wrath" (James 1:19). We are supposed to be slow to wrath and anger, and the way to control your anger is to control your words. "A soft answer turns away wrath, but a harsh word stirs up anger" (Proverbs 15:1).

We must watch what we say, because one word builds upon another, and things can get worse. You'll have the snowball effect.

You might say, "Well, I can't control it." You can control it, and I can prove it. For example, sometimes a husband and wife are just snarling, fighting, snapping down each other's throat in an argument—and right then the phone rings. They can answer it so sweetly..."Hello!"

"A wrathful man stirs up strife, But he who is slow to anger allays contention" (Proverbs 15:18). "An angry man stirs up strife, and a furious man abounds in transgression" (Proverbs 29:22). "A quick-tempered man acts foolishly, and a man of wicked intentions is hated" (Proverbs 14:17). "He who answers a matter before he hears it, It is folly and shame to him" (Proverbs 18:13). Learn to alleviate your anger. You can control it, and you had better learn to control it. If you don't control it, you will be out of control.

ACTION POINT This week, memorize Proverbs 29:20: "Do you see a man hasty in his words? There is more hope for a fool than for him."

18

The LORD will open to you His good treasure, the heavens, to give the rain to your land in its season, and to bless all the work of your hand. You shall lend to many nations, but you shall not borrow.

DEUTERONOMY 28:12

You are the servant of whoever you're in debt to. God doesn't want you, His child, to be the borrower; He wants you to be the lender. God wants to bless His people above all the nations of the world, and He wants to give His people financial freedom. But so many people are in financial bondage! The devil wants to keep you in bondage, and he doesn't care what kind of bondage you're in.

Let me give you some marks of financial bondage. Maybe you charge everyday expenses on credit because of lack of funds. You put off paying a bill until next month. You borrow to pay fixed expenses; i.e. taxes, insurance, house payments. You become unaware of how much you owe. You have creditors calling on you about past-due bills. You take from your savings account to pay current bills. You make new loans to pay off your old ones. Maybe you and your spouse argue over finances. (You know, "'til debt do us part...") You begin to entertain an idea about being dishonest or unscrupulous about some financial dealing. And maybe you find it difficult to return God's tithe to God's house on God's day.

God doesn't want His people to be in this kind of place.

ACTION POINT Are you in financial bondage? God wants you out of that so you can serve Him freely. Today we are blessed to have a number of godly Christian ministries guiding believers to sound, biblical teaching and freedom from debt. If you are under financial stress, contact one of them today. The Lord Jesus said, "If the Son therefore shall make you free, you shall be free indeed" (John 8:36).

May 19

For our light affliction, which is but for a moment, is working for us a far more exceeding and eternal weight of glory, while we do not look at the things which are seen, but at the things which are not seen. For the things which are seen are temporary, but the things which are not seen are eternal.

2 CORINTHIANS 4:17-18

A man may say, "It's hard for me to have faith—I deal in reality." So, what is real? Your house? Your car? Your money? No, reality is not in something you can see, taste, touch, smell, or feel. Those things are not real because they are not lasting. Reality is in God. It is only when we put God first that we come in contact with reality.

If you're putting your trust in things you can see, touch and count, you're living in a world of illusion. The things that are seen are temporal; the things that are not seen are eternal. The only "real" things are those things that will last eternally.

My hope is built on nothing less
than Jesus' blood and righteousness;
I dare not trust the sweetest frame,
*but wholly lean on Jesus' name.**

ACTION POINT When we put God first, then we will come in contact with reality. Are you putting Him first? Is He more real to you than things that seem so rock solid? Look up Matthew 6:33 in your Bible and commit to living by seeking His kingdom first.

*"My Hope is Built on Nothing Less" — Edward Mote, 1834

20

Preach the word! Be ready in season and out of season. Convince, rebuke, exhort, with all longsuffering and teaching.

2 TIMOTHY 4:2

Something that really bothers me is to go to a church and hear a pastor stand up and preach without an open Bible. Or, maybe he will quote a text, and then close the Bible and make a speech. And it may be a wonderful oration, it may even be inspiring, but the people are not learning the Word of God.

What we need to do is read the Book. If we're going to do it the way they did it in the Bible, we must read it distinctly and then explain it. If I or anyone else preaches and you don't understand, then frankly, I have failed. You ought to come away saying, "Yes, the Bible says so. It's there in the Word, and I'm able to understand it." Sometimes we hear a preacher and say, "He must be brilliant—I didn't understand him!" But just 'cause a river is muddy doesn't mean it's deep. Do you know what was said about Jesus Christ? "The common people heard him gladly" (Mark 12:37b). The plain folks, the common folks. You didn't need a PhD to understand the Lord Jesus because Jesus took the Word of God, analyzed it, organized it, and expounded it so that people could understand.

Oh, how we need teachers who will do this! I believe there is a famine in the land today for that kind of preaching. That's the kind of preaching that will ultimately build great Christians.

ACTION POINT When you heed the Word of God, it's going to produce three things: first sorrow, then joy, and then obedience. Until you know Jesus, you will never really understand the Bible. And until you understand the Bible, you are not really ready to live.

May 21

> For I am persuaded that neither death nor life, nor angels nor principalities nor powers, nor things present nor things to come, nor height nor depth, nor any other created thing, shall be able to separate us from the love of God which is in Christ Jesus our Lord.
>
> **ROMANS 8:38-39**

Once upon a time, a wife borrowed her husband's brand new car, and then she had a wreck. She wasn't hurt, but the car was totaled. She felt awful. She reached into the glove compartment where they kept the insurance papers and got them out.

When she opened the papers, there was a note right in the midst of them. The note was written by her husband. I think it's one of the sweetest things I've ever heard: he had written, "Remember, sweetheart, it's you I love." Isn't that great? He was saying, "This car is not important. Honey, you are the important one." God has the same love for you and me. Whatever mess you may have made, God says, "It's you I love."

One of God's greatest gifts to you and to me is forgiveness. The Bible calls our sins a debt—"And forgive us our debts, as we forgive our debtors" (Matthew 6:12). We've been created to serve God, to love Him, and we have not done it. We've been brought into heaven's court, been sued for damages, and we cannot pay. We're cast into a debtor's prison, and the only way we'll be set free is to be forgiven. "But God demonstrates His own love toward us, in that while we were still sinners, Christ died for us" (Romans 5:8).

ACTION POINT Remember that: It's you God loves. I want to tell you, you may have wrecked your life, but God loves you. Whatever mistakes you may make today, you must believe that.

22

Come to Me, all you who labor and are heavy laden, and I will give you rest. Take My yoke upon you and learn from Me, for I am gentle and lowly in heart, and you will find rest for your souls. For My yoke is easy and My burden is light.

MATTHEW 11:28-30

In Numbers 21, God taught His people Israel that it is a painful thing to rebel against God. Now, the world doesn't believe that—the world believes it's a painful thing to serve God. I've heard it said so many times, "It's hard to be a Christian." Where did we get that idea? We didn't get it out of the Word of God! It is not hard to be a Christian.

It's not hard to believe Christ. We didn't have to wait for it, work for it, pray for it, or pay for it. And don't you try to add one scintilla of works to your salvation, "For by grace you have been saved through faith, and that not of yourselves; it is the gift of God, not of works, lest anyone should boast" (Ephesians 2:8-9). That's the Gospel, friend, and it is easy to understand. Little children understand it.

The Bible says, "The way of the unfaithful is hard" (Proverbs 13:15), but it is not hard to be a Christian. You might ask, "Do you mean there's no suffering?" But there is suffering in this world whether you are saved or lost. You're not going to get out of life unbent, unbloodied, or unbowed. But there is joy in the Lord Jesus Christ, and Jesus is the One who makes the sufferings of this life worth it all.

ACTION POINT If you are struggling and straining today to "lead the Christian life," then something is out of whack. Jesus said, "I will give you rest." Come to Him right now in humility, and lay down the heavy burden.

May 23

> The Lord is not slack concerning His promise, as some count slackness, but is longsuffering toward us, not willing that any should perish but that all should come to repentance.
>
> **2 PETER 3:9**

Suppose you got sick and the doctor examined you. And he said, "It's very serious, and you're going to die. There is a remedy, but it is so rare and valuable that enough of it to save you would cost a king's ransom."

And you said, "Doctor, I don't have any money."

Suppose the doctor said, "Let me see what I can do." He was gone for several days. When he came back his hair was disheveled, his eyes sunken back in his head, his face white, his beard grown out, his hands trembling, his clothing torn and blood-stained.

You'd say, "Where have you been? What happened to you?"

The doctor holds out a little vial and says, "Do you see this? I went to every foundation to secure this medicine for you. I withdrew my savings from the bank in order to purchase it for you, and I was in such a rush to get down here to your bedside that on the way I wrecked my car. The blood that you see on my shirt is the blood of my only son, who was with me. I've just come from the morgue where I left his dead and mangled body in order to bring this medicine to you. Here it is, take it, and you will live."

Suppose you took that vial, looked at it, and then dashed it on the floor. The contents ran out into the rug, never to be recovered. Suppose you then pointed your finger in the doctor's face and said, "If I die, it will be your fault."

ACTION POINT This is exactly what God has done for mankind. God offered His Son, but you must accept His gift of salvation. Have you accepted it?

24

For the time will come when they will not endure sound doctrine, but according to their own desires, because they have itching ears, they will heap up for themselves teachers; and they will turn their ears away from the truth, and be turned aside to fables.

2 TIMOTHY 4:3-4

There are some people who say, "I come to church on Sunday to feel good. I don't want some man up there ranting, raving, and pointing his finger at me, telling me I've got to repent and get right with God and all that business."

Billy Sunday, a great fire-and-brimstone preacher of the 19th century, preached in tent revival meetings across America. Once, after he'd preached a blistering message against sin, somebody said, "Billy, you'd better tone it down a little bit. You're rubbing the fur on the cat the wrong way." Billy replied, "Well, the old cat is headed towards Hell! If she'd turn around, I'd be rubbing it the right way."

Today, we seem to think that God has no right to punish sin. I have a conviction that if the Supreme Court of America could vote upon it, they would outlaw Hell as "cruel and unusual punishment." They would say, "God has no right to do that." Let me tell you something: it's not that God is too good to punish sin, it is that God is too good not to punish sin. It is the goodness of God, the righteousness of God, and the holiness of God which say that sin must be punished, and if you die and go to Hell it won't be God's fault—it will be your fault.

ACTION POINT Does the truth of God rub you the wrong way? Then it's time to turn around. When you turn around 180 degrees and go the opposite direction, do you know what that is a picture of? Repentance. If what God says is upsetting to you, it's up to you to be the one to turn around.

May 25

> So when Jesus had received the sour wine, He said, "It is finished!" And bowing His head, He gave up His spirit.
>
> **JOHN 19:30**

The 19th century evangelist Billy Sunday was born into poverty in Iowa. His father had been killed in the Civil War when Billy was only five weeks old. He spent some time in an orphanage. But because he was a natural-born athlete, he became a major-league baseball player for the "Chicago White Stockings"—known as the White Sox, today.

One day, on a street corner, he and some fellow ballplayers stopped to hear a Gospel team from a local mission. Billy Sunday was saved. His teammates and even his fans noticed the change in him.

Soon he left baseball to become an evangelist himself. He was one of the most celebrated preachers of the early 1900s. He dined with Presidents, but his greatest appeal was to the common folks who came to his revival meetings.

After a meeting ended one day, a young man who had been in the service and under great conviction found Billy Sunday and earnestly pleaded, "Oh Mr. Sunday! I need to be saved! What can I do to be saved?"

Billy said, "I'm sorry. You're too late." The young man said, "Oh, but I wanted to be saved. I should have been saved. What must I do to be saved?"

And Billy Sunday said, "You're too late to do anything to be saved, for Jesus has already done it all. It's finished. All you need to do is receive what He's already done." Then and there, he led the young man to Jesus.

ACTION POINT Upon the cross, with His last word, the Lord Jesus Christ cried out, "It is finished!" The work of redemption was done. What must you do to be saved? There's nothing more for you to do than to receive what Jesus has already done.

26

> He who believes in Him is not condemned; but he who does not believe is condemned already, because he has not believed in the name of the only begotten Son of God.
>
> **JOHN 3:18**

People don't go to Hell only because they lie, steal, or cheat. People also go to Hell because of unbelief. Unbelief is the major sin—the mother sin, the father sin, the sin out of which all other sins grow. It is the one sin that will damn you and send you to Hell.

Unbelief is a terrible, horrible sin. It's never an intellectual matter; it's always a moral matter. There is no greater sin than to aim the gun of unbelief at Jesus Christ on the cross, dying in agony and blood for you, and refuse to receive Him.

The Bible says, "Beware, brethren, lest there be in any of you an evil heart of unbelief in departing from the living God" (Hebrews 3:12). "He who believes in the Son of God has the witness in himself; he who does not believe God has made Him a liar, because he has not believed the testimony that God has given of His Son" (1 John 5:10).

ACTION POINT Can you think of any sin greater than to point the finger of unbelief at God and say, "You lie!"? It's not a matter of your brain; it's a matter of your heart. It's not your intellect you first must overcome, it's your will. Set stubbornness aside and say, "Just as I am...I come."

27

> Do not love the world or the things in the world. If anyone loves the world, the love of the Father is not in him.
>
> **1 JOHN 2:15**

It stands to reason: if you love health, you're going to hate germs. If you love flowers, you'll hate weeds. If you love cleanliness, you'll hate dirt. If you love God, you will hate sin.

There is nothing wrong with loving "the world," as in God's creative act: the birds, the bees, the flowers, the trees. God said, "It is good." So don't equate sinfulness with physical, material things. And when the Bible says, "Do not love the world," it's not talking about the world of people. The Bible says concerning that world in John 3:16, "For God so loved the world that He gave His only begotten Son..."

And still the Bible says, "Do not love the world or the things in the world." What, then, is worldliness, and why should a Christian not love this world?

There are three reasons:

- Because of the character of the world—what it is.
- Because of the corruption of the world—what it does.
- Because of the condemnation of the world—where it's headed.

There is a satanic system that the Bible calls "this world." What is the purpose of this world? To oppose the Word of God. "For all that is in the world—the lust of the flesh, the lust of the eyes, and the pride of life—is not of the Father but is of the world" (1 John 2:16).

ACTION POINT If we're not to love this world, what then, are we to love? Jesus tells us. "'You shall love the LORD your God with all your heart, with all your soul, and with all your mind.' This is the first and great commandment. And the second is like it: 'You shall love your neighbor as yourself'" (Matthew 22:37-39).

28

I say then: Walk in the Spirit, and
you shall not fulfill the lust of the flesh.
GALATIANS 5:16

By "flesh," the Bible doesn't mean skin and bones. Our old nature, called "the flesh," takes the things of God and perverts and twists them and tries to get us to fulfill a legitimate desire in an illegitimate way. "For the flesh lusts against the Spirit, and the Spirit against the flesh; and these are contrary to one another, so that you do not do the things that you wish" (Galatians 5:17).

Everybody who has been saved has felt this battle going on, this civil war within the forces of man's soul. You've felt it, and so have I. You know that you love God and there is the Holy Spirit within you bearing witness that you are a child of God. You want to sing, and praise, and serve God, and yet you feel that old fleshly nature. Now the flesh is not the body, but the flesh often operates through the bodily impulse.

When God made you, He gave you certain impulses—the impulses of hunger and thirst, for example, and the need for rest, for achievement, and the need for pleasure and sex. All these are God-given instincts. There is nothing dirty or impure about any of these.

But the flesh takes these natural instincts and distorts, perverts, twists, and misuses them. Hunger turns to gluttony; sex turns to immorality; the need for rest turns to laziness; the need for recreation turns to debauchery.

ACTION POINT How can we keep the flesh from taking over? Look at our verse: "Walk in the Spirit, and you shall not fulfill the lust of the flesh." The Christian life is not a one-time event but a daily walk, step by step each day. When you are submitting moment by moment to the Holy Spirit, the flesh will not be in the driver's seat.

May 29

> I beseech you therefore, brethren, by the mercies of God, that you present your bodies a living sacrifice, holy, acceptable to God, which is your reasonable service. And do not be conformed to this world, but be transformed by the renewing of your mind, that you may prove what is that good and acceptable and perfect will of God.
>
> **ROMANS 12:1-2**

Some people say, "Oh, I'm searching to know the will of God." Listen: it's not your job to find the will of God. It's God's job to reveal His will to you. It is your job to simply present yourself to Him.

If you have been conformed to this world, you will not know the will of God, and therefore you will not do the will of God. A Christian needs to be transformed into the likeness of the Lord Jesus Christ. Here is the formula for knowing the will of God: *Presentation + transformation = revelation.*

- Present yourself to Him.
- Allow Him to transform you.
- He will reveal His will to you.

With your transformed, renewed mind, you will have wisdom. The will of God is not like a map; it's like a compass. God doesn't give you a map and say, "Here's where you're going to go for the rest of your life." Day by day, you use the mind that God has given you.

Why does He transform your mind? For you to use it!

ACTION POINT If you want to know the will of God, you must first present yourself to God in humility and submission. Let Him change you. Then you won't have to find the will of God—the will of God will find you.

30

Looking unto Jesus, the author and finisher of our faith, who for the joy that was set before Him endured the cross, despising the shame, and has sat down at the right hand of the throne of God.

HEBREWS 12:2

Tigranes the Great is believed to have been Armenia's greatest king. He ruled from about 95 B.C. to 55 B.C. He was once captured by the Roman army. They took Tigranes in chains, with his lovely wife and beautiful children, to stand before the Roman general to receive the sentence of death.

Tigranes was a brave, courageous warrior, but when he came before the Roman general, he fell on his face before him saying, "Take me and do what you will, but spare my wife and my children! Do with me as you will! Anything you want! But I plead with you, spare my wife and my children!"

The Roman general was so moved by his plea that he released them all—Tigranes himself, his wife, and his children. Later on, Tigranes was speaking to his wife, and he asked, "Did you notice the beautiful tapestries on the throne room wall?"

She said, "I didn't see them."

"Did you notice the ivory throne?"

"I didn't see it," she replied.

"Did you notice the look on his face?"

"I didn't see that, either."

"Woman," he asked, "where were your eyes?"

"My eyes were on the man who was willing to die for me. I had eyes for no one else but him."

ACTION POINT Are your eyes on the One who was willing to die for you—Jesus Christ? Bravely run the race, looking to Jesus and nothing else, because He is the Author and the Finisher of our faith.

May 31

Therefore we also, since we are surrounded by so great a cloud of witnesses, let us lay aside every weight, and the sin which so easily ensnares us, and let us run with endurance the race that is set before us.

HEBREWS 12:1

God has a plan for my life, and He has a plan for yours. It's an individualized plan. Do you know it yet? More importantly, are you willing to follow it? If so, you need three things: discipline, direction, and determination.

The old King James Version of the Bible says "run with patience" in Hebrews 12:1, but that is not the best wording, for that word as it meant when the KJV was translated did not mean "patience" as we think of it today. Instead, it meant endurance.

Are you up for this? Are you willing to develop endurance so you can run the race God has for your life? Are you on the racetrack? Listen, you're burning daylight if you're wandering around out there on the infield. You're wasting time if you're up there sitting in the grandstands. Time is short and doesn't care! Whether you're nine or ninety, man or woman, rich or poor, God has a course for you. He has a race He wants you to run and the Bible says you're to run the race that is set before you.

ACTION POINT Have you ever taken time to get alone with God about this? I've said before, God does business with people who mean business. Take out a blank sheet of paper. It represents your life from this day on. Say, "God, You fill it in. Whatever Your will is, I'll do it." And sign your name at the bottom. The will of God—nothing more, nothing less, nothing else, nothing but!

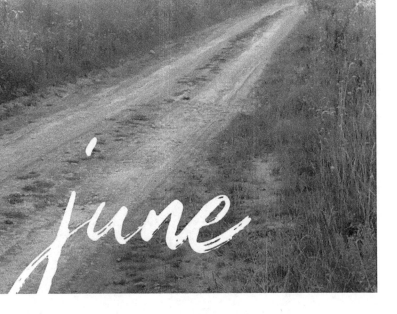

Don't put a question mark where God has put a period.

ADRIAN ROGERS

June 1

> Now about that time Herod the king stretched out his hand to harass some from the church...Peter was therefore kept in prison, but constant prayer was offered to God for him by the church...Now behold, an angel of the Lord stood by him, and a light shone in the prison; and he struck Peter on the side and raised him up, saying, "Arise quickly!" And his chains fell off his hands. Then the angel said to him..."Put on your garment and follow me."...He came to the house of Mary, the mother of John whose surname was Mark, where many were gathered together praying...Now Peter continued knocking; and when they opened the door and saw him, they were astonished.
>
> **ACTS 12:1-16**

Peter was in prison, and the Church was praying. They had no other recourse. They couldn't petition the government; they had no political influence, and no money to bribe Herod. But they could pray. The world might have laughed, but the devil did not laugh. The devil mocks at our schemes, laughs at our organizations, and ridicules our talents, but he fears our prayers.

Someone once wisely said, "The devil trembles when he sees the weakest saint upon his knees." The prayer is unto God, who controls the Universe. Notice that "constant prayer was offered to God for him by the church" (Acts 12:5). They prayed not only with intensity, but also with specificity.

What did you pray for this morning? Many of our prayers are so vague that if God were to answer them, we wouldn't know it. And If God did not answer them, we wouldn't have to admit it.

ACTION POINT Stop praying vague, general prayers. Get specific. When they prayed for Peter to be released, and the answer came, they could know it was an answer to their specific prayers.

2

Then he [Herod] killed James the brother of John with the sword. And because he saw that it pleased the Jews, he proceeded further to seize Peter also.

ACTS 12:2-3A

And we know that all things work together for good to those who love God, to those who are the called according to His purpose.

ROMANS 8:28

What do you do in times of crisis? One thing we all must do, before we panic or sin against God, is respect the mystery of God's providence. Throughout the pages of His Word, you see the hidden hand of God working in mysterious, inexplicable ways. God is in the shadows, arranging things, moving things that people cannot see.

That may be true in your life right now. God is working, but you cannot see Him working. You may be in the middle of chaos right now. Nothing seems to be making sense. Everything you thought you had nailed down is coming loose, and the devil is pulling nails.

Just because it doesn't make sense to you does not mean that it doesn't make sense. Many of us have questions. As we look at Acts 12, we say, "Well, how could God let a rascal like Herod be the king anyway? Isn't God, God? If I were God, I'd turn him into a frog. And why should James be killed, yet Peter be released? Does God have favorites? Has He lost control?"

ACTION POINT We do not live by explanations. Life is not a problem to be solved, but a mystery to be lived. Just because you cannot see the hand of God working today does not mean God is not working. Step back and see the hidden hand of God.

3

"For My thoughts are not your thoughts, nor are your ways My ways," says the LORD. "For as the heavens are higher than the earth, so are My ways higher than your ways, and My thoughts than your thoughts."

ISAIAH 55:8-9

Have you ever watched an artist paint a picture? He starts putting his colors on canvas, splashing them on, mixing this one and that one. You can almost hear him thinking, "A little more yellow here..."

And we say, "He is so good—how does he do that?" Then suddenly he'll dip his brush in some colors and go *swoosh* across the canvas. We say, "Oh, you ruined it! You've really messed up. Let's see how you get out of this!" Then a few more strokes, and suddenly it just comes together. It's a masterpiece!

Sometimes we look at what God does the same way. As He puts His colors on the canvas, we look and say, "Lord, you're really doing well." Then all of a sudden God goes swoosh! "Lord! You've messed things up! How did You let this happen?" Have you ever felt that way? Yes, you have. And so have I.

When I watch an artist at work, it may not make sense to me, but it makes sense to him. And just because things are not making sense to you, do not think that they don't make sense. In Acts 12 we see Herod's ungodly power, James' death, then Peter's release. Yet all of these things are working together. We call that the sovereignty of God. It is the providence of God. God sees the end from the beginning. In spite of the worst that man can do, God always has a plan.

ACTION POINT Find Acts 12 in your Bible, and in the margin, write the reference of Romans 8:28: "And we know that all things work together for good to those who love God, to those who are the called according to His purpose."

4

> Again I say to you that if two of you agree on earth concerning anything that they ask, it will be done for them by My Father in heaven. For where two or three are gathered together in My name, I am there in the midst of them.
>
> **MATTHEW 18:19-20**

God is pleased when His children pray, but God is more pleased when His children pray in fellowship. There's nothing that will bind us together as a Church more than praying together. If you've ever had a prayer partner, you know how your hearts are linked together.

There are times when the Church prays and God seems to come down, and it is glorious! That's what we call "the fellowship of prayer." This kind of prayer is the prayer we see happening in Acts 12, when the Church came together to pray for Peter.

Jesus had an "inner circle"—Peter, James and John. You need one, too. Every believer needs that special friend or group of friends whom you can call on at a moment's notice—"in season, out of season" (2 Timothy 4:2)—to encourage and uplift you in prayer.

ACTION POINT You also need to be that go-to person for a fellow believer. If you have this fellowship in prayer, praise God! If not, ask Him to bring that prayer partner into your life, and join together with other believers to pray this week. Request the ministry of God's people, and give that ministry to others.

June 5

> And you will seek Me and find Me,
> when you search for Me with all your heart.
> **JEREMIAH 29:13**

Many times, we pray trying to impress someone in our group. But the early Christians were not trying to impress anybody. They were desperate. They prayed with intensity, fervency, and specificity. They prayed to God, not to impress one another.

I wonder, what do we know about intense prayer? When you're in a crisis, you learn how to pray with intensity, don't you? If I were to ask, you might not be able to tell me specifically what you prayed for this morning—if it was just a general prayer with no real intensity.

One of the things that I'm to cure myself of is casual prayer—prayer that is not intense. Prayer that costs little. Do you know that the Bible calls prayer, wrestling? Paul said, "Now I beg you, brethren, through the Lord Jesus Christ, and through the love of the Spirit, that you strive together with me in prayers to God for me" (Romans 15:30). Have you ever thought of prayer as striving, as wrestling? How much genuine agonizing, which literally means "wrestling," do we do in prayer? If you really get into intercession, you are going to find out that the devil will fight and oppose you. Prayer is work.

I love Jeremiah 29:13, where God says, "And you will seek Me and find Me, when you search for Me with all your heart."

ACTION POINT Sometimes we don't feel like praying, so we say we'll "just skip it." You don't feel like praying? Continue in prayer until you do feel like it. Friend, if there is ever a time that you need to pray, it is when you don't feel like it. Pray—not only frequently, but fervently.

6

Then He spoke a parable to them, that men always ought to pray and not lose heart.
LUKE 18:1

I think the reason we don't pray with frequency and fervency today is because we think we can do things on our own without prayer. You know, perhaps the worst thing about us is not our prayerlessness, but our pride.

We have our plans, machinery, and methods. We have our pastors, choirs, Bible fellowships, and buildings. So we come to church thinking, "We'll get it done; we know how to do it."

And do you know what the devil does? He stands in the corner and smirks. He says, "You can have your buildings, your choirs, your preacher—have everything you want. You can even have your Bible studies, as long as you leave out prayer." Satan knows the power of God that comes with the kind of fervent prayer that will not take no for an answer.

When every door is shut, that's every door except one—and that one is the one that goes straight up. That is the door that no one can shut. In a crisis, there is always prayer. And when there's no hope in the horizontal direction, there is always hope in the vertical direction.

ACTION POINT We must get this in our heads: the devil was willing to go head-to-head in battle with the archangel Michael (Daniel 10:12-13), but he fears our prayers! He will do everything he can to keep you distracted and off your knees. Spend time in prayer—not only frequently, but fervently.

7

Behold, He who keeps Israel shall neither slumber nor sleep.
PSALM 121:4

I once heard about a man who was in a crisis and couldn't sleep. But then he thought about this verse of Scripture: "Behold, He who keeps Israel shall neither slumber nor sleep" (Psalm 121:4). So he said, "Well Lord, there's no need for both of us to stay up all night. Good night, Lord. I'm going to sleep while you stay awake."

The Bible says, "You will keep him in perfect peace, whose mind is stayed on You, because he trusts in You" (Isaiah 26:3). It may sound like a paradox: on one hand, we're supposed to "pray earnestly." "Continue earnestly in prayer, being vigilant in it with thanksgiving" (Colossians 4:2). On the other hand, we're told to get some sleep. (Psalm 121:4) But Philippians 4:6-7 tells us, "Be anxious for nothing, but in everything by prayer and supplication, with thanksgiving, let your requests be made known to God; and the peace of God, which surpasses all understanding, will guard your hearts and minds through Christ Jesus."

Now if you are in a crisis, let me give you four things to remember: Number one, don't demand to understand. You'll never figure it out. Number two, remember the resource of prayer. Number three, put your eyes upon God and rest in His love. And number four, expect God's power to move in His own time and in His own way. And friend, He will do it. He's the Christ of every crisis.

ACTION POINT Friend, turn your problem over to Him. Roll it on the Lord. I don't care how big it is—read and obey Philippians 4:6-7 and know the mastery of God's peace. Respect the mystery of God's providence. Rejoice in the majesty of God's power. God's peace will settle over your panic.

June 8

For all have sinned and fall short of the glory of God.
ROMANS 3:23

You may be a "righteous" sinner, a "moral" sinner, a "church member" sinner, a "fine up-standing" sinner, or an "educated" sinner; but you are a sinner. And until you confess your sinnership, you will never be saved.

If ever an age needed to hear about sin, our sophisticated but sin-sick age needs it. We have almost done away with the idea of sin. It's old fashioned to speak of sin, so we've gotten some new high-sounding phrases such as "error," "mistake," "psychological maladjustment"—anything but sin. We must come back to a place of accountability: all people have a sinful nature, and they do wrong because they're wrong.

And the Bible says Jesus, and Jesus alone, is the answer to man's sin. Without Jesus Christ, nothing can be done for your sin. And with Jesus Christ, nothing else needs to be done. We must confess our sins and be willing to admit we're sinners. We must believe Jesus is the only answer for our sin. We must believe He is the Savior.

Dear friend, if you will admit you're a sinner, then you are well on the road to being saved. If you offer God an alibi, or any excuse for sin, you will never be saved. First John 1:7 says, "... the blood of Jesus Christ His Son cleanses us from all sin." And Romans 5:20 says, "...where sin abounded, grace did much more abound."

ACTION POINT "So they said, 'Believe on the Lord Jesus Christ, and you will be saved, you and your household'" (Acts 16:31). Confess your sins, repent of them, and believe. Then, "...Though your sins are like scarlet, they shall be as white as snow."

June 9

And whoever lives and believes in Me
shall never die. Do you believe this?
JOHN 11:26

I heard a story years ago of a boy who was lying on a battlefield, mortally wounded. And the army chaplain was there, cradling this boy's head tenderly in his hands and looking down into those languid eyes, trying to give him comfort. And the boy looked at the chaplain and said, "Chaplain, am I going to live?"

The chaplain looked down at those grievous wounds and saw his lifeblood ebbing out onto the soil, and the chaplain knew that in just a few minutes the boy would be dead. So the chaplain said to the boy, "Son, are you a Christian?"

The boy gave a weak smile and said, "Sir, the happiest day in my life was in my little church back yonder in North Carolina, when I walked down the aisle of that church and gave my hand to my pastor and my heart to Jesus Christ. Yes chaplain, I'm a Christian."

The chaplain laid the dying head of that boy back down on the ground and said, "Then my son, you will live."

"Most assuredly, I say to you, he who hears My word and believes in Him who sent Me has everlasting life, and shall not come into judgment, but has passed from death into life" (John 5:24).

ACTION POINT "And this is eternal life, that they may know You, the only true God, and Jesus Christ whom You have sent" (John 17:3). Life is short, death is sure; sin is the cause, and Christ is the cure. Do you know Jesus, whom God has sent? Believe in Him. Trust in Him for your salvation. Then you too will live!

10

If we confess our sins, He is faithful and just to forgive us our sins and to cleanse us from all unrighteousness.

1 JOHN 1:9

A minister I once read said that bad behavior is the result of your environment and experiences, that the idea of sin is out of date. But I want to tell you that sin is a reality. Sin is Public Enemy #1. But if we don't make a proper diagnosis, we will never come up with the correct remedy. What's wrong with our society today? We're spending too much time sweeping down cobwebs when we need to be killing spiders. The spider is sin—the cobwebs are the results we see around us.

Behavioral psychologists say that man has all of these desires within him, and has been restrained by blocked memories that squeeze him in. They say that if he represses himself, he'll end up with a neurosis or psychosis. And so they say, "Live it up! Do your thing, and whatever feels good to you, express yourself!"

They claim that the opposite of repression is expression. But no, friend! Let me tell you, it is not repression, not expression—it is confession. "But if we walk in the light as He is in the light, we have fellowship with one another, and the blood of Jesus Christ His Son cleanses us from all sin" (1 John 1:7).

ACTION POINT Romans 10:8-10 makes it so clear: "But what does it say? 'The word is near you, in your mouth and in your heart' (that is, the word of faith which we preach): that if you confess with your mouth the Lord Jesus and believe in your heart that God has raised Him from the dead, you will be saved. For with the heart one believes unto righteousness, and with the mouth confession is made unto salvation."

11

For the wages of sin is death, but the gift of God
is eternal life in Christ Jesus our Lord.

ROMANS 6:23

When the Bible says "the wages of sin is death," it's not talking primarily about physical death, but spiritual death. You see, death means separation. Sin separated us from God. Remember, God told Adam in the Garden of Eden that if he were to disobey, "you shall surely die" (Genesis 2:17). Well, Adam disobeyed God, but did he die that day? Not physically. He and Eve went on to live for hundreds of years.

Adam and Eve spiritually died that day. Spiritual death is the separation of the soul from God. To cover Adam and Eve, God had to kill an animal and provide it's skin for a covering for them—a foreshadowing of the atoning death of Jesus on the cross.

If you are a child of God and this moment were to have a stroke or heart attack, and a doctor were to say, "I'm sorry, he/she is dead," the doctor would be "dead" wrong! You'd never be more alive!

Physical death is the separation of the soul from the body; spiritual death is the separation of the spirit from God. I can never die in that spiritual sense, because I can never be separated from God. Neither can you, a child of God, a Christian! Paul said there is nothing that "shall be able to separate us from the love of God which is in Christ Jesus our Lord" (Romans 8:39b).

ACTION POINT A lot of "dead" people will go to work tomorrow. They have existence, but they don't have life. But if you know Christ, you have life and you will never die. "He who has the Son has life; he who does not have the Son of God does not have life" (1 John 5:12). Accept His offer of eternal life today. Salvation is a gift, but you must accept it.

12

> Do you have faith? Have it to yourself before God. Happy is he who does not condemn himself in what he approves. But he who doubts is condemned if he eats, because he does not eat from faith; for whatever is not from faith is sin.
>
> **ROMANS 14:22-23**

What is this verse saying? It's saying that any action not motivated and done by complete faith in God is sin. Anytime you do anything without being absolutely confident that it's God's will for you to do that thing, if you have a doubt about doing that thing—whether the thing in and of itself is right or wrong—you have sinned.

Once upon a time, a man was in his bedroom getting dressed. His wife was out in the living room talking with a friend. He yelled out, "Is this shirt clean enough for me to wear?" Without hesitation, she said no, and went on talking. After a while he came out, buttoning up another shirt. He asked, "How did you know that shirt wasn't clean without looking at it?"

She said, "If you had to ask, it wasn't."

That's what God is saying in Romans 14:22-23: whatever you don't have confidence in (whatever you don't have faith in) is doubtful. Leave it alone. Often we wonder whether a course of action is right or wrong. Since we don't know absolutely, we do it anyway. But if we think it may be wrong, we should leave it alone until we're sure it's right. We ought to give God the benefit of the doubt. The old adage "When in doubt, don't" is often a good course to follow.

ACTION POINT When faced with a choice, ask: "Will this gladden the heart of God or grieve Him?" A good prayer for you to pray today is: "Lord, I want my heart to be grieved by those things that grieve Your heart and be gladdened with the things that give You joy."

13

> If we say that we have no sin, we deceive ourselves, and the truth is not in us. If we confess our sins, He is faithful and just to forgive us our sins and to cleanse us from all unrighteousness. If we say that we have not sinned, we make Him a liar, and His word is not in us.
>
> **1 JOHN 1:8-10**

Our culture rejects sin as "old fashioned." We've replaced it with new words in our vocabulary—error, mistake, misjudgment, weakness, psychological maladjustment, glandular malfunction, a stumble upward—anything but sin.

Some behavioristic psychology says that if a man does wrong it's simply because he has been "programmed" wrongly. And if evolution is true, there is no such thing as sin, because right and wrong will change; if man is the product of blind chance, then there's no God, and there's no ultimate standard of right and wrong. And then humanism tells our young people, "Sin is the product of 'priestcraft.' It's something the Church has conjured up to whip everybody into line." All of them try to downplay the idea of sin, and the problem is compounded by liberal clergy who no longer believe the Word of God.

We've gone through the medicine cabinet and put new labels on the old bottles of poison. So we have new terminology. We've tried to change things by changing the words, but they've not really been changed at all. Nothing has changed except how we see ourselves. We're lying to ourselves and to a holy God.

ACTION POINT Take inventory. Are you seeing your sin and dealing with it humbly and honestly before the Lord? We must come back to a place of accountability. People have a sinful nature, and they do wrong because they are wrong. Friend, I want to tell you, sin is a reality. Your great enemy is sin.

June 14

Therefore, just as through one man sin entered the world, and death through sin, and thus death spread to all men, because all sinned—
ROMANS 5:12

Some would say that man is but the sum total of his environment and his body chemistry. If he does wrong, it's because he's like a computer that's been wrongly programmed. If he was raised in a bad neighborhood, he shouldn't be blamed for breaking into stores or robbing people or selling illegal drugs. Or if he has a vile temper, perhaps he had an overbearing mother or father.

According to behavioral psychologists, people behaving badly may be pitied, but not blamed. They may be sick, but they're not sinful. They may be weak, but not wicked. They need some sort of a psychological adjustment rather than salvation.

But these social evaluators are wrong. If we don't make a proper diagnosis, we'll certainly never come up with the right cure. The diagnosis is sin. The original Greek word for "sin" here in Romans 5:12 means "missing the mark." There's the target out there; we shoot at it, but we come short of it. "For all have sinned and fall short of the glory of God" (Romans 3:23).

ACTION POINT Are you blaming others? Or instead, are you taking responsibility and coming to the Cross? "If we confess our sins, He is faithful and just to forgive us our sins and to cleanse us from all unrighteousness" (1 John 1:9).

15

> And there was a great famine in Samaria; and indeed they besieged it until a donkey's head was sold for eighty shekels of silver, and one-fourth of a kab of dove droppings for five shekels of silver.
>
> **2 KINGS 6:25**

In Samaria there was a terrible famine, and the result was a depraved diet. The same is true for us—a depraved diet is the mark of our day, only ours is a spiritual famine instead of a physical one.

Now look at this: "'Behold, the days are coming,' says the Lord God, 'That I will send a famine on the land, not a famine of bread, nor a thirst for water, but of hearing the words of the Lord" (Amos 8:11).

Today, we're feeding on all sorts of depravity and filth. And why? Why are millions of people feeding on pornography? Why are they going to see sick movies and so-called "adult" films? Why are these dens of iniquity, known as "gentlemen's clubs" and casinos and night clubs, filled with people?

Because there is a famine in our land—a famine for the Word of God. Any time a man, woman, boy, or girl is not properly fed, that person will start consuming a depraved diet.

ACTION POINT How do you change your diet and keep from feeding on fare that poisons your soul? Not simply by saying, "I'm going to be good." You must load up on the Word of God. Feast on the honey, the milk, the meat of God's Word. Then you won't be hungry for that which corrupts, yet does not satisfy.

16

> Then Abraham lifted his eyes and looked, and there behind him was a ram caught in a thicket by its horns. So Abraham went and took the ram, and offered it up for a burnt offering instead of his son.
>
> **GENESIS 22:13**

I don't know what your problem is today, but God already knows the answer. In our situation, today, God has already spoken. God already has a plan. God already knows what He's going to do, and what He wants us to do.

Abraham thought he had a problem when he was going up to Mt. Moriah to sacrifice Isaac. He didn't know how his need was going to be met. But the moment Abraham started up one side of that mountain with Isaac, a ram started up the other side—the ram that was going to be the substitute for Isaac.

Abraham never saw the ram, but God saw it. God sent it. God planned for the substitutionary sacrifice long in advance. And I want to tell you, God knows a way for you. God has a plan for you. God has a plan for all of us.

ACTION POINT We have a little saying: "Pray and believe, you'll receive. Pray in doubt, you'll do without." God's children are never to panic. Worry is an insult to Almighty God. Trust God—He already knows.

17

Then Jesus said to His disciples, "If anyone desires to come after Me, let him deny himself, and take up his cross, and follow Me."

MATTHEW 16:24

Do you want to be filled with the Spirit of God? Do you really? Are you willing to forsake self? God is not going to superimpose His mighty, dynamic power on your old self-life.

Some people think denying themselves is doing without certain kinds of food, going without sleep, or doing without certain pleasures. They think maybe if they go live in a monastery, they'll be denying themselves.

Friend, there's no holiness in a hole. It is not denying yourself things, it is denying yourself. Now, that may include denying yourself things. But you can deny yourself things without denying yourself. Simon Peter forsook his nets, but it was a long time before Simon Peter forsook Simon Peter. Self will plead eloquently for its life, but are you willing to say, "None of me, and all of Thee"? Are you so willing to be identified with the Lord Jesus Christ that you will go down with Him into the river of judgment and come up on resurrection ground, saying, "I'm willing that I should die, that Jesus Christ may live"? The apostle Paul said, "I have been crucified with Christ; it is no longer I who live, but Christ lives in me; and the life which I now live in the flesh I live by faith in the Son of God, who loved me and gave Himself for me" (Galatians 2:20).

ACTION POINT Self doesn't want to die. Take Self off the throne, and enthrone Jesus there instead. Tell Him, "None of me and all of Thee, Lord Jesus."

June 18

Honor and majesty are before Him;
Strength and gladness are in His place.
1 CHRONICLES 16:27

I once heard about a little girl who loved her daddy so much, she wanted to do something very special for him for Christmas. She decided to make him some house slippers. She went up to her bedroom every evening and worked. The times that she used to sit in her father's lap, when they use to talk together, disappeared. For days, she worked alone. Finally, she came down on Christmas Day with the slippers and presented them to her father.

He tried to smile, and he was appreciative of her nice gift. But he thought within himself, "Oh, how much more would I have valued her time, just sitting in my lap and being with me, than I value these slippers."

Jesus values the time that you spend with him far more than the things that you do for Him. Do you know that? Oh, how important it is that we learn to sit at the feet of Jesus! How important it is that we learn to follow Jesus. To be a disciple means first of all, that there is a person to please—and that is the Person who's called us to be a disciple.

ACTION POINT Are you occupied elsewhere doing things for God, rather than spending time with Him? Jesus values the time you spend with Him far more than the things you do for Him. Learn to sit at the feet of Jesus. Make a commitment to spend time in His presence each day.

June 19

> So the woman conceived and bore a son. And when she saw that he was a beautiful child, she hid him three months.
>
> **EXODUS 2:2**

A man once came into a little village. As he drove around, he saw one of the villagers and asked, "This is a beautiful village—any great men born here?" The man said, "No, just babies."

No one is born great; they have to be made, shaped, molded and guided. A great person is the result of Mama's and Daddy's faith, prayers, and instruction.

At the time that Moses was born, Pharaoh decreed that every baby boy born to the Hebrews must be killed. Children are a gift from God, and we need to look at them as great bundles of potentiality. And that is what Moses' mother and father did. They saw that he was a good little child with great potential. But he had to have the opportunity for training to develop to his full potential. They had a vision, and they protected Moses, so that he could grow up and be used of God.

Some people spend more time training their hunting dogs than their kids. They tie up the dog at night and let the kids run wild...and then wonder what went wrong. Train your children. Children who have been *taught* the way they should go may hear other teaching and depart. But when they have been *trained*, it becomes part of their lives.

ACTION POINT Are you consistently setting aside one-on-one time to teach each of your children the ways of God? Proverbs 22:6 says you are to "Train up a child in the way he should go, and when he is old he will not depart from it." Teach them to choose the right path, to live the right way, to make wise choices, and when they are old, they won't lose their way.

June 20

> But above all, my brethren, do not swear, either by heaven or by earth or with any other oath. But let your "Yes" be "Yes," and your "No," "No," lest you fall into judgment.
>
> **JAMES 5:12**

In June we take time to focus on fathers. I have discovered, in talking with teenagers, that many of them harbor bitterness and resentment. When you dig a little deeper, you find that much of that resentment is directed toward their fathers over the serious matter of broken promises.

Are you faithful? I mean, can you be counted on? "Confidence in an unfaithful man in time of trouble is like a bad tooth and a foot out of joint" (Proverbs 25:19). Today, there is a serious lack of genuine integrity and faithfulness among men. A man's word seems to mean little today, whether it's over a marriage contract, a business contract, or a treaty between nations.

A Gallup report once found out something that was sickening: 40% of Americans admitted to calling in sick when they were not sick, short-changing a customer, pilfering, stealing on the job, or cheating in examinations in school. We are facing a crisis...God give us faithful men.

If you are a dad who wants to restore your relationship with your children, whatever their ages, one of the best things you can do is remember those broken promises. Then go to them with a remorseful spirit and say, "I've asked God to forgive me, and I want you to forgive me." Ask them this question, "Have I ever made a promise to you that I've failed to keep? If so, I want you to tell me because I want to repent. I want you to believe that your dad is a faithful man."

ACTION POINT Are you a man of your word? If not, start fresh today and make a commitment that you will stand behind your word.

21

Blessed is every one who fears the LORD, who walks in His ways. When you eat the labor of your hands, you shall be happy, and it shall be well with you. Your wife shall be like a fruitful vine in the very heart of your house, your children like olive plants all around your table. Behold, thus shall the man be blessed who fears the LORD. The LORD bless you out of Zion, and may you see the good of Jerusalem all the days of your life. Yes, may you see your children's children. Peace be upon Israel!

PSALM 128

I am convinced that America's families will not be changed until the dads in America are changed. The key is the father. God has given us a survival manual, and it begins with the father. A father is to be a God-fearing, hard-working, worshipping man of God. He is to be bold, but he must also truly fear God.

What is the fear of God? It is not a cringing dread of God—it is love on its knees. And I am convinced that the man who fears God the most loves God the best.

Dads, your children need to see the fear of God—an awe-filled respect for God—in your life. I've made an observation of fathers: do you know what makes a good dad? A man who is both strong and tender at the same time. Strong, but not afraid to hug, to kiss, to love, and to speak softly and gently to his children.

ACTION POINT These children of yours are like olive plants round about your table. Dads, if you will do this, if you will put the emphasis upon your family, we are going to see goodness in this nation again.

Then Elisha said, "Hear the word of the LORD. Thus says the LORD..."

2 KINGS 7:1A

We speak of the Bible as being inerrant and infallible. When the Bible speaks, God speaks. I have noticed that the more liberal a preacher gets, the more he doesn't like to call the Bible, "the Word of God." But oh, dear friend, this is the Word of the Lord, spoken by His prophets, and it is authoritative.

Is it really important that we believe that the Word of God is true and perfect? Yes, it is. If any part of His Word is not true, then we must conclude that God is a liar. But God cannot lie! Every word in the Bible can be trusted.

Billy Graham came to this conclusion in the early years of his ministry and prayed, "I have seen enough of the transforming power of this Word to know that You are behind it....I take it by faith....and trust You to make clear to me what it means."

F. B. Myer, one of the greatest devotional writers of all time, said that if any promise of God should fail, "The heavens will clothe themselves in sackcloth, and the sun and moon and stars will reel from their seats. The universe will rock, and a hollow wind will moan through creation, bearing the tidings that God is mutable, that God can lie."

ACTION POINT A God of truth cannot inspire untruth. Praise God for His absolute trustworthiness. No need to argue or quibble about it. If it's the Word of God and God is a God of truth, then it can't contain error. A God of error cannot inspire, and a God of truth cannot inspire error. It is the product of the Spirit of God. It is thereby totally infallible because God is infallible. Thank God for the inerrancy of the Bible!

June

23

> So an officer on whose hand the king leaned answered the man of God and said, "Look, if the LORD would make windows in heaven, could this thing be?"
>
> **2 KINGS 7:2A**

This officer, a government official, acted like he believed in God, but he was a practical atheist. He spoke of God but doubted His power. To me the biggest fool is not the man who says there is no God, but the man who says there is a God, and then doesn't live like it.

Here was a man who had a sterile religion. He believed in God...in a way. He had a form of godliness, but he denied the power thereof. And he was the loser; he was robbed by the thief of unbelief. I want you to see, in the rest of the verse, what Elisha, God's prophet, said to this officer: "And he said, 'In fact, you shall see it with your eyes, but you shall not eat of it'" (2 Kings 7:2b).

Unbelief always withholds God's blessings from us. When we say we believe, but act as though God is not in the equation, we are practical atheists. "But without faith it is impossible to please Him, for he who comes to God must believe that He is, and that He is a rewarder of those who diligently seek Him" (Hebrews 11:6).

ACTION POINT Are you captured by the thief of unbelief? Your sins are withholding good things from you and unbelief is the chief among them. Renounce unbelief as a sin. Confess it to the Lord. Refuse to let it hold you captive.

24

> But God has chosen the foolish things of the world to put to shame the wise, and God has chosen the weak things of the world to put to shame the things which are mighty.
>
> **1 CORINTHIANS 1:27**

People say, "Well, I don't believe God can use me." They are insulting God. They are limiting Him. "Well," you may say, "all right then. I'll just serve God in my poor little old weak way." Quit it! He doesn't want you to serve him in your "poor little old weak way." God wants to take ordinary people and do extraordinary things through them!

This is the kind of people God wants to use. He delights to use them! He's done it from the dawn of time: Gideon, Deborah, young Samuel, Ruth the widow, David the shepherd boy, Esther the orphan, Matthew the tax collector. Don't forget Cornelius, the member of an occupying army; Saul, the church-persecutor; Peter, the denier; John Mark, the deserter.

- It's not about your fame; it's about your faith.
- It's not about your scholarship; it's about your relationship.
- It's not about who you know; it is Whose you are that counts.

ACTION POINT God takes what the world calls a foolish message, combines it with a weak messenger, and mixes these two in the crucible of His love and wisdom. The result is glory to God. Be willing to be used of God, no matter how weak you believe you are. Trust Him to empower you. Remember—God doesn't need your ability, only your availability.

June 25

> Now there were four leprous men at the entrance of the gate; and they said to one another, "Why are we sitting here until we die?"
>
> **2 KINGS 7:3**

Jim Elliot was a martyred missionary to the Aucas (now known as the Waorani tribe) in Ecuador. He wrote in the flyleaf of his Bible, "He is no fool who gives what he cannot keep to gain what he cannot lose." Jim Elliot was talking about giving his life for Christ and the Gospel.

I tell you, in these days, the most dangerous thing you can do is play it safe. You are safer out on the waves with Jesus Christ than you are in the boat without Him. These are desperate days, and we need to live like it.

Dear friend, you will never be a messenger that God can use until you yourself are convinced of Calvary's victory. You can't have a stutter, you can't have a stammer; you have got to blow the trumpet with certainty. Have you experienced that victory? Are you convinced? The reason that some of us don't witness, I'm afraid, is that we have yet to be convinced of the victory that is in the Lord Jesus Christ.

I want you to be convinced. God will convince you, but the devil will do all he can do to keep you from seeing the victory. The devil doesn't want you to see just how badly defeated he is.

ACTION POINT Even the lepers in 2 Kings had sense enough to ask, "Why sit here till we die?" You're going to die anyway. Don't just sit there and let life pass you by! Come to Jesus. You have everything to gain. You've got nothing to lose. You can't save your life, and you won't get out of life alive. So invest it in something important.

26

Then they said to one another, "We are not doing right. This day is a day of good news, and we remain silent. If we wait until morning light, some punishment will come upon us. Now therefore, come, let us go and tell the king's household."

2 KINGS 7:9

Andrew Murray once said, "There are two classes of Christians: soul winners, and backsliders." In my humble estimation, there are two great sins a Christian can commit:

The greatest is to fail to love the Lord Jesus.

The second greatest is not adultery, or drunkenness, but the sin of silence—to refuse to share the Gospel of Jesus Christ.

Suppose you knew the cure for cancer. Would you not tell it? Suppose you were on an island where people were starving to death and you knew where there was a vast hoard of food. Would you not tell it?

Ours is the greatest mission, the greatest message, the greatest Master that the world knows anything about. Our mission is the Great Commission. Our message is the saving Gospel of our Lord and Savior. Our master, Jesus Christ Himself, has told us we are to take the Gospel to every creature on earth. Yet many Christians are sinning against this command. They're committing what I call "the sin of silence." If you're not a witness, you're not right with God; I don't care what else you may do.

ACTION POINT It doesn't matter how faithfully you attend church, how eloquently you teach, how liberally you give, how beautifully you sing, or how many commandments you keep. What matters is, are you telling the good news? Stop committing the sin of silence. Share the Gospel. Witness to others about what Jesus has done for you.

June 27

> How beautiful upon the mountains are the feet of him who brings good news, who proclaims peace, who brings glad tidings of good things, who proclaims salvation, who says to Zion, "Your God reigns!"
>
> **ISAIAH 52:7**

When I was in seminary, our seminary president, Dr. Roland Q. Leavell, told a story that touched my heart. He told how, as a pastor in Georgia, he received a notice from The War Department. There was a certain young man who had been a member of his church and who had been reported as missing in action and was assumed to be dead. They had already informed his mother that her son was dead. But now, they had found him—alive! And they said to Dr. Leavell, "You are the pastor of this woman, and we want you to go and tell her that her son is not dead, but is alive."

Now what do you think Dr. Leavell did? Do you think he said, "Well, I've got a little vacation trip I'm going to take first, and I want to play around at golf or do some other things." Can you imagine being about to go into a home and tell a mother that her son—whom she had assumed to be dead, missing in action; a body somewhere on a battlefield, buried somewhere in a forlorn unknown grave—her son was indeed alive, and coming home! Dr. Leavell told of the joy, the happiness, the excitement and the thrill of going to tell that message.

I tell you, there ought to be that thrill in our hearts every time we tell a poor sin-sick, sin-cursed, undone sinner that there's good news: Christ died for our sins! This is a day of good tidings! The Gospel is good news!

ACTION POINT How could a person know the Gospel and not want to share it? Deliver the message! Tell those who feel hopeless that there is an answer. Share Jesus with them.

28

> And Moses said to the people, "Do not be afraid. Stand still, and see the salvation of the LORD, which He will accomplish for you today. For the Egyptians whom you see today, you shall see again no more forever."
>
> **EXODUS 14:13**

Three hundred and sixty-five times in the Bible—once for every day of the year—it says, "Do not be afraid," or the equivalent: "The Lord is my helper, and I will not fear what man shall do unto me" (Hebrews 13:6 KJV).

Sometimes we come to a place where things are out of our hands. There is nothing we can do. Oh, we hurry around, we're so busy manipulating, trying, conniving, and scheming. But finally we come to a place where God hems us in—the sea here, a mountain there, a mountain there, and the devil behind. And there is no way out but up.

Just stand still.

"Be still, and know that I am God; I will be exalted among the nations, I will be exalted in the earth" (Psalm 46:10)! We always think that we have to do something—even if it's wrong. So, sometimes God places us in a place where there is nothing we can do.

Read those words in Exodus 14:13 again: "...you shall see again no more forever. The Lord will fight for you, and you shall hold your peace" (Exodus 14:13b-14).

ACTION POINT God wants you to come to the place of dependence that you may learn there is nothing to fear, and He may say to you, "Do not be afraid" and "Stand still." Just stand still.

June 29

> Also Moses said, "This shall be seen when the LORD gives you meat to eat in the evening, and in the morning bread to the full; for the LORD hears your complaints which you make against Him. And what are we? Your complaints are not against us but against the LORD."
>
> **EXODUS 16:8**

The Israelites had just come through the Red Sea, and they were dancing with joy and praising the Lord.

But just three days later, they were murmuring and complaining! Moses said to them, "Your complaints are not against us, but against the LORD."

One of the greatest lessons you can ever learn is that when you murmur and complain, you are really murmuring against God. Murmuring is no little sin. God lists it with idolatry and fornication (1 Corinthians 10:6-11).

The Israelites were being led by the Lord. Moses was there. The Word of God was there. Why did they murmur? It was because of a lack of faith, but it was also lack of reason. Would God have brought them through the Red Sea just to let them die? If Jesus Christ died for you on that cross, do you think He saved you only to abandon you? The Israelites' murmuring ultimately cost them dearly. An entire generation of them never entered the Promised Land. Are you willing to pay that price just so you can continue murmuring?

ACTION POINT We murmur and don't even realize it. Try this: put a loose rubber band around your wrist. Each time today you catch yourself thinking or expressing a complaint, snap the rubber band. By the end of the day, you may be surprised the level of murmuring in your thought life. Now take steps to counter it with praise for all you do have. Will you follow Him and let Him have His way, and not murmur or complain?

30

Who has directed the Spirit of the LORD,
or as His counselor has taught Him?
ISAIAH 40:13

How often do we like to tell God how He ought to do things? Do you hear yourself doing that in prayer? I can imagine those early disciples when Saul was making havoc of the church, hauling Christians off to prison and death. I imagine many were praying, "Oh, God! Do something about Saul! Strike him dead!" But God didn't want to strike him dead. God struck him alive! And aren't you glad He did?

Out in the wilderness, when poisonous snakes entered the Israelite camp, people were crying, "God! God! Kill these snakes!" But God didn't kill the snakes. Instead, He had a bronze serpent placed high on a pole and had Moses tell the people that if they would look upon the bronze serpent that Moses lifted up, they would be healed. (See Numbers 21) None of the Israelites would have thought of that, but God raised up a solution—one which was also a foreshadowing of His Son raised on a cross. "And as Moses lifted up the serpent in the wilderness, even so must the Son of Man be lifted up, that whoever believes in Him should not perish but have eternal life" (John 3:14-15). Everyone who looks to Jesus, lifted high upon the cross, finds the cure for his sin and can be saved.

Never substitute your human reasoning for obedience. The Bible is not primarily a book to be explained; it is first and foremost a book to be believed and obeyed. Whether you understand it or not, when God says it, you just simply obey it.

ACTION POINT Isn't it strange how God works? Understand that our ways and God's ways are so different. Don't believe your way is better. In humility, say to God, "I will trust You, Father, and I will obey."

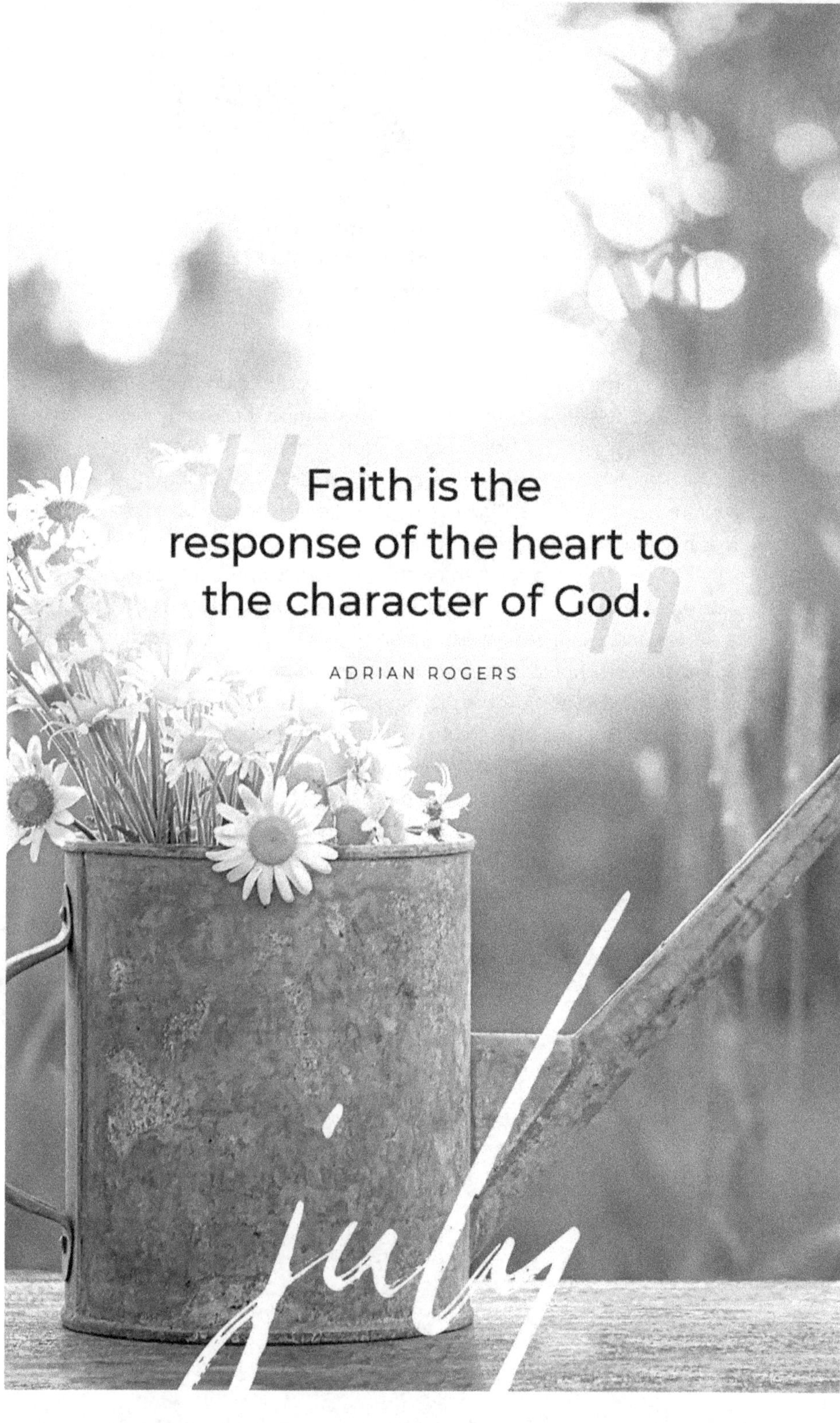
Faith is the response of the heart to the character of God.
ADRIAN ROGERS
july

1

The king's heart is in the hand of the LORD; like the rivers of water, He turns it wherever He wishes.
PROVERBS 21:1

Christian, we have five duties concerning our government. One: we're to pay for government. "For because of this you also pay taxes, for they are God's ministers attending continually to this very thing" (Romans 13:6). Jesus paid His taxes; you ought to pay your taxes. A Frenchman once said, "France fell when people got the idea that the government was a cow to be milked rather than a watchdog to be fed."

Two: to pray for our government. "Therefore I exhort first of all that supplications, prayers, intercessions, and giving of thanks be made for all men, for kings and all who are in authority, that we may lead a quiet and peaceable life in all godliness and reverence" (1 Timothy 2:1-2). You may ask, "Well, should I pray for my leader if he's wicked?" You ought to pray all the more for him. God can change a ruler, God can remove a ruler, and God can overrule a ruler.

Three: to praise our government when it does right. Patriotism is not bad. Four: to preach to our country when it does wrong. God's people dare not identify the Christian faith with the Democratic or the Republican Party—we need to be free to tell both parties to repent. Five: to participate in government—not on the basis of parties, politics, or policies, but on principles. It is inconceivable that God would ordain human government and then tell His people to stay out of it. If that's true, who does that leave to run it?

ACTION POINT The greatest responsibility in America is not in the White House, but in the church house. Pray for America right now: "Oh God, bless America. Lord, we deserve judgment, but we need mercy. Bring this nation, Lord, back to You. The troubles that we see in our land are tokens of Your love to bring us to our knees. Lord, it's beyond us. God, we need You in America."

2

Then He spoke a parable to them, that men
always ought to pray and not lose heart...

LUKE 18:1

Do not fret because of evildoers,
nor be envious of the workers of iniquity.

PSALM 37:1

Edmund Burke wrote, "All that is necessary for evil to triumph is for good men to do nothing." When it comes to the political scene and government, some have dropped out altogether. They have the idea that if you get involved in government, somehow that's the "social gospel." So they've just dropped out and hunkered down, trying to "hold on till Jesus gets here." Some have been intimidated by the great debate between church and state.

We can't drop out. It's impossible to think that God would have ordained government and told His people to stay out. Who else does that leave to run things?

Others with misguided zeal have tried to bring in the kingdom of God by political machinations. That cannot be done either. So where do we get the answers? Not from the politician who may have his personal ax to grind. Not from the ungodly or the humanists who don't believe the Word of God. Not from finger-bumping philosophers who don't know the Word of God. The only place we're going to get the answers is from the Word of God.

ACTION POINT What must we do as the Church? We must continue to pray. Pray for our President and pray for our nation, because we are in a crisis. I am calling you to set your face in prayer. I am calling you, dear friend, to see who God is. I am calling you to pray for the glory of God.

3

Therefore I exhort first of all that supplications, prayers, intercessions, and giving of thanks be made for all men, for kings and all who are in authority, that we may lead a quiet and peaceable life in all godliness and reverence. For this is good and acceptable in the sight of God our Savior, who desires all men to be saved and to come to the knowledge of the truth.

1 TIMOTHY 2:1-4

When I was a boy in Florida, we lived at the seaside. I love the water, and one of the things that always intrigued me as a boy was the changing of the tide. As we'd go out fishing, my brother and I would always be cognizant of the tides because we would come and go by the tides. The tides were important to us.

There are tides in nations too. America saw a tide of revival sweep in twice—in the First and Second Great Awakenings. But today we've seen a different tide. At this lowest point, when the tide is as low as it can get, may God grant that we see the tide begin to turn back the other way, back to decency in America.

ACTION POINT We need to look up. Only God can help us. We need to confess up and turn from our wicked ways. We need to speak up. We need to stand up for what is right. Pray 1 Timothy 2:1-3 today.

4

And He changes the times and the seasons; He removes kings and raises up kings; He gives wisdom to the wise and knowledge to those who have understanding.

DANIEL 2:21

What does the Word of God have to say about government? It teaches that God has ordained human government. The prophet Daniel said, "He is the one who removes kings. God is the one who sets up kings." And Romans 13 teaches that the powers that be are ordained of God.

What about wicked governments? Did God set them up? It may surprise you to learn, yes, He did. That does not mean they are God's will. God would much rather have righteousness. But by and large people get the kind of government they deserve. The nation Israel in the Old Testament is both a pattern and a warning. God gave them the leaders they deserved. Wicked leaders are God's reward for a wicked people.

ACTION POINT What are we to do as a church? What is my responsibility so far as government is concerned? First, we are to pray for our government. We need to pray for leaders even if they're wrong, for this is good and acceptable and right in the sight of God our Savior. I call upon you to confess your sins personally and our sins nationally. And I call upon you to pray for America as Daniel prayed for his people—in the power of the shed blood of our Lord and Savior Jesus Christ. It's prayer time in America.

5

> Then I set my face toward the Lord God to make request by prayer and supplications, with fasting, sackcloth, and ashes.
>
> **DANIEL 9:3**

It's one thing to criticize the fact that our children cannot pray in school. But I think that it is unmitigated hypocrisy to carp and criticize about children not being able to pray in school unless we ourselves are prayer warriors, don't you? It is hypocrisy unless we, ourselves, are teaching our children to pray in the home. We are unvarnished hypocrites to criticize that school policy and yet not to teach our children to pray in the home, and not to pray ourselves.

Only prayer can hold back the floodtide of sin in our nation and the floodtide of judgment. Only prayer can release the cleansing and healing hand of God—and not just any prayer.

- It's not the arithmetic of our prayers—that is, how many there are.
- It's not the geometry of our prayer—how long it might be.
- It's not the rhetoric of our prayer—how eloquent it may be.
- It's not the music of our prayer—how sweet our voice.
- It's not the logic of our prayer—how argumentative we become.
- It's not the method of our prayer—how methodical we are.

It is the faith and the fervency of our prayer that counts with God.

ACTION POINT Walk with Daniel through the school of prayer. Read Daniel chapter 9 today. See in action the "effectual fervent prayers of a righteous man" (see James 5:16).

6

And I prayed to the Lord my God, and made confession, and said, "O Lord, great and awesome God, who keeps His covenant and mercy with those who love Him, and with those who keep His commandments, we have sinned and committed iniquity, we have done wickedly and rebelled, even by departing from Your precepts and Your judgments."

DANIEL 9:4-5

The greatest thing we can do for America is pray for America. We must teach our children to pray in the home, by both gentle instruction and by example. Our children are watching us and will model our behavior.

The man who reads the Bible gets understanding, and the man who has understanding prays. There is no way that you can separate Bible study from prayer. When you read the Bible, the Bible impels you to pray. And when you pray, your prayer life will urge you to read the Bible. Prayer and Bible reading go hand in hand. Bible reading is God speaking to you. Prayer is your talking back to God.

In Daniel 9, not only did Daniel pray with resolution, but he prayed also with reflection. He kept talking to God, and about God. Look again at Daniel 9:4-5 and see how he describes God. Friend, when you pray with resolve, you also need to pray with reflection. You need to see who God is. When you see the character of God, the nature of God, you can hardly keep from praying. We need to only glance at our problems and gaze upon our God.

ACTION POINT Are you teaching your children how to pray? Are you taking them beyond "Now I lay me down to sleep"? If your children can talk, it is not too early to teach them how to pray.

7

> We have sinned and committed iniquity, we have done wickedly and rebelled, even by departing from Your precepts and Your judgments.
>
> **DANIEL 9:5**

In Daniel chapter 9, this golden chapter on prayer, when Daniel sought God he prayed with passion and repentance: "we have done wickedly and rebelled, even by departing from Your precepts and Your judgments." You might ask, "Did Daniel do all that?" No. Daniel simply included himself in his prayer for his nation.

- Does God hold me accountable for the abortion in America? Yes.
- Does God hold me accountable for the pornography? Yes.
- For the drug addiction, alcoholism, materialism, humanism? Yes, He does.

Friend, if the church had done what she ought to have done, and if we would do what we ought to do, these problems would be healed. And while we may not commit these sins, they are still our sins. Daniel 9:20 makes that so clear: Daniel says, "While I was speaking, and praying, and confessing my sin and the sin of my people Israel..."

Now, people who don't know God aren't going to confess the sins of this nation. Like Daniel, we must set our face and pray with resolve and repentance, confessing our sin and the sin of America. Only sin that is confessed is forgiven.

ACTION POINT Have you ever "set your face" to pray? So much of our prayer, I hate to say, is casual prayer, prayer that comes with almost a take-it-or-leave-it attitude. Set your face before God today to pray as Daniel did. Pray with fasting and determination.

8

> The instant I speak concerning a nation and concerning a kingdom, to pluck up, to pull down, and to destroy it, if that nation against whom I have spoken turns from its evil, I will relent of the disaster that I thought to bring upon it.
>
> **JEREMIAH 18:7-8**

In this passage, God is not just talking about the nation Israel. He's talking about nations in general. God says, "When I get ready to judge a nation, if that nation will repent, then I will turn from the judgment I had planned."

We must understand this about the great heart of our God: God is a God of justice, righteousness, and judgment, but God had rather show mercy than send judgment.

America is ripe for judgment. God will turn from judgment if a nation will repent. We are in the eleventh hour, the clock is about to strike midnight, and we need to pray, "Oh God, hold back Your hand of judgment upon America."

Remember, "If My people, who are called by My name, will humble themselves and pray, and seek My face, and turn from their wicked way, then will I hear from heaven and will forgive their sin and heal their land" (2 Chronicles 7:14).

ACTION POINT A church steeple points us to God. Notice that the closer the steeple gets to the top, the smaller it gets. The closer we get to God, the more we realize how insignificant and sinful we are. This isn't a time for finger-pointing in America but for repentance of personal sin, especially for the people in the pew. First Peter 4:17 says, "The time has come for judgment to begin at the house of God." Get alone with God. Confess your personal sin and repent. Be part of the answer, not the problem.

9

To the Lord our God belong mercy and forgiveness, though we have rebelled against Him....O my God, incline Your ear and hear; open Your eyes and see our desolations, and the city which is called by Your name; for we do not present our supplications before You because of our righteous deeds, but because of Your great mercies.

DANIEL 9:9, 18

Daniel is saying, "O God, please forgive us. Remove the guilt." Why does Daniel believe he can bring this passionate petition before the Lord? Not because of "our righteous deeds" but because of "Your great mercies."

Daniel prayed, "O Lord, according to all Your righteousness, I pray, let Your anger and Your fury be turned away from Your city Jerusalem, Your holy mountain; because for our sins, and for the iniquities of our fathers, Jerusalem and Your people are a reproach to all those around us" (Daniel 9:16). Friend, could that not be said about America? Daniel is praying for the removal of guilt, but also for the restoration of glory. "O Lord, hear! O Lord, forgive! O Lord, listen and act! Do not delay for Your own sake, my God, for Your city and Your people are called by Your name" (Daniel 9:19). In your Bible, underline "for Your own sake, my God." When we are concerned for the glory of God, then we see our prayers answered.

Isn't it wonderful that "to the Lord our God belong mercy and forgiveness"? You see, just as Daniel prayed, the basis of our prayer is the greatness and the mercy of God. It is impossible to see the greatness of God and the mercies of God and not pray with confidence.

ACTION POINT We need to pray, "God, cleanse us, restore us, revive us, renew us, refresh us. We need revival in America. Remove our guilt."

10

> Now therefore, our God, hear the prayer of Your servant, and his supplications, and for the Lord's sake cause Your face to shine on Your sanctuary, which is desolate. O my God, incline Your ear and hear; open Your eyes and see our desolations, and the city which is called by Your name; for we do not present our supplications before You because of our righteous deeds, but because of Your great mercies. O Lord, hear! O Lord, forgive! O Lord, listen and act! Do not delay for Your own sake, my God, for Your city and Your people are called by Your name.
>
> **DANIEL 9:17-19**

Be honest: when you cry out to God on behalf of our nation, what is foremost in your mind? Many of us pray "for America's sake." So often, we are simply trying to get out of difficulty. Rather than going to God in praise, seeking His glory, we say, "God, we're in a mess. Get us out so we can go right back on to our sinful lifestyle."

In Daniel 9, Daniel is praying, "Oh God, please forgive us. Remove our guilt." He's also praying for the restoration of God's glory. Notice in Daniel 9:17—"for the Lord's sake."

Most of us want revival so we can return to our own ways, once God gets us out of the mess we're in. Do you have a burning, yearning in your heart for the glory of God? Do you want to see God's glory spread over this land? I want to see God do something again that cannot be explained by pundits and news anchors.

ACTION POINT Daniel is praying for a restoration of God's glory. When you pray, it must be for His name's sake. Do you want your nation to bring honor to Him? Then pray for the glory of God. When you do, God will move in.

11

> So Samuel said: "Has the LORD as great delight in burnt offerings and sacrifices, as in obeying the voice of the LORD? Behold, to obey is better than sacrifice, And to heed than the fat of rams."
>
> **1 SAMUEL 15:22**

I once read an interesting story about Stephen Grellet, a pioneer evangelist to lumbermen in the Rocky Mountains. He felt the Spirit of God leading him to a particular lumber camp to preach. When he got there, the place was absolutely deserted. He said, "Lord, I don't understand, but I'm going to be obedient." So he opened his Bible and preached a full-length message. Then he pled for people to come to Christ.

Years later, a man walked up to him in England and said, "I was the foreman at a lumber camp. I had come back to the camp to get an ax, and I heard you preaching. I stood behind a pile of lumber and listened. As you preached, my heart was warmed, and I accepted Jesus Christ. I later witnessed to four other men. Now, all five of us are missionaries preaching around the world."

Do you know why we're not obeying God more than we are? Because we're not hearing what God is saying. We're not spending time listening to God. That's the importance of a quiet time; that's the importance of getting somewhere alone with God in a nook with this book, reading and listening.

ACTION POINT You can be good and obey in so many areas, but God is asking you to obey Him completely and minutely. Obey God in the seemingly small things as well as the big things. This is so important.

12

> And a servant of the Lord must not quarrel but be gentle to all, able to teach, patient, in humility correcting those who are in opposition, if God perhaps will grant them repentance, so that they may know the truth, and that they may come to their senses and escape the snare of the devil, having been taken captive by him to do his will.
>
> **2 TIMOTHY 2:24-26**

In order to be ordained as a missionary, a young man once had to appear before the superintendent of missions. His appointment was set for five o'clock in the morning. It was a snowy morning, but he was there on time.

He waited until eight o'clock. Finally, the superintendent arrived. He said, "I'm glad to see you. Are you ready for your interview?" The young man said, "Yes sir." So the superintendent said, "Spell baker." "Well," the young man said, "B-A-K-E-R." The superintendent said, "Thank you. Do you know mathematics? What is two plus two?" "Four, sir," the young man answered. The superintendent said, "Thank you, that's all. You're dismissed." The young aspiring missionary said, "Well, thank you sir for your time." He was perplexed, but he went away with a gentle spirit.

In his report, the superintendent wrote, "I asked him to come early on a snowy morning and he came without a murmur. That shows a spirit of self-sacrifice. Furthermore, he was there on time. That shows his character. He was made to wait for three hours and he did it without grumbling, and that shows his patience. When I came down, he was not angry. That shows his temper. I asked him very simple questions, and he answered them in a straightforward manner. That shows his humility. He'll make an excellent missionary."

ACTION POINT Sometimes God will ask you to do something that doesn't make sense or seem important. This is when faith and obedience are on the line. Let God determine what's important. Trust and obey.

13

I understand more than the ancients, Because I keep Your precepts.
PSALM 119:100

"The ancients" is a way of saying "the accumulative wisdom of the ages." David is saying, "I haven't been off to the university, I haven't studied abroad; but I keep God's Word, and therefore God reveals to me His truth."

People sometimes say, "I read the Bible, and it doesn't make sense to me." Well, the way to understand the Bible is to obey the Bible. The way to understand the verses you don't understand is to obey the verses you do understand.

The only way you can really understand the Bible is for God to reveal it to you, and God doesn't reveal it to rebels. Some of you know what God wants you to do, but you're not doing it. And you wonder why you've come up against a roadblock when you try to read the Bible!

Would you like for Jesus to be so real to you that He's not just someone you know about, but someone you know? Then look in John 14:21: "He who has My commandments and keeps them, it is he who loves Me. And he who loves Me will be loved by My Father, and I will love him and manifest Myself to him." Do you know why Jesus doesn't feel real to many of us? We are just not obeying His word. Do you want Him to manifest Himself to you? There is no way apart from obedience.

ACTION POINT The prerequisite to obedience is hearing the Word of God. The priority of obedience is that there is no substitute for it—not reason, resources, or any kind of human pride or achievement. The power of obedience is such that when we obey God, God's omnipotence links with our obedience, and peace, protection, power, purity, perception, and the presence of the Lord all become ours. Determine to keep God's Word, and through it, God will reveal His truth.

14

> To him who strikes you on the one cheek, offer the other also. And from him who takes away your cloak, do not withhold your tunic either.
>
> **LUKE 6:29**

The idea has gotten out today that being a Christian is going to make you prosperous and happy, and give you ease and joy through this life. We equate Christianity with success, and with popularity.

It is not so. You are not going to have that success, prosperity, and popularity just because you are a Christian. You need to learn that there may be adversity, and that people may hate you. (See John 15:17-19)

Someone once asked an army officer, "Why are you a Christian?"

The officer said, "One day we went out on a march. We slugged through the mud all day long. Our boots were dirty and our clothes were heavy. When we came into the barracks, we were cross and irritable. There was a young man who had already come in, cleaned up, and was kneeling down by his bed saying his prayers. When I saw that man, somehow I became so irritated, so aggravated at him, I took one of my muddy boots and I hit him in the head with it. The young man paused for a moment, and then continued praying. But when I awoke the next morning, my boots were polished and set by my bed—by that young man. That's what brought me to Christ."

ACTION POINT When God's people suffer persecution for their faith, the world begins to look at us. We may not want it. We may not ask for it. Certainly, I'm not asking for it. From the human viewpoint, it is misery. From the Satanic viewpoint, it is mystery. But from the divine viewpoint, it is ministry. Don't wait until persecution comes. Make your decision that, if you are called upon, you will suffer for Christ.

15

Do not fear any of those things which you are about to suffer.
Indeed, the devil is about to throw some of you into prison,
that you may be tested, and you will have tribulation ten days.
Be faithful until death, and I will give you the crown of life.

REVELATION 2:10

Polycarp was the pastor of the early church in Smyrna. He was asked to renounce Christ and worship Caesar. The Romans said to him, "If you will just offer incense to Caesar we will give you your liberty. We will let you go. You can go back and continue to live out your life. But you must deny Christ."

Polycarp refused, and said, "Eighty and six years have I served Him, and in nothing hath He wronged me; and how, then, can I blaspheme my King, who saved me?"

When they heard that, they clamored to burn him at the stake. They brought their wood and heaped it around his feet. And then Polycarp prayed:

> *"I thank Thee that Thou hast deemed me worthy of this day and hour, that I should have my portion in the number of the martyrs, in the cup of Thy Christ."*

And when that fire was kindled around his feet, he was heard singing and praising the Son of God.

ACTION POINT Most of us will not die at the stake, be carried to the wall and shot, or be imprisoned for the Lord Jesus Christ. But can we not die to this vile world? Can we not die to our plans and our ambitions? And can we not say that Jesus Christ is Lord?

16

...Be faithful until death, and I will give you the crown of life. He who has an ear, let him hear what the Spirit says to the churches. He who overcomes shall not be hurt by the second death.

REVELATION 2:10B-11

If others in past centuries—and some even today—have reddened the mouths of lions, faced firing squads, languished in prisons, and been scorched in the flames, can't we go out today, back to school, back to the office, and live for Jesus Christ? God help us if we don't. May God empower us to do it!

In this evil hour, sin-bound, self-bound, Hell-bound men and women need a Savior. And we need revival. We'll have it when there are Christians with burning hearts, brimming eyes, and bursting lips, who fear nothing but sin and who love nothing but Jesus Christ.

Who among us will be faithful unto death? We're not to be fearful; we're to be faithful. God help us that we shall!

ACTION POINT Pray this with me: We realize, Lord, that in most of our lives we have had it relatively easy. Help us not to be ashamed of Jesus. Help us not to deny Him. Help us to fear none of the things that shall happen, but to be faithful to death. Lord, we are so grateful for the good times we have and for the joy we have. We don't want to be morose about whatever is to come, but help us that we might see things clearly and understand Your Word. In the name of Jesus we pray, amen.

17

> But hold fast what you have till I come. And he who overcomes, and keeps My works until the end, to him I will give power over the nations—'He shall rule them with a rod of iron; they shall be dashed to pieces like the potter's vessels'—as I also have received from My Father; and I will give him the morning star.
>
> **REVELATION 2:25-28**

In these days there will be more temptation to get away from the Word of God, the blood atonement, and salvation by grace through faith. Churches will be under attack by seducing spirits and doctrines of demons. Here, in Jesus' message to the Church in Thyatira, He says, "You hold fast till I come."

Even though it seems to be tough, remember this, dear friend—one of these days Jesus is going to come and rule this world. The saints are going to have their day. Look at Revelation 2:26. "He who overcomes and keeps My works until the end, to him I will give power over the nations." God the Father has given to God the Son the right to rule and reign here upon this Earth.

And when He does, we're going to rule and reign with Him. If we suffer with Him, we'll also reign with him (2 Timothy 2:12). We are even going to judge angels (1 Corinthians 6:3). It may not be long before Jesus comes and His millennial reign begins on this Earth. The Bible clearly says that it's going to be a powerful reign (Revelation 2:27).

ACTION POINT Don't give up; don't let down. Hold fast, stick to it, stay with the Word of God. Hold fast that truth. Hold fast to this Book and don't let go.

18

And I will give him the morning star.
REVELATION 2:28

I remember reading a story about a wealthy Roman who had a lavish estate, and a servant named Marcellus. When the wealthy Roman died, his will left everything to his slave, Marcellus. The Roman also had a son, and for some reason there had been a disagreement with him, so in his will the Roman said, "I have left my entire estate to my slave Marcellus. To my son, I leave him only one thing. He can choose any one thing from my estate he wants, but that's all." The son said, "Very well; I choose Marcellus."

Here at the end of Revelation 2, our Lord gives a sweet promise to those who overcome: "And I will give him the morning star." The morning star is the star that appears in the heavens just after the darkest hour of the night.

Jesus is that morning star! What Jesus is saying is, "You will receive the greatest reward of all: you will receive Me, the morning star."

Don't let go, don't let down, don't back up, and don't shut up until you're taken up, because the Lord Jesus Christ is coming and He says, "Just hold fast, stand in there, stick in there, because one of these days you will be the possessor of that morning star that's going to come." And if you have Jesus, you have everything.

ACTION POINT It's getting very dark...But praise God, it's getting gloriously dark, and before long, that morning star, Jesus, is going to appear! Choose Jesus, for with Him comes all the Father's wealth.

19

Do not cast me away from Your presence,
and do not take Your Holy Spirit from me.
PSALM 51:11

When a person dies, his spirit departs. And I'm afraid that is what has happened to many churches: the Holy Spirit has departed. The living organism has become an organization.

Years ago, Dr. Carl Bates said something that shook me to my foundation: "If the Holy Spirit were to suddenly die—" (now, of course, you know that's impossible. He cannot die, but...)—"if the Holy Spirit were to suddenly die, most of our churches would meet next Sunday, go right on, and never know the difference." I wonder if that's not true about many churches—especially today, when "The Bible says..." has been switched out for "Well, in my opinion..."

The Holy Spirit has not died, but He has departed. The life of the church is gone. There's a difference between carnal emotion and spiritual sensitivity. I've been in some of these churches where you'd think Hallelujahs and Amens cost $100 apiece...there's a sort of barren stillness. I pray that God will help us have a spirit of love, of conviviality, that is the legacy of God. The Holy Spirit will never draw attention to Himself, but I just pray God we'll always keep our warmth.

ACTION POINT There is something contagious about the Holy Spirit of God. "Now the Lord is the Spirit; and where the Spirit of the Lord is, there is liberty" (2 Corinthians 3:17). Don't fry in fanaticism or freeze in formalism. Have a burning, passionate love for the Lord Jesus Christ.

20

> But none of these things move me; nor do I count my life dear to myself, so that I may finish my race with joy, and the ministry which I received from the Lord Jesus, to testify to the gospel of the grace of God.
>
> **ACTS 20:24**

Do you pay a "price"—as in, some extra time in the morning—to get into the Word of God? Do you pay the price of being ridiculed because you keep your Bible on your desk at the office, or bow your head and thank God for His gracious goodness when He gives you a meal? Are you willing to be different? Will you finish your course?

When you are running this race, you'll find out that you are running against the grain. Don't get the idea that there's a broad road, and a narrow road, and the narrow road runs alongside the broad road, and that over there a bunch of people are going this way, and you're over here, going in the same direction.

No. There's the broad way, and here you are—right in the middle of it, going the other way. Against the tide. Against the grain.

What we believe as Christians starts at a different source, follows a different course, and ends at a different conclusion...and there is a price to pay for that.

ACTION POINT We don't like the idea of a "price to pay." We say, "I'm saved by grace, so I'm just going to float on into Heaven on flowery beds of ease." No. A disciple is one who follows his Master. There is a price to pay. Get the sin out of your life. Fix your eyes on Jesus Christ. Don't slack up. Finish your course. Go across the finish line with a burst of energy.

21

Therefore we also, since we are surrounded by so great a cloud of witnesses, let us lay aside every weight, and the sin which so easily ensnares us, and let us run with endurance the race that is set before us, looking unto Jesus, the author and finisher of our faith, who for the joy that was set before Him endured the cross, despising the shame, and has sat down at the right hand of the throne of God.

HEBREWS 12:1-2

If you're going to run a race, how do you prepare? First, you lay weight aside. Notice athletes: they run in very light clothing. The less weight, the better. One thing you'll never see is someone in the Olympics running in an overcoat. It's not going to happen! They get as light as they possibly can.

The Greek word *weight* doesn't mean something sinful; it just means something that burdens you, that holds you down. There are some things that are not bad in themselves. There's nothing wrong with an overcoat. You just don't wear an overcoat when you're running a race. Paul said: "All things are lawful for me, but all things are not helpful" (1 Corinthians 6:12a).

Friend, this weight may be some recreational habit that you have. It may be some cottage in the woods. It may be some acquaintance, some hobby, or too much television or sleep. In 1 Corinthians 6:12, Paul is saying, "Some things may be lawful for me, but if it doesn't speed me on my course, then I need to lay it aside and leave it alone."

ACTION POINT Ask yourself, "Is there something in my life that's hindering my walk with Christ? Something holding me back, excess baggage keeping me from being all I ought to be for the Lord Jesus Christ? Whatever it is, if you want to win the race, lay it aside. Good things become bad things when they keep you from the best things.

22

> Therefore we also, since we are surrounded by so great a cloud of witnesses, let us lay aside every weight, and the sin which so easily ensnares us, and let us run with endurance the race that is set before us...
>
> **HEBREWS 12:1**

By the middle of Hebrews 12:1, Paul is no longer talking about good things that might become bad things. "...The sin which so easily ensnares us..." Now he's talking about bad things, period—things that ensnare you, tangle you up. Can you imagine someone trying to run a race with a long flowing robe around his legs? Or a rope around his feet? No; he wants to be free so he can run.

What sin most easily trips you up? You will never fulfill the destiny God has for you if you refuse to let go of the sin that so easily trips you up. Weights load us down, and sin trips us up. Either one—"weight" or sin—can make you a poor runner, and keep you from running the race.

In Hebrews 11 and 12, Paul is talking about faith. Hebrews tells us that we live by faith; therefore, we run by faith. The whole race we're running is the race of faith.

Most of us say, "I wish I had better faith, stronger faith." The reason you don't have more faith is sin. You might say, "Now wait a minute, Dr. Rogers..." No, friend. The Bible says, "Beware, brethren, lest there be in any of you an evil heart of unbelief in departing from the living God" (Hebrews 3:12).

ACTION POINT Unbelief is not a mental sin. It's a moral sin. It doesn't come out of the head; it comes out of the heart. Lay aside what weighs you down. Identify that sin in your life that so easily entangles you, then lay it down!

23

Therefore we also, since we are surrounded by so great a cloud of witnesses, let us lay aside every weight, and the sin which so easily ensnares us, and let us run with endurance the race that is set before us...

HEBREWS 12:1

The word "endurance" here literally means "endurance." It means bearing up under some load, or some challenge.

Are you looking for an easy way, a cheap way, a lazy way to serve God? All honey and no bees? A life of ease? You just want to say, "Oh, I'm so happy in Jesus." Listen, this business of running this race means that you're going to go at it with all your heart.

You may be on a sick bed or in a wheelchair, but no one is excluded. We are to run with endurance. When you watch someone running, do you notice how intense he is? If you're in this race, you need to pray over it, you need to weep over it, you need to study over it, you need to work over it. And if we possess it, it must possess us.

So many people run and then quit. Some of you used to run, but don't anymore. You might say, "Well, the church is doing fine now. It's time for me to pull back the throttle." It is never time for you to pull back the throttle. You say, "I don't need to give now like I used to give." You're right...you need to give more. I don't care how far ahead you are in any race; if you stop running, you're going to lose the race. You are to finish your course.

ACTION POINT I've learned that God does business with those who mean business. Being saved and running your race is a full-time occupation. Don't settle any longer for being a part-time Christian. Commit fully to following Jesus.

24

> Looking unto Jesus, the author and finisher of our faith, who for the joy that was set before Him endured the cross, despising the shame, and has sat down at the right hand of the throne of God.
>
> **HEBREWS 12:2**

If we will look to Jesus, Jesus will be the author and finisher of our faith. The word "author" in the Greek literally means "example," "leader," or "originator." Jesus is the example of faith, but He's also the originator of our faith. Faith comes from beholding the Lord Jesus Christ, from looking at Him.

All the other heroes of the faith mentioned in Hebrews chapter 11 can cheer us on, but they are not our chief examples. Jesus is the One who never sinned, who never failed. The more you behold the Lord Jesus Christ, the more you will know that He is the author and finisher.

He is the one who originates the race. He is the one who fires the starting gun. He is the goal toward which we run. He is the coach who runs alongside us and gives us courage and strength to run.

ACTION POINT It is not so much great faith in God that we need, as it is faith in a great God. What a wonderful Savior we have in the Lord Jesus Christ. This phrase in Hebrews 12:2, "looking unto Jesus," means looking away from everything else and looking at Jesus. It is Jesus all the way! If you want faith, fix your eyes upon Jesus Christ. Keep "looking unto Jesus." Your faith will grow!

25

> Looking unto Jesus, the author and finisher of our faith, who for the joy that was set before Him endured the cross, despising the shame, and has sat down at the right hand of the throne of God.
>
> **HEBREWS 12:2**

Jesus is our example. He is a champion who, at the end of His race, received a crown of joy. When an athlete runs, he runs to win a trophy. In our verse today, what is "the joy set before Him"? It's winning the race. He "endured the cross, despising the shame, and has sat down at the right hand of the throne of God."

The crown gave Him the ability to endure. If you keep the crown in mind, you can bear the cross. But you cannot have the crown if you despise the cross. We are crucified with the Lord Jesus Christ.

I have a few trophies I won back in high school on a championship football team: a gold football, a letterman's sweater and a silver cup. Do you know what happened to all those trophies? Someone broke into the house and got the gold football. The moths had a camp meeting in the sweater, and it's gone—no more letters on the letter sweater. What happened to the silver cup? I haven't the foggiest.

ACTION POINT Athletes run "to obtain a perishable crown, but we for an imperishable crown" (1 Corinthians 9:25). There is a prize for you to possess. Follow your Lord and walk as Jesus walked.

26

For what is our hope, or joy, or crown of rejoicing?
Is it not even you in the presence of our Lord Jesus Christ
at His coming? For you are our glory and joy.

1 THESSALONIANS 2:19-20

Paul tells the church in Thessalonica, "When Jesus comes, my crown will be those I've led to Him." Now that is a crown that doesn't rust or tarnish. When you die and go to Heaven, are you taking precious souls with you, or are you going to Heaven alone? I don't want to hurt your feelings, but I am concerned, because most people are not active soul winners. That's tragic.

You could say, "But Dr. Rogers, I give my money!" I don't care how much money you give. If you are not endeavoring to bring souls to Christ, you are not right with God. You say, "Well, I teach." I don't care how eloquently you teach! If you are not trying to bring souls to Jesus, you are not right with God. You say, "Well, I attend church faithfully." I don't care how much you attend. If you are not trying to bring souls to Jesus Christ, you are not right with God.

Andrew Murray said, "There are two classes of Christians: soul winners and backsliders." You are one or the other. If you don't have a passion to see people come to the Lord Jesus Christ, I wonder if you know the Jesus I know.

ACTION POINT We cannot win people every time we try, because that is the work of the Holy Spirit, and people must yield their hearts to Jesus Christ. You cannot control what they do. But I am telling you, dear brother, dear sister, that there is a crown: the soul winner's crown. I want the soul winner's crown. I want the victor's crown.

27

Grace and peace be multiplied to you in the knowledge of God and of Jesus our Lord...

2 PETER 1:2

Have you ever noticed how God puts things in sequence in the Bible? For example, the Bible says, "Grace and peace be multiplied to you." It never says "peace and grace"—always "grace and peace." Why? Because you will not know peace until you know grace. Here's another: "repentance and faith." (See Acts 20:21, Hebrews 6:1) If you're having difficulty with faith, first try repentance.

The Bible also says "Believe and be baptized," not "Be baptized and believe." The Bible teaches believers' baptism. "Now as they went down the road, they came to some water. And the eunuch said, 'See, here is water. What hinders me from being baptized?' Then Philip said, 'If you believe with all your heart, you may.' And he answered and said, 'I believe that Jesus Christ is the Son of God.'" (Acts 8:36-37)

If you were baptized before you gave your heart to Jesus and truly believed, you haven't been baptized at all. True baptism follows true belief. Believer's baptism signifies that you are "Buried with Christ in death, and raised to walk in the newness of life." If you are baptized before you truly come to know Jesus Christ as Savior, that's like having your funeral before you die. God's order is "believe, and be baptized."

ACTION POINT There's nothing more debilitating or more smothering to faith than a sin that you are harboring in your heart. We all have our "besetting sin." Do you know what it is? Have you confessed it to God and repented from it? If you're going to run the race of faith, you've got to do some personal conditioning.

28

> And do not be drunk with wine, in which is dissipation; but be filled with the Spirit...
>
> **EPHESIANS 5:18**

To be filled with the Spirit of God means first, repentance, then resistance of the devil, and then renewal. It means there's not one room in your body, soul, or spirit that's off-limits to God. There's not one closet He doesn't have a key to. It means you are filled with the Spirit in your church life, your business life, your sex life, your political life, and your social life, in the big things and the little things, in your money, exercise, sleep, eating, in your lying down, and in your waking up.

You have a choice: you can grieve the Spirit of God and be filled with the devil, or you can put the devil out and be filled with the Spirit of God. "...And be renewed in the spirit of your mind, and that you put on the new man which was created according to God, in true righteousness and holiness" (Ephesians 4:23-24). It's not enough to put off the old man—put on the new man. Don't you love that phrase, "true holiness"? God forgive us for this icky, gooey, syrupy kind of holiness, this pretense which is not holiness at all.

"And do not grieve the Holy Spirit of God, by whom you were sealed for the day of redemption" (Ephesians 4:30).

Give Jesus the keys to it all. Then when you're filled with the Spirit, there's no more room for Satan, no place for the devil. Where can the devil go? He has no place. If there's room for Satan, the Spirit is grieved and you're not filled with the Spirit.

ACTION POINT Repent, resist, renew! Don't try to repent until you're honest and face your sin. Don't try to resist until you've repented. And don't try to be filled until you renew—until you choose against Satan and yield to God's blessed Holy Spirit.

....

....

....

29

Two things I request of You (Deprive me not before I die):
Remove falsehood and lies far from me; give me neither
poverty nor riches—feed me with the food allotted to me;
Lest I be full and deny You, and say, "Who is the LORD?" Or
lest I be poor and steal, and profane the name of my God.

PROVERBS 30:7-9

You may encounter in this life both the tests of poverty and of riches. If so, the Lord has some advice for you:

See poverty in the proper perspective. In the Lord Jesus Christ, you are highly exalted, no matter how poor you are. Having Christ, you are richer than the richest man on Earth without the Lord Jesus. As a Christian, you have gone from rags to riches in Him.

It's hard to be poor, and even harder to be rich. The rich man may have an easier time in life, but he has a harder time passing the test. Many people would do better being poor than rich. Some people can stand almost anything but prosperity.

The Lord doesn't tell the rich to renounce their riches, but to properly assess them. It is not wrong to have money. Some of God's choicest saints—Abraham, for example—were wealthy. But the rich are to see their wealth from a proper perspective.

ACTION POINT It's better to have balance, neither wealth nor poverty, but enough food for our daily bread. If we have too much, we may think we don't need God. If too little, we might be tempted to steal and dishonor the Lord. Remember to thank the Lord today for His daily provision.

30

> He who loves his life will lose it, and he who hates his life in this world will keep it for eternal life. If anyone serves Me, let him follow Me; and where I am, there My servant will be also. If anyone serves Me, him My Father will honor.
>
> **JOHN 12:25-26**

You know, sometimes it is hard to look at people and know whether they're saved or not saved.

One way to illustrate it is, if a group of people is standing around and there's a dog in the midst, it's hard to tell which man that dog belongs to. Let's say two men are having a conversation, and the dog is sitting on the floor. When the two men part, you're going to find out who the dog belongs to, because the dog will follow his master, right?

I made up my mind long ago that if a dog can follow his master, I'm going to follow mine. You will be known by which master you follow.

ACTION POINT In high school, some kids will go this way and Jesus will go a different way, and you'll go His way because Jesus is your Master. In business, some men are going to go this way, and Jesus is going to go that way. Mr. Christian Businessman, you will go that way, because Jesus is your Master. You will be known by the Master you follow. Make it your purpose to do what Jesus said so long ago: "Follow me."

31

> And the Spirit and the bride say, "Come!" And let him who hears say, "Come!" And let him who thirsts come. Whoever desires, let him take the water of life freely.
>
> **REVELATION 22:17**

You don't have to pay one blessed cent for the water of life. Take it, and drink freely. You will never have your heart's deepest thirst satisfied until you are satisfied with Jesus. I promise, on the authority of the Word of God, that He will save you.

Let's say a Mr. Sam Smith asks, "But Pastor Rogers, what if I'm not one of the 'elect'? How can I know for sure I'm one of the 'elect'?"

Would it help Sam to believe he's one of the elect if Jesus had said here in this verse, "Let Sam Smith come and take of the water of life freely"? No; there's more than one Sam Smith.

What if this verse said, "Samuel D. Smith"? There might be another Samuel D. Smith. It might not refer to our Sam.

What if it said, "Samuel D. Smith, born in Sam's hometown on July 4, 1990"? There could be another Samuel D. Smith born in his town on July 4, 1990. By now you're saying, "Adrian Rogers, you're getting ridiculous."

Let me solve this. Let's forget all that and just put one word in that verse: "whosoever." That's exactly what it says: "Whosoever will, let him come..." That is better than anybody's name spelled out in detail.

Who are the elect? I can settle that in a second: the elect are the "whosoever wills."

ACTION POINT If you want to be saved, come to Jesus. He's reaching His nail-pierced hands to you, saying, "Come." Jesus says come. The Spirit says come. The bride says come. The individual says come. You can come and drink.

Just because you cannot see God working does not mean He is not at work.

ADRIAN ROGERS

august

1

For by grace you have been saved through faith, and that not of yourselves; it is the gift of God, not of works, lest anyone should boast.

EPHESIANS 2:8-9

A man is saved by grace, through faith in the Lord Jesus Christ, and by nothing else. It is grace plus nothing. You are not saved by doing good works, and if you feel that you are saved by doing good works, if you feel that good works ever helped save you, then you can never, ever have assurance of your salvation. If somebody asks you, "Are you saved?" the very best you could say is, "Well, I hope I'm saved."

If you were to ask me, "Adrian Rogers, are you saved?" I'd say, "Yes, praise God! I *know* I am saved!" And you could say, "Well you have a lot of confidence in yourself!" Well, if you knew me like I know me, you'd know that I don't have any confidence in me. But I've got a wonderful confidence in my Savior, and I'm trusting the Lord Jesus Christ and the Word of God that says, "Believe on the Lord Jesus Christ, and you will be saved, you and your household" (See Acts 16:31).

But if works have anything to do with my salvation, and you were to ask me, "Adrian Rogers, are you saved?" I'd have to say, "Well, now, let me think. Yes, I believe I'm saved. I prayed today and I studied the Bible. I didn't curse today, and I didn't steal. But...uh-oh...I *did* lose my temper today. Well, let me see. I *hope* I'm saved."

ACTION POINT If you depend upon works to get you to heaven, either a little or a lot, then you will never be able to say, "Praise God, I know that I know that I'm saved." But you are not saved by works—you're saved by grace, through faith. It is the gift of God.

2

> You lust and do not have. You murder and covet and cannot obtain. You fight and war. Yet you do not have because you do not ask.
>
> **JAMES 4:2**

Once upon a time, a little boy was trying with all his might to move a huge stone. His little muscles were straining, and there was perspiration on his face. His father, who was watching, said to him, "Son, are you using all of your strength?" The little boy said, "Yes, Daddy, I'm using all of my strength." And his dad said, "No, you're not. You haven't asked me to help you."

Sometimes we're burdened down with weighty problems, and we strive, we cry, and say, "I'm doing everything I know to do!" Well...have you asked your Father to help?

Oh, friend, the presumption of unoffered prayer! Did you know that prayerlessness is a sin? It's a sin. The Bible says, "Moreover, as for me, far be it from me that I should sin against the Lord in ceasing to pray for you; but I will teach you the good and the right way" (1 Samuel 12:23). Did you know the Bible tells us that we're to pray all the time? "Rejoice always, pray without ceasing, in everything give thanks; for this is the will of God in Christ Jesus for you" (1 Thessalonians 5:16-18). "Then He [Jesus] spoke a parable to them, that men always ought to pray and not lose heart" (Luke 18:1; word in brackets added).

ACTION POINT It may be that God wants to bless you, but that the reason He has not is very simple: "You do not have because you do not ask." Decide today to link your life with His. Tap into His power. When you don't pray, you're not just simply missing a blessing: you're committing a sin. You're doing without the things that God wants you to have, and you are sinning against the Lord.

3

Therefore submit to God. Resist the devil and he will flee from you.
JAMES 4:7

Suppose you own a piece of property, and right in the middle of it you sell me an acre, and I have access in and out. Let's suppose all night long I'm playing loud music, I throw trash around, I desecrate your property. After a while you say "I want you out of there. Move out. You're defiling my land."

But I say, "I'm not going; you can't make me go. You sold me this piece of property; I've got a legal right to it and I'm not moving." Dear friend, you would not be able to move me out, because you sold it to me.

Some of you have done almost the same thing with Satan. Certain things in your life have become strongholds, and you have given a place to the devil. You cannot dislodge him unless you *legally* dislodge him. How can you do that?

ACTION POINT Even after you repent from sin, the devil isn't just going to walk out. You're going to have to run him out. You still have to clean house. You have to say, "Satan, I've given you a place, but I take it back in the name and the authority of Jesus. Satan, I don't shout at you, I don't plead with you, I don't argue with you, I don't beg you. I bring Jesus Christ against you. You have no right here, no authority here. This body of mine is the temple of the Holy Spirit of God. You are trespassing on my Father's property, and in the name of Jesus, Whose I am and Whom I serve, *be gone*!" He will flee from you.

4

He who is faithful in what is least is faithful also in much;
and he who is unjust in what is least is unjust also in much.

LUKE 16:10

Look carefully at this verse. Jesus is saying that when a person is unfaithful in the small things, he will be unfaithful in greater things as well. He didn't say "may be" or "could be" unfaithful. It says he *is*. If you would steal so much as a 15-cent pencil and carry it home from the office, you've made a place for the devil.

You might say, "Now wait a minute..." No. This is what the Bible says. A person who would steal a 15-cent pencil has the *potential* of stealing a $150,000 payroll. When you are unfaithful in that which is least, the Bible says you are *unfaithful*. Period.

That dawned on me the other day. I used to say, "Well, if I'm capable of stealing a little, then I'm *capable of* stealing a lot." But that isn't what God says: He says that if you are unfaithful in that which is least, you *are* unfaithful in that which is much, because with God thievery is thievery. It makes no difference.

ACTION POINT If there's an area of dishonesty in your life, that area will be the devil's campground. Examine your heart. Does any part of your life fall short of impeccable, indisputable, complete honesty? Repent of that today and change it.

5

The Lord is not slack concerning His promise, as some count slackness, but is longsuffering toward us, not willing that any should perish but that all should come to repentance.

2 PETER 3:9

"Seeing then, that all these things shall be dissolved, what manner of persons ought ye to be in all holy conversation and godliness" (2 Peter 3:11)? Folks, that is a big question. If there's a new world coming, as 2 Peter 3 says there is, then what should I be like? What should you be like? The job, the duty that we have is to get as many folks saved as we can. The only reason that Jesus is not yet come is, according to 2 Peter 3:9, "The Lord is not slack concerning His promise, as some count slackness, but is longsuffering toward us, not willing that any should perish but that all should come to repentance."

Some people believe there is a set number of certain persons who are going to be saved and that number has been fore-ordained—already settled, nothing we can do about it. They believe God has predestined some for Heaven and some for Hell. Don't get the idea that God created a little baby and said, "You, child, are going to go to Hell, and there's absolutely nothing you can do about it." I don't believe that for one second!

I believe God wants everybody to be saved. Read today's verse—black print on white paper. Listen, God is not willing that *any* should perish, but that all should come to repentance.

ACTION POINT It's one thing to believe this...it's another to get out there and start sharing the Gospel with people. What are you doing to present them with the opportunity to be saved? Are you sharing the Lord Jesus Christ?

6

> And a servant of the Lord must not quarrel but be gentle to all, able to teach, patient, in humility correcting those who are in opposition, if God perhaps will grant them repentance, so that they may know the truth, and that they may come to their senses and escape the snare of the devil, having been taken captive by him to do his will.
>
> **2 TIMOTHY 2:24-26**

I've heard it told that in the South Sea Islands, they catch a monkey by taking a coconut, making a hole in the top, and putting a handful of rice in. A monkey will reach his paw in and grab a fistful of rice—and then his fist is bigger than the hole, and he can't withdraw it. Then, when the captor comes, the monkey will scream and plead, but he will never let go of the rice.

You might say, "Foolish monkey!" Yet are you a foolish person who will not relinquish the sin you're clinging to, that you might have the blessings of God? Foolish person, taken captive by Satan, who will not have power with God because of some handful of rice—some sin, some habit, some grudge—that you hold onto.

ACTION POINT What sin is holding you captive? Let go of it. Relinquish the sin you're clinging to. Are you living day by day, obeying the commandments as well as quoting the promises? Are you righteous? Are you living a pure life, a clean life? If I regard iniquity in my heart the Lord will not hear me. How foolish we are not to relinquish our sins.

7

...Who, in the days of His flesh, when He [Jesus] had offered up prayers and supplications, with vehement cries and tears to Him who was able to save Him from death, and was heard because of His godly fear.

HEBREWS 5:7

My Savior prayed with "vehement cries and tears." How that rebukes me. Does it rebuke you? When was the last time you shed a tear over some soul that is mortgaged to the devil? When was the last time you, like Jacob, said to God, I will not let You go unless You bless me"? (See Genesis 32:26) When was the last time you "labored fervently" in prayer? (See Colossians 4:12)

Prayer is hard work! For the energy it takes, I'd rather preach than pray. I'd rather study than pray. It takes work to pray. And here is our Savior, who was praying passionately. We need that same passion in our prayers.

The effect of my preaching is not measured by how my sermons are outlined or illustrated, but by the power of Almighty God upon my life because I've been alone with God in prayer. A choir may entertain, a choir may amaze, it may amuse, but it will never bless until that music is soaked in prayer.

ACTION POINT The life of the Lord Jesus shows us by His example how we should pray. Set aside a time every day to get alone with God in prayer.

8

> To me, who am less than the least of all the saints, this grace was given, that I should preach among the Gentiles the unsearchable riches of Christ.
>
> **EPHESIANS 3:8**

The Apostle Paul, who penned these words to the church in Ephesus, left a rising career as one of the brightest up-and-coming Jewish scholars. He left his standing among the religious leaders of the day, setting aside His reputation, laying all that down for "the unsearchable riches" of life in Jesus Christ.

Have you been complaining about your poverty? Listen, you may not have much money in the bank, but you are immensely wealthy. You're in the King's family! "The Spirit Himself bears witness with our spirit that we are children of God, and if children, then heirs—heirs of God and joint heirs with Christ, if indeed we suffer with Him, that we may also be glorified together" (Romans 8:16-17).

"For you know the grace of our Lord Jesus Christ, that though He was rich, yet for your sakes He became poor, that you through His poverty might become rich" (2 Corinthians 8:9). "I thank my God always concerning you for the grace of God which was given to you by Christ Jesus, that you were enriched in everything by Him in all utterance and all knowledge" (1 Corinthians 1:5).

ACTION POINT I want you to remember that you're a prince, a royal blueblood, if you're born again. No matter how poor you may be in this world's eyes, in Jesus Christ, you are rich. You are a child of the King!

9

> Against You, You only, have I sinned, And done this evil in Your sight—that You may be found just when You speak, and blameless when You judge.
>
> **PSALM 51:4**

Two kinds of wounds can come to the human psyche: guilt and sorrow. I was talking with a precious member of our church whose husband had died. Her heart was wounded by sorrow but not guilt. Sorrow, you see, is a clean wound. Though it's deep and raw, a clean wound will heal. But guilt is a dirty wound. It festers. It soils the soul, saturates the mind, and stings the conscience. It will never heal until it is cleansed.

David's great sin was the latter kind—the one that soils the soul. When David committed adultery with Bathsheba, he cried out against the sin, knowing he had done evil before a holy God. You see, David had not only sinned against Uriah, Bathsheba, and his own family, but his sin was an affront to a Holy God who loved him and had redeemed him. With a guilt-laden conscience, David wrote Psalm 51, crying out for cleansing.

If all you're afraid of is punishment for your sin, I doubt you've been saved. Children of God weep not primarily because of punishment, but because they've disgraced God. "Not only did I break Your law, Father. I broke Your heart." That's the difference between a slave and a son. A slave fears his master's whip. A son fears the father's displeasure.

ACTION POINT When we sin against God, we break His heart, and that should break ours. Are you willing to truly repent? Pray this prayer: "Lord, may my heart rejoice with those things that gladden Your heart, and Lord, may my heart be broken with that which breaks Your heart. In Jesus' name, Amen."

10

Oh, that they had such a heart in them that they would fear Me and always keep all My commandments, that it might be well with them and with their children forever!

DEUTERONOMY 5:29

Our little 4-year-old grandson was at our house, and I was up in my study. I was busy—busy-and-a-half. Well, he walked in there, looked me in the face and said, "You know, Papa, I'm going to have to go home in a little while." Then he said, "Now, Papa, if we're going to do any playing, we don't have a lot of time."

I looked at that little guy, and I looked at my desk. I laid down my pencil and shoved all that stuff aside and went outside and played, and then we came back in and watched a movie.

It's so important that we understand God's plan for the home and the family. Let me tell you why family is so important. A child gets his idea of himself from his family. Children are dependent upon their parents and grandparents, the home, the environment, the people around them, to get some concept of who they are and what they're worth. A child gets a picture of life from the family. A child gets a picture of God from the family. You see, if the family does not provide an environment of love, forgiveness, mercy and grace, it's so much harder for a child to understand those concepts in God. What are your priorities? What are your core values? What things are you willing to die for?

ACTION POINT It's been impressed upon me more and more that I am leaving to my children a legacy. I'm handing off the baton, I'm passing the torch. One day, you will be gone. What is your wife going to say about you, sir? What are your children going to remember about you? "The righteous man walks in his integrity; His children are blessed after him." (Proverbs 20:7).

11

I have no greater joy than to hear that my children walk in truth.

3 JOHN 1:4

What are the desires that you have for your children? What are you praying for them? Are you praying for their health, their wealth, that they might be famous, or that they might have a life of ease? Even the pagans want healthy, successful children—children who are going to be free from care and worry. Is that what concerns you most about your children?

How many of you would say, "Dear God, what a blessing if You were to call my son into the ministry or my daughter to be a missionary?" Some people think that would be a colossal waste. But the Bible says, "Like arrows in the hand of a warrior, so are the children of one's youth. Happy is the man who has his quiver full of them; they shall not be ashamed, But shall speak with their enemies in the gate." (Psalm 127:4-5), and arrows are to be shot at the enemy.

What is your ambition for your children? I want to be like the Apostle John, who said in 3 John 1:4, "I have no greater joy than to hear my children walk in the truth."

ACTION POINT I've told God many times, "I don't care whether my children are wealthy or successful; I want them to know and love You." What is your greatest desire for the children in your life? Pray that for them every day. Ask God to bring it to fruition in their lives.

12

Though one may be overpowered by another, two can withstand him. And a threefold cord is not quickly broken.
ECCLESIASTES 4:12

The other day, as we were getting dressed, I told my wife, Joyce, "You know, the great miracle is not love at first sight; it's love after a long, long look. It's a miracle that you can continue to love." I've had a good look at Joyce, and I love her with all of my heart.

But Joyce knows that she's not first in my life—she knows that God is. She doesn't mind being second. She knows I can love her more by putting her second than I ever could by putting her first. And I know I'm not first in Joyce's life. I'm second. And I don't mind, because she loves me with a love that she could not love me with had she not fortified her faith in the Lord,

Joyce and I were at the Billy Graham Conference Center called "The Cove," a beautiful place, and I was preaching on the home. Afterward, in a Q&A session, a little lady got up. She said one of the wisest things I've ever heard: "Ladies, I want you to remember, you may marry a shining knight on a white horse, but somebody's got to clean up after the horse...and enjoy doing it." I thought, now that's a wise woman. You may have married a shining knight, but I'll tell you, he's riding a horse that's going to leave some mess around.

ACTION POINT The Bible says, "A threefold cord is not easily broken." What is that threefold cord? A man, a woman, and God Himself. Marriage is much stronger when you both love the Lord first. If you want a strong, unbreakable marriage, trust in Christ. Make Him Lord of your life and Lord of your home.

13

For "He who would love life and see good days, let him refrain his tongue from evil, and his lips from speaking deceit."

1 PETER 3:10

Homes are going to experience attacks. Ours has, and yours will. Some attacks come from without, and some will come from within. Let's think about some attacks that could come:

Earthquakes come. We've known some earthquakes. I mean some things that shook us to the very foundation. And then there are woodpeckers, always beating on your home. You know the woodpeckers—they just hammer away. But it's easier to deal with the earthquakes and woodpeckers than the termites... those little things in which bitterness comes. Termites get into the foundation, and just silently eat away.

You must banish bitterness!

Don't go to bed angry. "'Be angry, and do not sin': do not let the sun go down on your wrath" (Ephesians 4:26). Don't be getting back at one another. Continue communication. Look at 1 Peter 3: "Finally, all of you be of one mind, having compassion for one another; love as brothers, be tenderhearted, be courteous; not returning evil for evil or reviling for reviling, but on the contrary blessing, knowing that you were called to this, that you may inherit a blessing. For 'He who would love life and see good days, let him refrain his tongue from evil, and his lips from speaking deceit'" (1 Peter 3:8-10).

ACTION POINT One of the greatest dangers to your home comes from within. It's bitterness. Bitterness, like a swarm of termites, eats away at your home's foundation, destroying your marriage. Banish bitterness. Give your spouse and your family the grace you yourself also need.

14

For what will it profit a man if he gains the whole world, and loses his own soul?

MARK 8:36

I read a story that deeply touched my heart. A young preacher came to a mill town. He went to see the owner of the mill, who literally owned the town, to invite him to come to the church. The man answered, "Young man, you've not seen me in church, and you will not see me until my funeral. I own this town and this mill. It is my pot of gold. When I came here as a young immigrant, I heard that in America there was a pot of gold at the end of the rainbow. I have found the gold, but I have lost the rainbow."

Now, I wonder if you're working for that pot of gold and forgetting the rainbow. Work is necessary, but life can't be all work and no play. "It is vain for you to rise up early, to sit up late, to eat the bread of sorrows; for so He gives His beloved sleep" (Psalm 127:2). What he's saying is, don't be so busy making a living that you forget to live! So many people are doing that. God says that is vanity. There's a time to work. There's also a time to rest.

ACTION POINT If this describes you, life is passing you by! Your children are failing to have the joy and happiness God wants for each of you. Someone said, "If you're burning the candle at both ends, you're not as bright as you think you are." Don't forget to live! Work not solely for that gold. There's a rainbow to behold.

15

> Not that I speak in regard to need, for I have learned in whatever state I am, to be content: I know how to be abased, and I know how to abound. Everywhere and in all things I have learned both to be full and to be hungry, both to abound and to suffer need.
>
> **PHILIPPIANS 4:11-12**

One of the most valuable things you can learn for yourself—and teach your children—is contentment. Let your home ring with love, laughter, conversation, and fun, and be content with the simpler things of life.

You say, "Well, I want my kids to have things I never had, things my dad never gave me." Okay. But are you giving them the things your dad did give you: the desire to work, honesty, decency, learning to get along with the basics, and contentment? Would to God we'd get this in our hearts.

What is contentment? It is an inner sufficiency that keeps us at peace in spite of outward circumstances. Paul taught his son in the faith, Timothy, "Godliness with contentment is great gain" (1 Timothy 6:6).

In Philippians 4:11, Paul says contentment must be learned. Develop contentment within your children and you will be strengthening their character. Teach them to trust the Lord and be humbly grateful. Families need to learn to thank God. God has been so good to you.

ACTION POINT Is your family a God-centered family? It would be good for you to get a family diary and write in it the blessings of God. Sit down and rehearse with your children day after day after day the things that God has done for them.

16

Every good gift and every perfect gift is from above, and comes down from the Father of lights, with whom there is no variation or shadow of turning.

JAMES 1:17

A Congressman once told his pastor about a time he took his son to McDonald's for some father-son fellowship. He said:

"My son ordered a large order of fries. As I sat there, the fries smelled so good, I reached out my hand to get a couple. But my son said, 'Hey! Those are mine!' It flew all over me. I started thinking, 'Doesn't he know who bought those fries and gave them to him? Doesn't he know I could go up there and order twenty orders of fries and bury him in French fries? And that I could take them away or go buy some for myself? Doesn't he know that I'm just trying to have fellowship with him?'

Then God spoke to my heart. 'My son, that's the way you are with Me sometimes. I've given you blessings, and when I ask for a part of that blessing, you say, "Hey, that's mine." Son, don't you know I could take that whole thing from you if I wanted to? And don't you know, if I wanted to, I could give you more? And don't you know that I don't need that? I am God. I have anything I want, for "the earth is the LORD's, and all its fullness" (Psalm 24:1). And don't you know that I was wanting to have some fellowship with you?'"

ACTION POINT Oh, friend, may God have mercy upon the spirit of greed that's in our hearts! May we understand that all that we have has come from God—and thank Him for all He has done for us.

17

Now whom you forgive anything, I also forgive. For if indeed I have forgiven anything, I have forgiven that one for your sakes in the presence of Christ, lest Satan should take advantage of us; for we are not ignorant of his devices.

2 CORINTHIANS 2:11

A friend of mine once told me about a film he saw. I haven't seen it, but he explained it to me: He said they went up to the Canadian lakes and got one of these great northern pikes, a big fish, and put it in a huge aquarium with buckets of minnows. That pike thought he had died and gone to pike heaven!

But then they dropped in a glass cylinder, invisible to the pike. This time, they poured the minnows into the cylinder. The pike started for the minnows, but bumped his snout. He backed off and tried again. And again. And again. Finally he made up his mind. "I'll never have another minnow." And he settled down to the bottom of that tank. They pulled the glass tube out, and the minnows swam free, right up to his face, but the pike never moved. They had messed with his mind. He believed something that wasn't true.

Child of God, the devil will mess with your mind. He'll lie to you, just like he lied to Eve in the Garden of Eden (Genesis 3). "...When he speaks a lie, he speaks from his own resources, for he is a liar and the father of it [lies]" (John 8:44b).

ACTION POINT You're surrounded with the blessings of God, but Satan has you believing they're not yours. You say, "That might be for Pastor Rogers, but it's not for me. God doesn't expect me to live in victory." Yes, He does. The devil has never done anything but lie to you. Stop believing the devil's lies. Start believing Jesus, who said, "I've come that you may have life and have it more abundantly" (John 10:10).

18

If we say that we have no sin, we deceive
ourselves, and the truth is not in us.

1 JOHN 1:8

Consider this:

- The evolutionist believes man is on his way up.
- The educator seems to believe that man can be taught to live without sin.
- The scientist seems to think that in solving the problems of the natural world, we will do away with sin.
- The sociologist thinks sin comes from an unhealthy environment.
- The psychologist believes that if you talk about yourself long enough, you'll erase your guilty feelings about sin.

All of them want to ignore God and deny sin. If sin is seen as just a "mistake" or a "sickness," then there is no reason to have God. Sin is not a mistake or a sickness; it is part of man's nature since the Fall in the Garden of Eden. It has been atoned for by the blood of Jesus Christ, must be turned from when a sinner confesses, repents and comes to faith in Jesus, and must be progressively eradicated in the believer's life through submission to the Holy Spirit of God.

ACTION POINT How do you view sin in your life? If you try to ignore it, you'll never have fellowship with God. See it for what it is: an affront to a Holy God. Ask God to let you see it as He sees it. Then confess it. Call upon Him to help you abandon it.

19

> For we do not wrestle against flesh and blood, but against principalities, against powers, against the rulers of the darkness of this age, against spiritual hosts of wickedness in the heavenly places.
>
> **EPHESIANS 6:12**

We are in a great spiritual struggle. Right now we see colossal forces colliding, and this is no time to be asleep.

Dr. James Dobson shared this true story about a missionary in the jungle: One day the missionary entered his hut, and a gigantic snake—one of those that can swallow a whole pig—was inside. He went out to his truck and got his revolver. He only had one shell. He went in and carefully aimed at the head of that monstrous snake and pulled the trigger. The snake was mortally wounded, but he didn't die right away. He began to writhe and thrash around, going this way and that. He literally tore up everything in that hut as he was dying.

I want to tell you something: Jesus at Calvary put a bullet right in Satan's head. And what we're seeing now are the death throes of one who has been mortally wounded by the cross of Jesus Christ.

Friend, we're in a battle. But it's not that we're going to win; we already have won. That old serpent can twist and writhe, but thank God, we're on the winning team. Jesus said, "All authority has been given to Me in heaven and on earth" (Matthew 28:18). "In heaven" means "in the heavenlies" where the battle is. He has unlimited authority in every realm.

ACTION POINT Understand this: "For the weapons of our warfare are not carnal, but mighty in God for pulling down strongholds, casting down arguments and every high thing that exalts itself against the knowledge of God" (2 Corinthians 10:4-5). We're up against demonized, mobilized, powers of Hell. Understand your enemy. Exercise your spiritual authority.

20

My Father, who has given them to Me, is greater than all; and no one is able to snatch them out of My Father's hand. I and My Father are one.

JOHN 10:29-30

When discussing the issue of whether or not you can lose your salvation, I hear people use an interesting argument. They will say, "Well, you know, I don't think I believe in the security of the believer. I just believe that the devil could take you out of God's hands." And they use John 10 as a "proof-text." They say, "Jesus said no person could snatch them out of God's hand, but it doesn't say that the devil couldn't. He hasn't taken me out, but I believe he could. He could snatch you out of God's hand, and you'd be lost."

Now that is a strange doctrine, isn't it? They give Satan so much credit.

Think about it. If Satan *could* snatch you away, then why hasn't he? And if he could snatch one of us, why hasn't he snatched all of us? If he hasn't, then hasn't he been good to you! You are going to Heaven by the goodness of the devil!

Don't you think that if he could, he *would*? The only reason he hasn't is because he can't. The "no one" in John 10:29 is pretty clear. No one can pluck you out of the Father's hand.

ACTION POINT Read Romans 8:38-39 and underline in your Bible the words "angels" and "any other created thing." Meditate on what this means for you: "For I am persuaded that neither death nor life, nor angels nor principalities nor powers, nor things present nor things to come, nor height nor depth, nor any other created thing, shall be able to separate us from the love of God which is in Christ Jesus our Lord."

21

But lay up for yourselves treasures in heaven, where neither moth nor rust destroys and where thieves do not break in and steal.

MATTHEW 6:20

In Luke 16:1-9, the Lord Jesus gave one of the strangest parables in the Bible. At the end of the parable, He explained to His disciples how it applies to us. If the people of this world are so shrewd that they plan ahead for themselves, how much more should the child of God? So, what our Lord is saying is, "I want you to be a good steward of what I have placed in your hands. If you haven't been faithful in material goods, I can't trust you with the real riches. If you haven't been faithful in that which is least, I can't give you that which is more." Take what God has put into your hands and make friends for God. Win souls to Jesus. And when you die, they'll welcome you into Heaven. Have some people waiting on you there.

We often hear people say, "You can't take it with you." But I'll tell you what you can do: you can send it on ahead! And the only way you can send it on ahead is to invest it in something that's going to Heaven. And the only things I know of that are going to Heaven are the souls of men. So if you take the unrighteous mammon that God has put into your hands and invest it in eternity, bringing men, women, boys and girls to faith in Jesus Christ, think of the welcome when you get to Heaven.

ACTION POINT Take the money you have, make plans for the future, and invest your money in something that is going to Heaven. Then when you die and go to Heaven, someone is going to say, "Welcome home! Oh, I'm so glad to see you. I'm here because of your faithfulness."

22

"For My thoughts are not your thoughts, nor
are your ways My ways," says the LORD.

ISAIAH 55:8

God says, "My thoughts and your thoughts are different. My ways and your ways are different." We need to understand that God works on a different thought level than we do.

I once heard of a man who was criticizing the way the Lord made things. He said, "It doesn't make sense to me: a great big oak tree only has little acorns on it, but a weak watermelon vine has to bear those heavy melons. It would make sense for the watermelons to be on the oak tree, and the acorns on the vine." About that time an acorn hit him on the head...and he said, "I'm glad it wasn't a watermelon."

Have you ever heard someone say, "Well, if I were God, I would..."? Maybe you've said it yourself. But how foolish—you don't know what God knows! When you face something you can't understand, ask God to help you understand. In the meantime, trust Him for the answer.

ACTION POINT We may not understand, but "We know that all things work together for good to those who love God, to those who are the called according to His purpose" (Romans 8:28). He is making you what He wants to make you. He'll turn every Calvary into an Easter. He'll turn every midnight to noonday. He'll turn every sigh into a song. And He'll take all your tears and string them and make a diadem of pearls for you. God knows what He's doing, and God is working. The turning of the wheel of life and the touch of the Master's hand are in God's plan to make out of you a beautiful and a fitting vessel for His use.

23

> And we know that all things work together for good to those who love God, to those who are the called according to His purpose.
>
> **ROMANS 8:28**

Sometimes we say, "Now if I were God, I would have done it this way..." But we just don't understand the ways of God. God put this world together the way He wanted it.

If you ever learn this secret to getting into the ways of God, it will open up so many things to you. The Bible says, "So the LORD spoke to Moses face to face, as a man speaks to his friend" (Exodus 33:11a). Psalm 103:7 says "He made known His ways to Moses, His acts to the children of Israel." There is a significant difference between His ways and His acts. A lot of us just see the acts of God, but don't understand the ways of God.

When the Israelites were in the wilderness, being bitten by the fiery serpents, I imagine they were saying, "God, kill the serpents!" (See Numbers 21.) But He didn't do that. Instead, He told Moses to put a fiery serpent upon a brass pole, and whoever looked at it would live—a foreshadowing of His only Son lifted high upon a cross to save all mankind. "And as Moses lifted up the serpent in the wilderness, even so must the Son of Man be lifted up" (John 3:14).

People ask, "Why doesn't God kill the devil? If there's a God, and the devil's so bad, why doesn't God just kill him?" God doesn't kill the devil; God puts His Son on the cross. We need to understand the ways of God.

ACTION POINT Some things you will never understand until you reach Heaven. One of the greatest promises in the Bible is Romans 8:28. Stop trying to figure it all out. In faith, trust Him to form you into the vessel He wants you to be.

24

Then I went down to the potter's house, and
there he was, making something at the wheel.

JEREMIAH 18:3

A man once bragged to Abraham Lincoln that he was a self-made man. Abraham Lincoln said, "I'm glad to hear that. That relieves the Almighty of a fearful responsibility."

The Bible often uses the picture of a potter taking clay and shaping it into a beautiful vessel to describe the way God works in our lives. We like to think we can mold our own lives. But helpless clay could no more mold itself into a vessel of beauty than a human being could, without the touch of the finger of God.

Two things form the vessel from this unlovely lump of clay: the touch of the Potter's hand, and the turning of the wheel. The wheel represents the daily round of our lives, the constant turning of circumstances. God is seeing to it that our lives are revolving around certain events. And the whole time, God is touching our lives to make out of our lives what He wants to make. Now we may not understand every turn of the wheel. We look at things and say, "I don't know why this happened to me."

ACTION POINT You're not going to know why the Potter's wheel turns as it does. But God knows, and He is working. The turning of the wheel of life is His plan to make you a beautiful, fitting vessel for His use. Trust the Master's hand.

25

> Now the word of the Lord came to Jonah the second time, saying, "Arise, go to Nineveh, that great city, and preach to it the message that I tell you."
>
> **JONAH 3:1-2**

Have you stumbled in your walk with God? Then you have come to the right place: the Bible is filled with people who stumbled badly and needed a second chance.

- When Jacob got away from God, Jacob went back to Bethel, and God gave him another chance.
- When God told Jonah to go to Nineveh, Jonah went the other way. But God had a plan for Jonah, and He gave him another chance.
- God wasn't through with Simon Peter when Peter cursed and denied Christ. Thank God He gave him another chance.
- Saul of Tarsus was persecuting the early church, arresting believers. Jesus stopped him on the road to Damascus. A new man, Paul, became the author of much of the New Testament.

"And the vessel that he made of clay was marred in the hand of the potter; so he made it again into another vessel, as it seemed good to the potter to make" (Jeremiah 18:4). That's glorious. I've got great news for you: there is still hope for you! Why could the potter make this vessel again? Because the clay was still soft enough. It had not finally hardened. It was still pliable enough. You are still in the hands of God the Potter, and so the Potter can make it over again. God is the God of the second chance.

ACTION POINT Study the Bible and see how its pages are filled with those who got a second chance from Him. God can mend a broken life if you will give Him all the pieces. He wants to give you a second chance.

26

> And do not be drunk with wine, in which is dissipation; but be filled with the Spirit, speaking to one another in psalms and hymns and spiritual songs, singing and making melody in your heart to the Lord, giving thanks always for all things to God the Father in the name of our Lord Jesus Christ, submitting to one another in the fear of God.
>
> **EPHESIANS 5:18**

What will it take to heal our world? I'm convinced we're facing one of three things: revival, ruin, or the return of Jesus Christ. I pray God it will be either spiritual revival or the return of the Lord Jesus. But if it is a spiritual revival, how will it come about?

People have tried everything. There is only one answer for a world in the need our world is in. The will of the Lord is that the Church of the living God be filled with the Spirit of the living God. This alone is the answer.

What does it mean to be filled with the Spirit? It implies continuous control by the Holy Spirit. The emphasis is on "*be* filled," not "get filled." "Be" implies a continuous control by the Holy Spirit. The fact that you *were* filled with the Spirit doesn't necessarily mean that you *are* filled with the Spirit.

ACTION POINT Oswald Sanders said, "There is no such thing as a once-for-all fullness. We may, and should, be filled with the Spirit again and again." Yesterday's experience is no good for today. Being filled is a day-by-day experience. Ask God to fill you with His Spirit today.

27

Then He brought us out from there, that He might bring us in, to give us the land of which He swore to our fathers.

DEUTERONOMY 6:23

Can you imagine a young Israelite boy born in the wilderness, born during the Israelites' forty years there? He hears people talk about Egypt, what it used to be. He hears about Canaan, what it ought to be. His folks have come out of Egypt, but God brought them out that He might bring them in...to Canaan. But now for forty years, they are going around in circles! This kid looks around—his mom and his dad are not living in Canaan; they're not living in victory. What is he to think?

What about in your home? In your life in Christ, are you just circling around? Stuck in a rut? Off in the ditch? Or do your children see a vibrant, personal relationship with the God who parted the Red Sea and is answering your prayers today? Do your children catch you on your knees?

I'm convinced the reason the devil ensnares kids from good Christian families is, the parents have come out of Egypt, but they've never gone into Canaan. They're stopped in the desert, going 'round and 'round in circles. Live in the victory Jesus died to give you. Make sure your children see you living in victory.

ACTION POINT What are your core values? What are you willing to die for? Do your children know what your core values are? Do your children, your grandchildren, believe there are certain things that you would die for? The greatest testimony you can possess is to have those who know you the best respect you the most. Is that true in your life?

28

> This Book of the Law shall not depart from your mouth, but you shall meditate in it day and night, that you may observe to do according to all that is written in it. For then you will make your way prosperous, and then you will have good success.
>
> **JOSHUA 1:8**

Many people have the wrong idea about success. Someone overheard this conversation:

"You know you're successful if you're invited to the White House."

"No, you're successful if you're in the Oval Office and the red phone rings, but the President is so interested in talking to you, he doesn't even answer it."

"No, success is if you're talking to the President, the red phone rings, he picks it up and says, 'Here—it's for you!'"

Now that, in the eyes of the world, is success.

But not necessarily so. You can be important, or rich, or notorious—even have power and still not be successful. What is success? Listen very carefully. One definition of failure is "succeeding in the wrong thing." That's failure. A wise man has said, "Whatever a man does without God, in that situation he will do one of two things: either fail miserably or succeed more miserably."

May I ask you three questions about what you're doing right now? Everybody's going somewhere. If you get to where you're going, where will you be? I'm not just talking about Heaven or Hell; I'm talking about what where you're going in this life. Second question: If you accomplish your goals, what will you have? And here's the big question: are the things you are living for worth Jesus dying for?

ACTION POINT Success is simply the progressive realization of the will of God for your life. Ask yourself, "Am I actively seeking to know God's will?" Be diligent to find out what it is.

29

Epaphras, who is one of you, a bondservant of Christ, greets you, always laboring fervently for you in prayers, that you may stand perfect and complete in all the will of God.

COLOSSIANS 4:12

To "stand perfect and complete in all the will of God" will mean you are not only under His control, but subject to Him. Some people think being filled with the Spirit is like being filled with a substance, like intelligence, or enthusiasm. Or like a vessel being filled with water; that God's Holy Spirit is poured into the vessel and the vessel is filled.

That's not quite the idea in the Bible. The Holy Spirit is not a substance; the Holy Spirit is a Person. When the Bible says "being filled with the Spirit," it means our bodies are a temple, a dwelling, and the Holy Spirit is the person possessing every room, holding the key to every closet. It means we are in submission to the Holy Spirit.

ACTION POINT Some people don't understand this. They talk about wanting more of the Holy Spirit. The problem is not for you to get more of the Holy Spirit, for the Bible says God doesn't give His Spirit by measure. You have all the Holy Spirit you're ever going to get. At salvation, you have Him within you. But when you're filled, He has all of you. Let the Holy Spirit have full sway in you. Turn everything over to the Holy Spirit.

30

Then Philip opened his mouth, and beginning at this Scripture, preached Jesus to him.

ACTS 8:35

Philip was participating in a large revival in Samaria. People were being saved and baptized. But suddenly he is called away. Acts 8:26-29 tells what happened:

"Now an angel of the Lord spoke to Philip, saying, 'Arise and go toward the south along the road which goes down from Jerusalem to Gaza.' This is desert. So he arose and went. And behold, a man of Ethiopia, a eunuch of great authority under Candace the queen of the Ethiopians, who had charge of all her treasury, and had come to Jerusalem to worship, was returning. And sitting in his chariot, he was reading Isaiah the prophet. Then the Spirit said to Philip, 'Go near and overtake this chariot.'"

Philip ran to him, heard him reading a prophecy in Isaiah about the coming Messiah, and explained the passage to him. You can read the rest of the account in Acts 8:30-37.

Returning home from Jerusalem, the most religious city on earth, the Ethiopian had come away empty. Now when the Holy Spirit sees the Ethiopian is ready, He looks for a man, in this case Philip, whose heart is committed to the Spirit's mission. And the Holy Spirit gets Philip and the Ethiopian together. Salvation takes place!

ACTION POINT The Bible says the eyes of the Lord are searching, looking for men, women, boys, and girls He can use. Are some folks being used of God, but you're not? Get yourself usable. Be completely available to Him, and God will wear you out.

31

> The fruit of the righteous is a tree of life,
> and he who wins souls is wise.
> **PROVERBS 11:30**

It's amazing what gets folks all excited. A Russian once came to the United States during football season, and friends took him to a great bowl game. Afterward, they asked him what he thought about it.

Do you know what he said? "I've never seen so much first-rate enthusiasm for such a second-rate cause."

What is the first-rate cause? What's the most important thing? "For the Son of Man has come to seek and to save that which was lost" (Luke 19:10). Getting souls saved is what it's all about. "Those who are wise shall shine like the brightness of the firmament, and those who turn many to righteousness Like the stars forever and ever" (Daniel 12:3).

You may have members in your family who are lost. One day they will die, and you'll say, "My God, why didn't I witness?" Why don't you say this week, "I'll make my life a life of one thing; this one thing I do." It's time we got excited about what excites God, our Father, and that's winning people to Jesus Christ, committed to the cause of the Holy Spirit.

ACTION POINT Make three commitments this morning, and make them anew every morning this week: One, be inclined to the cause of the Spirit. Two, be insistent for the cause of the spirit. Three, be instant to the commands of the spirit.

"You cannot confess to God what you will not admit to yourself."

ADRIAN ROGERS

september

1

Woe to you, scribes and Pharisees, hypocrites! For you are like whitewashed tombs which indeed appear beautiful outwardly, but inside are full of dead men's bones and all uncleanness.

MATTHEW 23:27

I once read an article about Art Linkletter. Everyone in America would recognize Art Linkletter, a man who for 40 years entertained millions on stage, screen, and television. Art Linkletter said he was a professing Christian. But one day, he had a great tragedy—his daughter took her own life. He really needed help.

In a hotel lobby in San Francisco, he met with some young people who were on-fire Christians. There was no pretense with them; no holds barred. It came time to pray, and those young people got down on their knees in that hotel lobby. And Art Linkletter got down on his knees with them in this public place. He said:

"I looked around and hoped no one would recognize me. But I was on my knees for only a second before I no longer cared what anyone else thought. Until that time, I was self-sufficient. I thought I didn't need anybody. I thought of myself as being a good person...but I was a cardboard Christian. I humbled myself before God, got on my knees, broke through to God, and met reality."

Our world is sick and tired of make-believe, cardboard Christians. It hungers for reality, not hypocrisy. The greatest argument *for* Christ—or the greatest argument *against* Christ—is the life of a Christian!

ACTION POINT There have always been hypocrites. There always will be. But how wonderful to know Jesus Christ—to serve and love Him with reality in your heart. Jesus devoted the sixth chapter of Matthew to the problem of hypocrites. Examine your heart. Would you have knelt and prayed in that hotel lobby?

2

And He said, "My Presence will go with you, and I will give you rest."
EXODUS 33:14

Is a counselor someone you go to who solves your problems? No! What is the purpose of all true counseling? The purpose is to bring people into the presence of God.

Israel knew the *works* of God, but they didn't know the *ways* of God. God was bringing His people into problems—actually engineering their problems! God brought them to Mt. Moriah, a place where there was no water. And He did that, the Bible says, to prove them. All the difficulties of life are meant to bring us to God. He wanted them to find out not only that He is necessary, but also that He is enough.

Do you know what a good counselor does? He just brings people to God. That doesn't mean he won't help them with their problems, but if helping with their problems is all he does and he does not bring them to God, then the problem was wasted. The purpose of all counseling and preaching is not to solve problems for people, but to bring them into God's presence so that they come to know God face to face. You allow them to have an intimate relationship with Almighty God in which they begin to learn the ways of God and the nature of God.

A good counselor has the ways of God in his or her heart. And only those who know the ways of God make good counselors.

ACTION POINT When looking for a counselor, do some research. Ask questions. Look for one who is as solidly grounded in Scripture as he or she is educated in how our minds and emotions work. Look for one who knows the *ways* of God.

3

Through the Lord's mercies we are not consumed,
because His compassions fail not. They are new
every morning; great is Your faithfulness.

LAMENTATIONS 3:22-23

Has it ever occurred to you that, for you to cease living, God would not have to *take* your life? All that He would have to do is just stop *giving* you life! Every day is a gift from God. Time is something God gave you today and will give you tomorrow. God is the Creator, the Possessor of time.

So I am a steward of the time God has given me, and one day I will have to answer to God for what I did with this day and every day. Twenty-four hours in the day, 1,440 minutes, 86,400 seconds. And every one of them is a precious gift from God. I've heard these words since I was a teenager:

I have only just a minute,
Only sixty seconds in it.
Forced upon me, can't refuse it.
Didn't seek it, didn't choose it.
But it's up to me to use it.
I must suffer if I lose it,
Give account if I abuse it.
Just a tiny little minute...
*But eternity is in it.**

ACTION POINT Don't go around saying, "Well, he/she has more time than I have." That's wrong. We all have the same amount of time. Everybody has 24 hours a day—the difference is how people use the time God has given them. I want you to see this time as a provided opportunity that God wants you to awaken to. My dear friend, how are you planning to use your 24 hours today?

*From the poem "Just a Minute" — generally attributed to Dr. Benjamin E. Mays

4

> "Come now, and let us reason together," says the LORD, "Though your sins are like scarlet, they shall be as white as snow; though they are red like crimson, they shall be as wool."
>
> **ISAIAH 1:18**

Do you know what a cynic is? A cynic is one who knows the price of everything and the value of nothing. Many people today scorn the Gospel and have not discerned the inherent goodness in Jesus Christ because they are cynics. The Pharisees and Sadducees—quick to dispute everything the Lord Jesus said—were poster-child cynics. Many today are their spiritual descendants.

There are some who will not kneel before Jesus—or anything, for that matter. They are so proud, so arrogant, and that's the reason they are going to miss Heaven and go straight to Hell. Most of the people in America are egomaniacs, strutting their way to Hell, thinking they're too good to be damned.

Cynicism is a terrible thing. Mr. Cynic, let me tell you something: God loves you, and Jesus loves you, but if you are a cynic, you will probably never know the love of Jesus because of your cynicism.

ACTION POINT Read again Isaiah 1:18, today's passage. You can hear the appeal of God, who with the heart of a loving father wants to forgive your sins no matter how crimson they may be—and make you whole once more. This is the desire of God for you. What will you do with His offer?

5

"Be angry, and do not sin": do not let the sun go down on your wrath...
EPHESIANS 4:26

Not all anger is bad or sinful. There are many things in our world that should move you to anger. The Lord Jesus Himself was moved with righteous anger when it was called for—but only when He saw others being misused and abused, and never when someone harmed Him. Jesus never *retaliated*. Righteous anger is aimed not at the person, but at the injustice; not at the sinner, but at the sin.

If you are angry, God warns people to stay away from you! "Make no friendship with an angry man, and with a furious man do not go, lest you learn his ways and set a snare for your soul" (Proverbs 22:24-25).

You may think that you can't be angry at the sin without being angry at the sinner. But sure you can! We get angry with ourselves over something we've done, yet we still love ourselves.

God has much to say about anger and how we must govern it. "And do not grieve the Holy Spirit of God, by whom you were sealed for the day of redemption" (Ephesians 4:30). The Holy Spirit is present in your situation, and He will give you the power you need.

Some of you have been angry for a long time. Someone hurt you, and you've been nursing a grudge. Quit. It's not worth it. Ungodly anger is an acid that destroys its own container. It harms anything it's poured on.

ACTION POINT What can we do? "And be kind to one another, tenderhearted, forgiving one another, even as God in Christ forgave you" (Ephesians 4:32). Dear friend, you must get into Ephesians chapter 4 and the book of Proverbs and learn how to deal with this thing of stubborn anger.

September 6

Then he showed me Joshua the high priest standing before the Angel of the LORD, and Satan standing at his right hand to oppose him.

ZECHARIAH 3:1

Do you like people talking behind your back? You have someone who not only talks behind your back, but will also accuse you to your face. He is constantly accusing you before God, pointing the finger of accusation. His name is Satan. He is your adversary—the very word Satan means "adversary." Here, in Zechariah 3:1, he stands before the Lord like a prosecuting attorney.

Revelation 12:10 makes it clear: Satan is constantly accusing you. He wants you to sin, encourages you to sin, and then he wants you to suffer the consequences. He points out your sin so you'll get into the guilt trap. He rejoices in your suffering. Satan wants to cripple you, and then blame you for limping! That's what he does!

Warren Wiersbe said, "Before you sin, Satan whispers, 'You can get away with it.' And after you sin, he shouts, 'You'll never get away with it.'"

ACTION POINT Every soldier will tell you: you have to know your enemy. Learn the difference between Satanic accusation and Holy Spirit conviction. You may be under the accusation of Satan, and you think you're under the conviction of the Holy Spirit, because you don't know the difference. Satan is the adversary; the Holy Spirit is the comforter. Satan accuses; the Holy Spirit convicts. Satan accuses to drive you to despair. The Holy Spirit convicts to draw you to Jesus Christ, forgiveness, freedom and liberty.

7

Hide Your face from my sins, and blot out all my iniquities...
Restore to me the joy of Your salvation,
and uphold me by Your generous Spirit.

PSALM 51:9, 12

Do you want to find out whether you are backslidden or not? Let's take your spiritual temperature with the "Joy Test." Do you have joy in your heart all the time—"Joy inexpressible and full of glory" (1 Peter 1:8)—whatever may happen?

You may say, "Dr. Rogers, no. I don't have *that* kind of joy. Nobody is supposed to be joyful all the time. I've had some tough times."

I think you are thinking about happiness, not joy.

True joy doesn't depend upon your circumstances. *Happiness* depends on circumstances—what "happens" to you. We're not talking about happiness. Joy, on the other hand, is an inside job. True joy shines best in tough times. You can radiate joy in spite of circumstances or what happens.

Did you know that the New Testament book that radiates the most joy—Philippians—was written by Paul from a Roman prison? He said (Philippians 4:4), "Rejoice in the Lord always, and again I say, rejoice." And you rejoice not in your circumstances but in the Lord.

ACTION POINT Paul didn't say "be happy always." He *did* say, "Rejoice always" (1 Thessalonians 5:16). You can't be happy always, because your circumstances change. Joy comes from your relationship with Jesus. You can have joy all the time because you can have Jesus all the time. Remember, "The joy of the Lord is your strength" (Nehemiah 8:10). Turn your eyes upon Jesus and away from your circumstances, and in Him you can "rejoice always."

September 8

Then they remembered that God was their rock,
and the Most High God their Redeemer.

PSALM 78:35

It's amazing—the things the devil will try just to get you to examine yourself and start doubting. You might say, "I know I'm saved."

The devil replies, "No, you're not."

"Why? Why am I not saved? I believe in Jesus."

"Oh, yeah, a person's saved by faith in Jesus," the devil says, "but your faith isn't good enough."

Has that devil ever pulled that on you? "You don't believe enough. Your faith isn't strong enough. Your faith is such a low-class faith—if it's faith at all—that it's not going to get you there, because you're not a true believer."

Now, how are you going to argue with the devil over that?

Here's how I do it: When the devil tells me, "Adrian Rogers, your faith is no good," I say,

"That's right...but isn't Jesus wonderful?"

ACTION POINT Sometimes we hear sermons on "saving faith." There is no such thing. Faith doesn't save you; *Jesus* does. It's "by grace, through faith" that you're saved (See Ephesians 2:8). Faith is necessary for salvation, but you're saved *by Jesus*! How much faith does it take? Just enough to say, "Lord, I trust You." Stop agonizing over whether your faith is strong enough. Instead, when doubts arise say, "Lord, I trust You." Don't put faith in faith; put faith in Jesus.

9

> But when the kindness and the love of God our Savior toward man appeared, not by works of righteousness which we have done, but according to His mercy He saved us, through the washing of regeneration and renewing of the Holy Spirit.
>
> **TITUS 3:4-5**

Theoretically, there are three ways you can get to Heaven:

1. Die before you reach the age of accountability. Precious little children who die before they know right from wrong go immediately to Heaven. But if you understand what I'm saying, this opportunity is already passed for you. (Strike one.)
2. Be perfect and never sin. Keep all the commandments perfectly. Never commit an evil deed or have an evil thought. If you could keep them, that would show that you had no sinful nature; you wouldn't need to be saved. But no one can keep them. Ever since Genesis 3, we are *born* with a sin nature. Is there anyone reading this who has never sinned at all? No. (Strike two.)
3. Give your heart to Jesus Christ. Receive Him and His death on Calvary as full payment for your sin.

You see, you already have two strikes against you when you come to the plate. One last opportunity: Receive Jesus Christ. If you don't, strike three—you're out. You can't do anything to merit eternal life in and of yourself.

ACTION POINT The only way to Heaven is to receive Christ as your personal Savior. Are you certain you're saved, your sins forgiven? Salvation is not something you inherit; it's a gift of God you receive by faith in the Lord Jesus Christ. If you have never taken that step, visit **lwf.org/discover-jesus** today.

September 10

> There is therefore now no condemnation to those who are in Christ Jesus, who do not walk according to the flesh, but according to the Spirit.
>
> **ROMANS 8:1**

Think for a moment about what it was like for Noah and his family to be in the ark while the waters raged outside and the entire world faced destruction. What would you feel? What would you be glad of? First, that the ark was waterproof. Second, that it held every provision you needed. Thirdly, that you were safe in God's hands. He had shut the door and sealed you inside.

It's the very same to be "in Christ Jesus." He is our Ark of safety. God told Noah, "Put pitch on the inside and on the outside" of the ark (Genesis 6:14). The word "pitch" in the Hebrew is *kapar*—and it's exactly the same word translated as "atonement." To Noah it was pitch—a tar-like substance. For us, He has said, "Put atonement on the outside, atonement on the inside," because the ark was a picture of the Lord Jesus Christ. The water was judgment, but not one drop of judgment could come through that atonement in that ark of safety, which was the Lord Jesus Christ.

You see, we are in Jesus as Noah was in that ark. Just as the storms of God's wrath beat upon that ark, the storms of God's wrath beat upon the Lord Jesus. But we are on the inside, and not one drop of judgment can come through.

ACTION POINT Read Romans 8:35-39. Reflect on the list of things Paul says will never separate you from God's love. Give glory to God that your sins have been fully forgiven by the righteous blood of the Lord Jesus Christ.

11

But immediately Jesus spoke to them, saying,
"Be of good cheer! It is I; do not be afraid."
MATTHEW 14:27

Sometimes I ask a friend, "How are you doing?" He'll say, "Oh, I'm doing pretty well under the circumstances." How did he ever get under there?

Dear friend, don't look at circumstances. If you look at circumstances, you're going to fall.

Remember when Peter and the other disciples were in the boat on the Sea of Galilee, the waves were dangerous, and Jesus came walking toward them on the water? Peter saw Him and said, "Lord, if it be Thou, bid me come to Thee on the water." The Master said, "Come."

Peter got out of the boat and started walking. I can imagine his heart was jumping with joy. "This is wonderful!" Then an unkind wave slapped him in the face. He looked around and said, "This is impossible." And it was. He started to sink. What happened? Peter simply failed to keep looking to Jesus. He looked at circumstances, that's all.

Listen, there are plenty of waves around us, but you'd better get your eyes off them and on Jesus. Don't look at yourself. Some Christians are always looking at themselves, examining themselves, taking themselves apart piece by piece—morbid introspection. Just take one glance to see that you're no good—no one is—and that'll do. From there on, look to the Lord Jesus!

Everything that threatened to be over Peter's head was already under Jesus' feet. Don't forget: Jesus was walking on that water!

ACTION POINT Circumstances are like a mattress. You're supposed to be on it, not under it. Under the circumstances, you suffocate; above them, you rest pretty well. Take your eyes off self and circumstances. Fix your eyes only on Jesus.

September 12

> He will sit as a refiner and a purifier of silver; He will purify the sons of Levi, and purge them as gold and silver, that they may offer to the Lord an offering in righteousness.
>
> **MALACHI 3:3**

You're probably not aware of some things that are lurking in your heart. Let me explain: a while back, my wife Joyce said something to me that upset me. I might as well be honest—it made me mad because it was true. She pushed a hot button somewhere, and what was in the murky recesses of my heart came up. Joyce didn't put it there. She only brought it out. I was surprised and ashamed at the pride, arrogance, and insensitivity in my own heart.

I got alone with God and let Him say, "You're not quite like you think you are, are you? There are some things in that old heart of yours that need to be refined out."

When the refiner's fire touches us, we're going to think God is a thousand light-years away. My dear friend, we need to trust the goodness of God and rest in the goodness of God, because Malachl says He's just sitting there during our refining with a sovereign, sympathetic, steadfast purpose.

Our refiner is the ruler and the Redeemer. He knows exactly what He's doing to burn away the superficial and give us the supernatural. In the middle of your trial, trust His sovereign purpose.

ACTION POINT Receive the grace of God. Recognize the goal of God. Rest in the goodness of God when you're in the fire. Then you will reflect the glory of God.

13

For He says: "In an acceptable time I have heard you,
and in the day of salvation I have helped you."
2 CORINTHIANS 6:2

When I preach, I preach to bring people to a decision. Some say, "I won't decide today." Oh, yes, you will—you will decide about Jesus Christ. You might say "I'm not going to decide." Well...you just decided.

I was witnessing to a young lady one day. I asked her if she would receive Christ. She said, "No. I can't do it today." I said, "Don't you realize that if you don't receive Him, you're denying Him?" "Oh," she said, "I wouldn't deny Him for anything." I countered, "Well, Jesus said, 'He that is not with Me is against Me.' Either you crown Him or crucify Him, you accept or reject Him. There's no middle ground."

She said, "I'm just not going to do anything." I said, "All right. Before I go, will you shake hands with me?" "Well, certainly." "Good. If you'll take Christ as your personal savior, and Heaven and all that goes with it, take my right hand. If you refuse Christ and take Hell and all that goes with it, take my left hand." "Oh then—I won't. I don't want to shake hands with you." "But you said you'd shake hands." I wanted that young lady to see there's no neutral ground.

ACTION POINT Maybe people you know think they aren't deciding—they're just delaying their decisions. Help them see that when you choose not to decide, you just made a decision. Joshua challenged God's people: "Choose you this day whom you will serve....but as for me and my house, we will serve the Lord" (see Joshua 24:15). What is your decision?

September 14

> Now as He was going out on the road, one came running,
> knelt before Him, and asked Him, "Good Teacher,
> what shall I do that I may inherit eternal life?"
>
> **MARK 10:17**

This young man mentioned in Mark 10:17 seemed to have it all:

- Youth and enthusiasm—he came running to Jesus.
- Humility—he publicly kneeled before Jesus.
- Discernment—he recognized that Jesus was no ordinary man.
- Position—he was a ruler, according to Luke 18:18.
- Morally upright—all his life he had kept the commandments. (See Mark 10:19-20)

But he did not have life. Jesus got below the surface. "Then Jesus, looking at him, loved him, and said to him, 'One thing you lack: Go your way, sell whatever you have and give to the poor, and you will have treasure in heaven; and come, take up the cross, and follow Me'" (Mark 10:21). How the young man responded exposed the hidden loyalties of his heart. His commandment-keeping was only outward. He walked away grieving.

All the commandments are summed up in loving God with all your heart, mind, soul and strength, and loving your neighbor as yourself (Luke 10:27). By turning away, the young man revealed that he had broken all the commandments, because "On these two commandments hang all the Law and the Prophets" (Matthew 22:40).

ACTION POINT This young man had another god in his life. Do you? Or is Christ your undisputed Lord with no rivals? Pray: "Jesus, I recognize that I cannot be saved by keeping commandments. I will have no other god before me, and I come to You and yield my life, my heart, my soul, my all—forever."

15

> Then Jesus, looking at him, loved him, and said to him, "One thing you lack: Go your way, sell whatever you have and give to the poor, and you will have treasure in heaven; and come, take up the cross, and follow Me."
>
> **MARK 10:21**

As Jesus was talking with the young man known as "the rich young ruler," He brought the young man to a place where he had to make a decision. Jesus challenged him, "Why do you call me good? There is none good but God."

Was Jesus saying that He was not good? No—He was asking, "Do you understand the source of My goodness, and what drew you to Me? The goodness I have is inherently Mine because I am God. Do you understand that I am God?" This young man, with prestige, and possessions, had to choose. No more fence-sitting.

The young ruler didn't realize the depth of sinfulness and wickedness in the human heart—even his own. "The heart is deceitful above all things, and desperately wicked; who can know it" (Jeremiah 17:9)?

We don't think our hearts are wicked—not us, our hearts are pretty good—but what about all these other people? Oh, how our hearts can deceive us!

ACTION POINT If you think you can go to Heaven without being born again, you're ignorant of two things: how wicked your heart is and how holy God is. Have you stopped recently to examine the condition of your heart? Even those who are saved need check-ups. Are you counting on the goodness of your heart or on His saving grace?

16

> Then Jesus, looking at him, loved him, and said to him, "One thing you lack: Go your way, sell whatever you have and give to the poor, and you will have treasure in heaven; and come, take up the cross, and follow Me." But he was sad at this word, and went away sorrowful, for he had great possessions.
>
> **MARK 10:21-22**

In this one-on-one encounter with the young man in the Bible known as "the rich young ruler," Jesus peeled back the layers to reveal the wickedness at the core of the young man's heart. Little did the young man dream what was there. That's why Jesus began talking about keeping the commandments.

Two things become abundantly clear:

1. None can be saved by keeping the commandments.
2. None can be saved by giving what he has to the poor.

Jesus shows the young man just the opposite. That's why He brought it up: so the young man could see he was trusting in his own self-righteousness.

Salvation isn't a reward for the righteous; it's a gift for the guilty. It rests not upon the goodness of man but on the grace of God. There's none good but God. You cannot be saved by commandment-keeping. "By the works of the law no flesh will be justified" in God's sight. (See Galatians 2:16.)

ACTION POINT The law serves as a teacher to bring us to Christ. It condemns us so we will come to the Gospel and be saved. Do you think you're fine just as you are? There's only one thing wrong with you—you're dead. "And you, being dead in your trespasses....He has made alive together with Him, having forgiven you all trespasses, having wiped out the handwriting of requirements that was against us. ...And He has taken it out of the way, having nailed it to the cross" (Colossians 2:13-14). What are you depending on for your salvation?

17

> Jesus answered him, "The first of all the commandments is: 'Hear, O Israel, the Lord our God, the Lord is one. And you shall love the Lord your God with all your heart, with all your soul, with all your mind, and with all your strength.' This is the first commandment.
>
> **MARK 12:29-30**

Jesus called for a decision from the rich young ruler, but the young man made a disastrous decision. Jesus didn't lower the standards of the Kingdom of God in order to get him. He didn't say, "Well, that's all right, come on back. We'll talk it over—let's negotiate this thing." No, Jesus let him go.

The young man had another god in his life—gold. He worshipped money more than the Master. There's nothing wrong with having money, but this young man's money had him. It meant more to him than Jesus Christ.

We're not saved by keeping the Ten Commandments or supporting the poor, as good as those things are. As believers in Christ, we *should* do them. But with good works or not, if you love anything or anybody more than Jesus Christ, you are not saved. "Jesus said to him, 'You shall love the Lord your God with all your heart, with all your soul, and with all your mind'" (Matthew 22:37; also see Deuteronomy 6:5).

God will never be a moonlighting deity with a duplex for a throne. He must be Lord of all if He's to be Lord at all. Jesus knew this young man had enthroned an idol in his heart and wasn't even aware of it. The young man thought, "The Bible says 'You shall have no other gods before Me.' I've never had any!" But he did.

ACTION POINT Do you sit in church on Sunday morning, listen to a sermon, and think that you have done God a favor? Examine your own heart. Make certain there are no other gods sitting on the throne there.

september

18

Then Jesus looked around and said to His disciples, "How hard it is for those who have riches to enter the kingdom of God!"

MARK 10:23

Not all stories have a happy ending. I like stories that end, "...And they lived happily ever after." But this one in Mark 10 has a tragic ending. It is the story of a rich young man who blew it. He lost his soul. I call it "the suicide of a soul."

This young man had so much going for him. He had riches, rank, and religion. But he was also humble—he came kneeling. He wanted to inherit eternal life. He recognized Jesus' authority and called Him "master." He recognized Jesus' goodness. He saw something in Jesus he'd not seen in anyone else: Jesus alone had the answer to eternal life.

Yet the account ends with, "But he was sad at this word, and went away sorrowful, for he had great possessions" (Mark 10:22).

A soul is the most precious thing on earth, the most valuable thing you have. Jesus said, "What will it profit a man if he gains the whole world, and loses his own soul? Or what will a man give in exchange for his soul" (Mark 8:36-37)? I'm convinced that Jesus would have died for you if you had been the only soul needing salvation. That's how much He loves you.

ACTION POINT What was it that kept this young man from leaving all behind to fully follow Jesus? For you, it may not be possessions. What do you need to lay aside to fully follow Jesus?

19

But the Jews who were not persuaded, becoming envious, took some of the evil men from the marketplace, and gathering a mob, set all the city in an uproar and attacked the house of Jason, and sought to bring them [Paul and Silas] out to the people. But when they did not find them, they dragged Jason and some brethren to the rulers of the city, crying out, "These who have turned the world upside down have come here too."

ACTS 17:5-6

Ours is the greatest mission on the face of this earth: the salvation of lost souls. Our message is the greatest message: the glorious Gospel of our Lord and Savior Jesus Christ. Our Master is the greatest Master: Jesus Christ Himself. The church that's not interested in evangelism and soul winning is not worthy of the ground it occupies. We are to evangelize, or we will fossilize. Our mandate is to preach the glorious Gospel of Jesus Christ to every creature.

What was the early church like? "Then the word of God spread, and the number of the disciples multiplied greatly in Jerusalem, and a great many of the priests were obedient to the faith" (Acts 6:7).

They did so much with so little. We do so little with so much. They didn't have Christian colleges, seminaries, radio and TV stations, or printing presses. They had no finances, no prestige. They went out to tell the message of a carpenter's son who was crucified. Against the imperial might of Rome, the intellectual sophistry of Greece, and the stiff-necked resistance of Jewish leaders, it was said of them, "These people turned the world upside down."

ACTION POINT Do you have a sincere concern for souls? You might answer, "I do." But would you feel a twinge of conscience as you did so?

20

> Jesus answered and said to him, "Most assuredly, I say to you, unless one is born again, he cannot see the kingdom of God." Nicodemus said to Him, "How can a man be born when he is old? Can he enter a second time into his mother's womb and be born?" Jesus answered, "Most assuredly, I say to you, unless one is born of water and the Spirit, he cannot enter the kingdom of God.
>
> **JOHN 3:3-5**

If you know people who are not Christians, do not try to argue with them. Nobody was ever argued into the Kingdom of Heaven. Anything someone can argue you into, you can be argued out of.

The problem is, they cannot see. Would you scold a blind man for not seeing? But a blind man would be foolish to say there's no light just because he cannot see it. There is light, but man needs more than light. He needs sight.

He may have 20/20 sight, but spiritually, he is blind. "Having their understanding darkened, being alienated from the life of God, because of the ignorance that is in them, because of the blindness of their heart" (Ephesians 4:18). The eyes may be fine, but the heart is blind.

Are there people you have shared the Gospel with—perhaps even members of your own family—but they still haven't a clue as to what it's all about? They never will, until the Holy Spirit opens their understanding.

ACTION POINT Before I preach, I pray, "O, God, give sight to those who need Jesus," because I know it takes the work of the Holy Spirit for someone to be saved. When you want your loved ones to come to Christ, pray for them "whose minds the god of this age has blinded, who do not believe, lest the light of the gospel of the glory of Christ, who is the image of God, should shine on them." (See 2 Corinthians 4:4.)

21

I will lift up my eyes to the hills—from whence comes my help?
My help comes from the Lord, who made heaven and earth.
PSALM 121:1-2

Are you facing problems that seem insurmountable? It may be in your marriage. It may be with your children. It could be at work. Some problems seem larger than any mountain when we face them.

In 1921, British Army officer George Mallory took part in the first expedition to climb Mt. Everest, this huge—some thought unconquerable—mountain. The expedition failed.

Mallory made a second attempt in 1922 and his last one in 1924. They got to 25,000 ft. No one is sure what happened, but Mallory and a friend slipped and fell—and died on the slopes of Mt. Everest. Soon, another group failed in tragedy.

Years later in London, a man was giving a speech on how hard Everest was to conquer. Behind him, a huge photograph of Everest covered the wall. Then he turned around and started talking to Mount Everest.

"Everest, we tried once to conquer you, and we failed. We tried again to conquer you, and we failed. But, Everest, we will conquer you, because you can't grow any bigger, but we can. We can."

Friend, your problems may seem like an unconquerable mountain, but you can grow in the power of the Holy Spirit.

ACTION POINT We can conquer. We can grow in the grace and knowledge of our Lord Jesus Christ. We can be filled with the Spirit. Our prayers can increase in power. Submit yourself to God. Pray the armor of God over yourself and your family (Ephesians 6:10-18). Begin today—overcome your Everest.

22

> I, wisdom, dwell with prudence, and find out knowledge and discretion. The fear of the Lord is to hate evil; pride and arrogance and the evil way and the perverse mouth I hate. Counsel is mine, and sound wisdom; I am understanding, I have strength. By me kings reign, and rulers decree justice. By me princes rule, and nobles, all the judges of the earth.
>
> **PROVERBS 8:12-16**

Which is more important for a leader—to be smart, or to be wise? How much better to have someone at the helm who is wise rather than just smart! When God offered Solomon anything he wanted, Solomon knew enough to ask for wisdom. Wisdom is the gift of God.

In your church, are those in leadership wise? Do you sense that they're trusting in the Lord for every decision, and are devoted to prayer and study of His Word? Many leaders today, both in the nation and the Church, are not statesmen. Politicians make decisions by polls: "If I find out what people want and give it to them, they'll vote for me." They lead by finding out which way the wind is blowing, then going that way. They're leading not by godly wisdom, but by human opinion. Former President Harry Truman said, "I wonder how far Moses would have gone if he'd taken a poll in Egypt?"

What would Jesus Christ have preached had he taken a poll in Israel? Would the Reformation have happened if Martin Luther had taken a poll? What's more important: polls of public opinion or right and wrong and leadership?

ACTION POINT People with fortitude and honesty, guided by what is right, make history. What about you? You can't have wisdom *from* God unless you are *under* God in service and worship. Devote yourself to prayer and the study of the Word. Wisdom will be the result.

23

> I beseech you therefore, brethren, by the mercies of God, that you present your bodies a living sacrifice, holy, acceptable to God, which is your reasonable service.
>
> **ROMANS 12:1**

I have a friend named Josef Tson, a dear man who is like the Billy Graham of Romania. Josef is a man of great faith. Once I was in Romania preaching crusades. One day, as we were riding along, I asked him for his opinion of American Christians.

He answered, "No, Adrian, I'd rather not." I said, "Josef, I'm a big boy—tell me." "Well, Adrian, in America, the big word is commitment." "That's good, isn't it, Josef?" "No, not necessarily. When you make a commitment, you're in control. But when you surrender, you're no longer in control."

The word "commitment" didn't even really come into vogue in the United States until about the 1960's. It's a popular word today. People are telling God what they're committed to: memorizing the Bible, tithing, soul-winning. People like to be in control. We like to make commitments, but the true word is *surrender*. Jesus is Lord. Don't say, "Lord, I'm committing myself to building a great church, to more Bible study," to more of this or that. Instead, say, "I surrender. I am yours, Lord."

ACTION POINT Only when you lift your hands in ultimate surrender will you know the power of God at work in you. You will never, ever be over those things God wants under you until you get under those things God has set over you. Start with complete surrender. Study the Word of God. Surrender fully to the lordship of Jesus Christ in your life.

September 24

> And I also say to you that you are Peter, and on this rock I will build My church, and the gates of Hades shall not prevail against it.
>
> **MATTHEW 16:18**

ny great church is built on these four things that begin with the letter B:

1. The *Book*—the inspired, infallible Word of God.
2. The *Blood*—the shed blood of the Lord Jesus Christ.
3. The *Birth*—the new birth.
4. The *Blessed Hope*—the coming again of the Lord Jesus Christ.

You need to be part of a community of faithful believers. Don't be "a bone on your own," like the dry bones in Ezekiel 37. "And let us consider one another in order to stir up love and good works, not forsaking the assembling of ourselves together, as is the manner of some, but exhorting one another, and so much the more as you see the Day approaching" (Hebrews 10:24-25). God wants us to find a Bible-believing church and to connect with the people there.

ACTION POINT If you are looking for a church, find out if the church you are considering takes a stand on the Book, the Blood, the Birth, and the Blessed Hope. If not, then saturate that place with your absence. Look for a church that does.

25

For we have become partakers of Christ if we hold the beginning of our confidence steadfast to the end, while it is said: "Today, if you will hear His voice, do not harden your hearts as in the rebellion."

HEBREWS 3:14-15

We hear people say, "Well, get right with God—you may die." Let me change that: "Get right with God—you may live." And if you live, you can live with Jesus.

Don't get the idea that being a Christian is paying some sort of penalty to get into Heaven, like taking bad medicine to get well, as if you don't like the way it tastes, but you choke it down.

I would be a Christian even if there were no Heaven or Hell, just to be able to serve the Lord Jesus Christ in this life. Now, there is a Heaven and there is a Hell, but serving Jesus is so wonderful that I would do it even if there weren't. Jesus said, "I have come that they may have life, and that they may have it more abundantly" (John 10:10b).

Oh, there are sorrows. We have troubles. Persecutions, certainly. Unsaved people have them too. But God's child has Someone to bring his sorrows to. A Christian has a hope and a strength and looks forward to the day when there'll be no more sorrows, no more suffering, when Jesus takes every tear and turns it to a pearl, the day He takes every hurt and turns it to a hallelujah.

ACTION POINT We have a loving Savior. How wonderful to know the Lord Jesus Christ in this life. Every day with Jesus is sweeter than the day before. Get right with God now, because you may live!

26

> Therefore you shall lay up these words of mine in your heart and in your soul, and bind them as a sign on your hand, and they shall be as frontlets between your eyes. You shall teach them to your children, speaking of them when you sit in your house, when you walk by the way, when you lie down, and when you rise up.
>
> **DEUTERONOMY 11:18-19**

When your children are little, it's always good to have family worship, to start the day with the Word of God. But how do you do it successfully?

My wife, Joyce, and I tried all kinds of things with our kids for family worship. I want to give you one of the simplest, easiest forms of family worship. You can also do this with your grandchildren, and with your grown children when they're with you at breakfast.

We let one of the little children who is old enough to read take the Bible and choose a proverb. The child can choose it at random. Since Proverbs has 31 chapters—the same as the number of days in a month—it's easy to choose a proverb from the corresponding day. If it's the seventh day of the month, the child might choose from the seventh chapter of Proverbs, and read a proverb—just one. And let that child explain what he thinks that proverb means. Then everyone else talks about it for a few moments.

It is so simple! But when your children are learning those proverbs and having to think about what they mean, you're giving them distilled wisdom, nuggets of truth they can carry with them to school and to work.

ACTION POINT Give your children and grandchildren wise instruction, but let that instruction be joined with training. "Train up a child."

27

For it is impossible for those who were once enlightened, and have tasted the heavenly gift, and have become partakers of the Holy Spirit, and have tasted the good word of God and the powers of the age to come, if they fall away, to renew them again to repentance, since they crucify again for themselves the Son of God, and put Him to an open shame.

HEBREWS 6:4-6

Have you ever been to the supermarket when they're giving away little samples of cheese? You may love it, and say, "Give me a pound of that!" You carry it to the register, and the checker says, "That'll be $30, please. It's imported from lower Mongolia. Very rare." You say, "Well, just put it back. I know what it is and how it tastes, but I'm not going to pay that high a price."

Our passage from Hebrews 6 talks about something impossible: it's 100% impossible for some people to be renewed to repentance and get right with God. Who is it talking about? Those who at one time were enlightened, whose eyes were opened. They have tasted the power of the Word of God.

These aren't saved people who've lost their salvation, but people who come up to the brink of salvation. After they know the truth and have nibbled at it, with eyes wide open they say "no" to God, refuse Christ, trample beneath their feet His precious blood, and—as it were—crucify Jesus again. In so doing, they commit a greater sin than those who nailed Jesus to the cross at Calvary.

ACTION POINT Here's the good news: If you want to be saved, that means the Holy Spirit is working in you. Anyone who wants to be saved can be. "...If you confess with your mouth the Lord Jesus and believe in your heart that God has raised Him from the dead, you will be saved" (Romans 10:9).

28

Therefore a man shall leave his father and mother and be joined to his wife, and they shall become one flesh.

GENESIS 2:24

You may have heard of the famous South African diamond mines. It is said that they were discovered when a man saw some little boys playing on the ground with shiny rocks. He watched how they sparkled in the sunlight—he stooped down, picked up one of them, and found out it was a diamond. Here were little boys playing marbles with diamonds!

I'm afraid that is what some people today are doing when it comes to sexual purity. God has given something so beautiful, so wonderful, to us and yet we misuse it and transgress every protection He placed around this sacred gift.

Since the fall of Adam and Eve in the Garden, man has trampled on this treasure. In modern times, things began to spin out of control with the moral and sexual revolution of the 1960's. We were told the parameters found in the Word of God concerning the physical relationship between a man and a woman were no longer applicable. Truths and commandments revealed to us in Holy Scripture were labeled ridiculous and out of date.

What has been the result of our grasping this valuable treasure and playing with it in the dirt like marbles? Children at younger and younger ages are stripped of their innocence. Our homes are coming apart at the seams. We are witnessing the slaughter of millions of precious unborn babies who are being put to death. Depression has skyrocketed. As the family unit falls apart, more young people are taking their own lives, and our nation is in chaos.

ACTION POINT This is the reason the Bible says, "You shall not commit adultery" (Exodus 20:14). God was saying, "Don't adulterate or contaminate something so precious and lovely." Marriage, as God created it, is to be honored and protected. Value purity. Treasure it as a rare diamond.

29

Therefore if the Son makes you free,
you shall be free indeed.
JOHN 8:36

You may say, "I don't want to belong to Jesus; I want to be free." Well, you will only become free when you belong to Jesus Christ.

If a train says, "I don't want to run on these tracks; I want to be free," how far do you think it will go? Here is a kite tied to a string—it says, "I don't want to be tied to a string; I want to be free!" The string breaks...and down it goes. If a tree planted in the earth said, "I don't want to be planted in the earth; I want to be free," and it was jerked up from the earth, would it live? Freedom is found in Jesus Christ.

Everything that is truly free is functioning as God made it to function. Just as a train was made to run on rails, God made you to serve the Lord Jesus Christ—to know Him, love Him, and keep His laws. Freedom is found in Jesus Christ, "for in Him we live and move and have our being" (see Acts 17:28).

ACTION POINT You are free to sin, but that is not freedom. It's only freedom to die and go to Hell. Real freedom comes from Jesus Christ. Yield your life to Jesus Christ. Then you will know the true freedom only He can give you.

30

He who loves silver will not be satisfied with silver; nor he who loves abundance, with increase. This also is vanity.

ECCLESIASTES 5:10

I can say without a shadow of doubt that money is a root of all kinds of family problems. Many of our families are in financial bondage, and it is the devil's plan to keep you there.

One of the most helpful things American families can learn is the difference between needs and wants. We have wants that aren't genuine needs, and the desire for more and more things isn't making us happy.

Surveys of married couples show that the number one problem in homes is not sex, children, or in-laws, but finances. Many young couples today think they have to get in three years what it took their parents thirty years to accumulate, and they think they can go out and get it with the false god of credit.

Your personal value is revealed not by money but by godliness. You don't need wealth to give you contentment, and what you do accumulate, you're not going to be able to keep. You'll never see a hearse going along with a U-Haul attached behind it. There are certain things we cannot keep and certain things we cannot lose.

What are you leaving behind? The greatest wealth you have is not in the bank. If you have children, your greatest wealth is your children. Prosperity is posterity.

ACTION POINT What legacy are you leaving in the hearts and lives of your children? Faithfulness to God? Love for His Word? Knowing how to pray and hear from God? Missionary statesman Jim Elliott said, "He is no fool who gives what he cannot keep to gain what he cannot lose."

Don't let your conscience be your guide unless God guides your conscience.

ADRIAN ROGERS

october

1

> And seeing the multitudes, He went up on a mountain,
> and when He was seated His disciples came to Him.
> Then He opened His mouth and taught them...
> **MATTHEW 5:1-2A**

Whatever your circumstances, Jesus' teaching in chapters 5-7 of Matthew tells you how you can go from spiritual rags to spiritual riches. We call it the "Sermon on the Mount." It begins with the Beatitudes. He's talking about how to live from the inside out: how to be saved, satisfied, and sanctified, how to enter the kingdom, enjoy the kingdom and express the kingdom to the world.

That's what serious followers of Jesus want. But it won't happen without inward change. If all we have are those outer trappings the world thinks are so important, we're spiritually bankrupt. So what do we do? A good place to start is with what Jesus taught in the Sermon on the Mount.

- "Blessed are the poor in Spirit..." We are spiritually bankrupt before a holy God. Give up any idea of self-reliance. Rely completely on Him.
- "Blessed are they that mourn..." Come in broken-hearted repentance.
- "Blessed are the meek..." Surrender control of your life. Give it to the Lordship of Jesus Christ.
- "Blessed are they which do hunger and thirst for righteousness..." Jesus Christ is our righteousness. Desire Him above all else.
- "Blessed are the merciful..." Let His love flow through you to others.

ACTION POINT The Christian life is a marathon, not a sprint. These five blesseds are the basics. Each one of these Beatitudes is an action for you as a believer. The time to begin is now.

2

> Therefore, if anyone is in Christ, he is a new creation; old things have passed away; behold, all things have become new.
>
> **2 CORINTHIANS 5:17**

Happiness doesn't come from what you have, but from what you are. That's why the social gospel will never work. Some well-meaning Christians think that if they could just change people's conditions, they could somehow change their character and thus change society. That's never going to work. Listen, I want to ask you a question: Where did mankind get into trouble in the first place? In the Garden of Eden. Where are you going to find a better environment than that? Yet Eden was where people decided to rebel against God.

Don't buy into the idea that a better or even a perfect environment is going to save the world. Better living conditions improve people's lives in the sense of meeting their physical needs, and we should want to help people have clean water, sufficient food, clothing and shelter. But that's not what we're talking about here. We're talking about character.

This is the difference between the social gospel and the saving gospel. The saving gospel realizes you're not going to build the knowledge of God, His character and His principles into people by providing a nicer environment, any more than you could purify water by painting the pump handle. The Bible puts the emphasis not on what man has, not even primarily on what man does, but on what man *is*.

ACTION POINT If you want this world to become a better place, help people understand that what they need is inward change. To provide the best environment for people to change, share with them the life-changing Gospel.

october

3

But seek first the kingdom of God and His righteousness,
and all these things shall be added to you.
MATTHEW 6:33

There's a certain discipline that the child of God must have. He doesn't always have time to participate in *good* things, because there are too many *best* things.

People sometimes ask, "Oh, have you read this book? It's so good." I say, "No, I haven't." And I think, "Where on earth did you ever get time to read that? I haven't even gotten to the best books yet. How am I going to have time to read good books?"

I'm amazed at how many people spend so much time doing good things. But good things are bad things when they keep you from best things. Life would be easier if it were a choice between good and bad. But it's a choice between good and best.

How we need to learn the best! There are some ambitions, some activities, that don't serve to speed you on your way. They must go if you want to win in this race.

Many people spend far more time with television or screen time than with the Word of God, and then wonder why they're not growing. Screen time has become a drag, a weight in your life. You're online till your brain is the size of a pea and your eyes are big as coconuts—yet you don't study the Word of God!

ACTION POINT I want you to ask God, "Are there legitimate, lawful things in my life still keeping me from running the race of life?" It might be a cabin at the lake, a hobby, a friend—and in and of themselves they're not bad things, but you're going to have to make a judgment. If that thing keeps you from maximizing your life for the Lord Jesus Christ, you must have the discipline to lay it aside!

4

Now I beg you, brethren, through the Lord Jesus Christ, and through the love of the Spirit, that you strive together with me in prayers to God for me.

ROMANS 15:30

One thing I am trying to cure myself of is casual prayer—prayer that's not intense. Prayer that costs little.

Do you know that the Bible calls prayer "wrestling"? When Paul said "that you strive together," the picture is one of a wrestling match. When the Roman Christians were praying for Paul, they were making unto God in faith. They were not praying to one another. They were not praying to impress one another. So many of our prayers are little memorized prayers.

But have you ever thought of prayer as wrestling? If you really get into intercession, you are going to find out that the devil will fight you and oppose you. Prayer is work. I'd rather preach for an hour than to pray for a half an hour, as regards the labor that genuine prayer takes.

How much genuine agonizing do we do in prayer? I love Jeremiah 29:13, where God says, "And you will seek Me and find Me, when you search for Me with all your heart." Seek Him in prayer with frequency and fervency of the prayer. Sometimes we don't feel like praying so we pass it by. But friend, if there's ever a time you need to pray, it's when you don't feel like it.

ACTION POINT Ask yourself: "How much genuine agonizing do I do in prayer?" Search for God with all your heart. Pray even when you don't feel like it. Pray not only frequently, but fervently.

5

Purge me with hyssop, and I shall be clean; wash me, and I shall be whiter than snow. Make me hear joy and gladness, that the bones You have broken may rejoice.

PSALM 51:7-8

Sin stings the conscience and saddens the heart. In the first century A.D., the Roman poet Juvenal wrote:

Trust me, no tortures which the poets feign
Can match the fierce, unutterable pain
He feels, who, night and day, devoid of rest,
Carries his own accuser within his breast.

Only one thing can take the joy that Jesus gives, and it's not your circumstances, it's your sin—not someone else's sin, but your own. A disobedient child, an unfaithful husband, an ungodly government—these can't take your joy. They didn't give it to you. Jesus gives it. It's joy in the Lord.

When David wrote Psalm 51, he wasn't lost, or looking to be saved. He was a saved but miserable child of God, praying, "Restore to me the joy of Your salvation" (see Psalm 51:12).

The most miserable man on earth is not a lost man but a saved man out of fellowship with God. Many unsaved people are having a ball, living high, wide and handsome. Never tell people they can't have pleasure if they're not saved. That is a lie. The Bible speaks of "the pleasures of sin." They last only for a season, but for that moment, they're pleasurable.

ACTION POINT When God saves you, God doesn't fix you where you can't sin anymore. He just fixes you where you can't sin and enjoy it anymore. If your joy is gone, you've been looking for it in the wrong places. You need to confess your sin and lay it down. Pray with David, "Restore to me the joy of Your salvation."

6

Do you not know that those who run in a race all run, but one receives the prize? Run in such a way that you may obtain it.

1 CORINTHIANS 9:24

I press toward the goal for the prize of the upward call of God in Christ Jesus.

PHILIPPIANS 3:14

Everybody knows that a runner is going to win or lose primarily by his endurance. When it hurts, you cannot quit. When your lungs are on fire, you cannot quit. When your feet are like lead, you cannot quit. When your sides ache, you cannot quit! When your head throbs, you cannot quit!

You can tell the size of a Christian by what it takes to stop him. How little it takes to stop some weak-kneed soldiers!

You will never be a spiritual athlete if you're a quitter! You must "run with endurance the race that is set before you" (See Hebrews 12:1). There must be determination! Being a Christian is not a Sunday afternoon stroll.

Every great athlete is possessed with a desire to win. I look sometimes at the Olympics and watch some of these young people as they've trained. I watch the swimmers and the runners, and sometimes tears come to my eyes. I say, "Oh, God! I want to be that kind of a Christian! I want to live in the spiritual realm the way these are willing to live in the physical realm!" They are people possessed! But not so for so many Christians.

ACTION POINT If we are to possess it, it first must possess us. This matter of being saved, of leading others to Jesus Christ, is a full-time occupation. We must pray over it. Weep over it. Study over it. Work over it!

October 7

> For this is the will of God, your sanctification: that you should abstain from sexual immorality; that each of you should know how to possess his own vessel in sanctification and honor, not in passion of lust, like the Gentiles who do not know God; that no one should take advantage of and defraud his brother in this matter, because the Lord is the avenger of all such, as we also forewarned you and testified.
>
> **1 THESSALONIANS 4:3-6**

What has led to the moral impurity we see today? In the first place, it is due to the attitude of modern parents who cannot wait for their children to grow up.

We see boys and girls dating at the age of ten, "going steady" by the time they're thirteen, and then we're shocked when they're in some sort of life-altering situation before they're old enough to vote. Schools with sex education classes have done a lot of enabling in this issue. Unmonitored screen time is another culprit.

We're told that America is going through a "moral and sexual revolution," that the ideas found in the Word of God and the truths, prohibitions, and commandments revealed to us in Holy Scripture are no longer applicable—they are old fashioned, outmoded, and out-of-date. And the result is this: our young people are being sucked down into swirling sewers of sin, our homes are coming apart at the seams, we see the slaughter of millions of precious little unborn babies, and our nation is in chaos. It is time to come back to the Word of God. May God have mercy upon us!

ACTION POINT We're pushing young people into situations they're not emotionally and mentally capable of handling. Young people today find themselves playing with matches in dry grass. And we, as parents, must take responsibility. Are we protecting them, or are we asleep at the wheel?

8

> ...As Sodom and Gomorrah, and the cities around them in a similar manner to these, having given themselves over to sexual immorality and gone after strange flesh, are set forth as an example, suffering the vengeance of eternal fire.
>
> **JUDE 1:7**

No society that takes a loose view of sex can long endure. That is a proven historical fact. Edward Gibbon, in his book *The Rise and Fall of the Roman Empire*, listed the causes of the fall of Rome in order of their importance. Number one on the list was sexual immorality. In fact, immorality also led to the downfall of Greece, Egypt, and Babylon. Immorality may well be the sin that destroys America.

Immorality causes us to sin against society. People who treat sex lightly, treat other human beings lightly also. Immorality is the enemy of the home, and the enemy of the home is the enemy of the nation. Faith that doesn't begin at home rarely gets a chance to begin. I'm concerned that in America we see God-centered Christian homes, and the nuclear family as an institution, quickly disappearing.

None of us live to ourselves, and none of us die unto ourselves. "And what agreement has the temple of God with idols? For you are the temple of the living God. As God has said: 'I will dwell in them and walk among them. I will be their God, and they shall be My people'" (2 Corinthians 6:16), and "If anyone defiles the temple of God, God will destroy him. For the temple of God is holy, which temple you are" (1 Corinthians 3:17). When a member of a church lives in sexual immorality, he sins against the body of Christ. This should cause us to fall on our faces and weep before Almighty God.

ACTION POINT We need to teach our children and warn them, clear and plain. And we need to demonstrate purity, modeling this before our children.

A faithful man will abound with blessings, but he who hastens to be rich will not go unpunished.

PROVERBS 28:20

The one thing that money cannot buy is poverty—you need credit cards for that. And many are buying it! Dr. James Dobson, founder of Focus on the Family, was telling some of us in a small meeting about a time when he was playing Monopoly with his family, and he had all the great properties, Boardwalk and Park Place, and he had hotels on all of them. He owned the railroads. You couldn't get around the board without paying him.

He was just raking in the money, and making everybody in the family mad. After a while, he had it all stacked up and finally just wiped everybody out. They were so mad at him, they got up and went to bed, and he sat there looking at that pile of play money and those properties.

There he was, the winner. Dr. Dobson said, "I had to put it all back in the box. I thought to myself, 'Isn't that like life? We spend all our lives getting it all away from everybody else, and when it's over, they don't like us. And we put it all back in the box."

ACTION POINT One day you're going to put it all right back in the box. And one day you'll be put in a box. The greatest legacies have nothing to do with money. What will your children remember about you? Leave them a godly example to follow. Teach them the power of prayer and how to pray.

10

For the LORD God is a sun and shield; The LORD will give grace and glory; no good thing will He withhold from those who walk uprightly.

PSALM 84:11

Did you know that you can be wealthy and also be in financial bondage? If you are wealthy and seek satisfaction in your money, then you are in financial bondage, because you'll never find satisfaction there.

A poor man has an advantage over a wealthy man because he hopes that if he could get enough, he'd be happy. The rich man says, "I have it and I'm still not happy." He doesn't even have the hope anymore.

The wealthy are in financial bondage when their wealth increases their worries. Think about it. If what you take in is a result of your inordinate desire to get rich, all you've bought for yourself is trouble. Some people today can't get a good night's sleep, not because of their poverty but because of their wealth. "In the house of the righteous is much treasure, but in the revenues of the wicked is trouble" (Proverbs 15:6).

The luxury of wealth brings responsibility. The Bible says, "Do not overwork to be rich; because of your own understanding, cease" (Proverbs 23:4)! Money is a wonderful servant but a poor master.

ACTION POINT Is your security in your possessions, income, or savings? You know they could be gone in a heartbeat. God wants you to trust in Him for your security. If you haven't yet, memorize Hebrews 13:5 this week: "Let your conduct be without covetousness; be content with such things as you have. For He Himself has said, "I will never leave you nor forsake you."

11

> Command those who are rich in this present age not to be haughty, nor to trust in uncertain riches but in the living God, who gives us richly all things to enjoy.
>
> **1 TIMOTHY 6:17**

Warren Wiersbe once told of an old Quaker who was in his house, and next door a new family was moving in, unloading all the stuff they'd gathered and accumulated. Toys, tools, finery, gadgets, furniture—all were going into the house. The old Quaker was standing there, having watched all this. A Scripture came to his mind: "And having food and clothing, with these we shall be content" (1 Timothy 6:8). Finally, when they got it all inside, he went over and said, "Friend, if thou dost ever have anything that thou thinkest thou needest, come and see me, and I will tell thee how to get along without it."

Are you content? You may know the story of John D. Rockefeller, who died as a billionaire in 1937. Can you imagine how much that would be in today's money? Someone once asked Rockefeller, "How much money is enough?" He answered, "Just a little bit more." Our old nature is never satisfied. We crave "just a little bit more." Covetousness is not God's plan for His child.

Now, God is not a cosmic killjoy. He doesn't want to keep you poor, down in the dust. God is a good God. "For the LORD God is a sun and shield; the LORD will give grace and glory; no good thing will He withhold from those who walk uprightly" (Psalm 84:11). The devil, however, will try to make you believe that God doesn't want you to have a good time. But He does!

ACTION POINT God gives us richly all things to enjoy. If God has given you a fine house, a nice car, a bank account, that's wonderful! Just don't trust in it. Trust instead "in the living God, who gives us richly all things to enjoy."

12

> Your wife shall be like a fruitful vine in the very heart of your house, your children like olive plants all around your table. Behold, thus shall the man be blessed who fears the LORD.
>
> **PSALM 128:3-4**

The greatest wealth you have is not in the bank. If you have children, then your greatest wealth is your children. "Like arrows in the hand of a warrior, so are the children of one's youth. Happy is the man who has his quiver full of them; they shall not be ashamed, but shall speak with their enemies in the gate" (Psalm 127:4-5).

I've heard it said that "children make a rich man poor." But they have got it exactly backward: children make a poor man rich! Friend, no one—rich or poor—can take his money to Heaven. But I am taking my children to Heaven. We need to think about what Jesus Christ has done for our families, and we need to add up everything that we own that money cannot buy and that death cannot take away—and then we need to praise God for that. It needs to be a family affair. Get your children together, have a praise service!

ACTION POINT Thank God for a Christian family! Thank God for the things that really matter. "Godliness with contentment is great gain" (1 Timothy 6:6). That godliness comes when we give our hearts to Jesus Christ and trust Him as our Lord and Savior.

13

He is a double-minded man, unstable in all his ways.

JAMES 1:8

Do you want to know the secret of true success in any realm? It is to bring your life into one, burning focus. Jesus said in Matthew 6:24, "No one can serve two masters; for either he will hate the one and love the other, or else he will be loyal to the one and despise the other. You cannot serve God and mammon (money)."

To be successful, you've got to narrow your interests.

Paul said, "All things are lawful for me, but not all things are helpful; all things are lawful for me, but not all things edify" (1 Corinthians 10:23). There is nothing wrong with friends, relationships, diets, vacations, jobs, or this or that thing. Paul is saying, "It may be lawful—but, if it doesn't bring me to my goal, then for me it is bad."

Good things are bad things when they stand in the way of best things. Every relationship, every ambition, every plan—all of it—if it hinders your knowing Jesus Christ supremely, preeminently, passionately, and powerfully, then for you it is wrong. You may say, "Dr. Rogers, that's narrow." You're getting it! We are talking about power. Now if you don't want power, that's fine. But if you want power, you're going to have to say with the Apostle Paul, "This one thing I do." (See Philippians 3:13)

ACTION POINT Have you brought all your ambitions down to one burning ambition? Concentration is the key to power: a river channeled within its banks is powerful, but water spread out over the ground is just a stagnant swamp. If you want to know real power in your life, your devotion to Jesus Christ must be your focus and concentration. You'll know true success when everything in your life is under the Lordship of Christ.

14

A merry heart makes a cheerful countenance,
but by sorrow of the heart the spirit is broken.
PROVERBS 15:13

A merry heart does good, like medicine,
but a broken spirit dries the bones.
PROVERBS 17:22

When I was a kid down in Florida, we had a terrible hurricane come through. My dad was out with the other men in this fierce, cold wind, nailing up plywood over our windows. I remember wondering if our house was going to blow away.

My dad came in shivering and shut the door against the wind. All the electricity was off, and I was a little boy there, eyes wide, wondering, "Is our house gonna blow away? Is this it?" My dad looked at my mother and said, "I would give five dollars for a cup of coffee."

My mother went to the tap, filled the pot with water, put it on the gas stove, and made him a cup of coffee. He had forgotten we had a gas stove! He looked at her, reached in his pocket, gave her five dollars, and we had a big laugh that eased all the tension.

Does God believe in laughter? Let me give you a verse: Genesis 21:6, "And Sarah said, 'God has made me laugh, and all who hear will laugh with me.'" God gave her a son. Do you know what she named her son? Isaac. Do you know what Isaac means? "Laughter."

ACTION POINT Learn to laugh at yourself. You'll have plenty to laugh at. One of the best gifts you can give your child is the gift of laughter. It will make a difference in your home.

october

15

Cast your burden on the LORD, and He shall sustain you;
He shall never permit the righteous to be moved.

PSALM 55:22

If you were carrying around $100,000 in cash, you would want to get it into the bank as soon as possible. You would say, "Boy, I hope I don't lose this. I hope somebody doesn't find out I've got it. I hope I don't get robbed—anything could happen!"

The word *commit* is a banking term, meaning to put something with someone else for a safe deposit. So you go down to the bank, make out a deposit slip, and deposit that $100,000 cash. You hand it to the teller and she gives you a receipt. Then you say, "Whew, I feel better."

Once it's safely in the bank, a burden lifts. It's still your money, but you see it differently. You've committed it to someone you know can take care of it. You don't get a couple of pistols and sit on the front steps of the bank to protect your money, do you? If you didn't believe they could take care of it, you wouldn't have given it to them in the first place.

That's the way it is with the Lord. The problems are still ours; we've just committed them to His keeping. He doesn't say He'll take the burden away. He says He will sustain you.

ACTION POINT That's the idea here. Just commit your burden to the Lord, "casting all your care upon Him, for He cares for you" (1 Peter 5:7). Don't worry about it; rather, commit it to God. He will take care of it. You can bank on it.

16

I have been crucified with Christ; it is no longer I who live, but Christ lives in me; and the life which I now live in the flesh I live by faith in the Son of God, who loved me and gave Himself for me.

GALATIANS 2:20

Here is one of the greatest secrets I know for living a victorious life: Holiness is not the way to Christ—Christ is the way to holiness.

Many times we think, "If I could pray enough, live purely enough, study my Bible thoroughly enough, or get my life holy enough, that would bring me closer to Jesus. It would bring me into a relationship with Him."

Not so! It is Jesus Christ who *enables* you to pray. It is Jesus Christ who *enables* you to study the Bible. It is Jesus Christ who *enables* you to live the pure life. Holiness is not the way to Christ—Christ is the way to holiness.

The way to be like Him is to see Him, to worship Him, and to praise Him. Then you're changed; you're made like Him. "As for me, I will see Your face in righteousness; I shall be satisfied when I awake in Your likeness" (Psalm 17:15). You become like what you spend time with.

ACTION POINT Claim now the fullness of God's power. We can never work ourselves into being "holy enough" to qualify for closeness with Jesus. Just as Elisha was identified with Elijah, so you must be identified with the Lord Jesus Christ. It happens in relationship—you must spend time with Him because, remember, we become like those we spend time with.

> And he who had died came out bound hand and foot with graveclothes, and his face was wrapped with a cloth. Jesus said to them, "Loose him, and let him go."
>
> **JOHN 11:44**

Do you remember the story of when Jesus raised Lazarus from the dead? Jesus said, "Lazarus! Come forth!" Lazarus came out. One preacher once said, "If Jesus hadn't specifically said 'Lazarus,' everybody would have come out!"

But Lazarus was still wrapped up like a mummy. He had life, but he didn't have liberty. Certain graveclothes were still clinging to him, impeding his freedom. Jesus told them, "Loose him, and let him go."

Some of you are saved, but you're still wearing the old filthy graveclothes of life before Christ—your old sinful nature. You're still wearing the smock that you wore in the hog pen. There's still spiritual wax in your ears, and certain unclean garments. You're not ready to receive the word. Get rid of those unclean garments! We're to be swift to hear the Word of God, but some of us don't hear because something unclean from the old life is clogging up our spiritual ears. People are saved, born again, have received the Lord Jesus Christ, and their sins are forgiven, and yet there seems to be sort of a hangover sin holding on from the old life.

ACTION POINT Do you want the Bible to speak to you? To be alive to you? Then willingly repent of those old hangover sins from your past life. When you repent, you'll be free from those old graveclothes that bind you.

18

And He said to me, "My grace is sufficient for you, for My strength is made perfect in weakness." Therefore most gladly I will rather boast in my infirmities, that the power of Christ may rest upon me.

2 CORINTHIANS 12:9

An evangelist named Paul Hutchins was greatly used of the Lord in large citywide campaigns. But just when his ministry began to be the most fruitful, he learned that he had tuberculosis and had to be shut away from the public for a long time.

Paul Hutchins then wrote:

> *"If blind John Milton could write* Paradise Lost, *if John Bunyan in the Bedford Jail could write* Pilgrim's Progress, *if Martin Luther imprisoned in Wartburg Castle could translate the entire New Testament into the German language, if Paul confined to a Roman prison and chained to a guard twenty-four hours a day could still proclaim the gospel; if these men under such mighty handicaps dared to make progress and history, why should not we?"*

God's strength is made perfect in weakness!

ACTION POINT Have you ever had the privilege of experiencing this? You sensed you were being empowered by the power residing in Christ Himself, experiencing the miraculous grace of God specifically for you at that season. In spite of circumstances, God was working in a way you could not explain apart from His divine hand. Think about one of the hardest times in your life. How did God show up in ways that have no human explanation? Write it down in a journal. Thank him for His amazing grace.

19

Then the serpent said to the woman, "You will not surely die. For God knows that in the day you eat of it your eyes will be opened, and you will be like God, knowing good and evil."

GENESIS 3:4-5

The devil is not against religion. In fact, he uses religion to damn and doom souls. The first temptation in the Garden of Eden was not for Eve to be ungodly but to be *more* godly. He said, "Do this, and you will be like God." It was not a temptation to fall down, away from God; it was a temptation to step up, toward God—but with one catch: *do it the devil's way*. Very interesting. See how clever the devil is?

The devil is the master liar of all liars, and the best lies sound the most like the truth. Every good lie has *some* truth in it. If it didn't, we'd reject it out of hand. So the devil takes a lie and cloaks it in enough truth that we'll take the bait. Satan's lies have just enough worm curled around the sharp hook of deception that we say, "Okay, I'll bite."

Which is more dangerous—a clock five hours wrong or five minutes wrong? You answer: "The one five hours wrong." No—if it's five hours off, you say, "Hey, that's wrong! Somebody tell me what time it is." But five minutes? Those could make you miss your plane.

ACTION POINT Proverbs 4:23 tells you to guard your mind: "Keep your heart with all diligence, for out of it spring the issues of life." "Beloved, do not believe every spirit, but test the spirits, whether they are of God; because many false prophets have gone out into the world" (1 John 4:1). Hell is having a holiday, as we draw closer to the end of an age. God will never deceive you. Jesus said, "I am the way, the Truth and the life..." (John 14:6a).

20

> Know that the LORD, He is God; it is He who has made us, and not we ourselves; we are His people and the sheep of His pasture.
>
> **PSALM 100:3**

God calls us His sheep, but like sheep, we have a tendency to get away from God our Shepherd. "All we like sheep have gone astray; we have turned, every one, to his own way; and the LORD has laid on Him the iniquity of us all" (Isaiah 53:6). Sheep don't have a good sense of direction; they get easily lost. Sheep will browse here, nibble there, while getting further and further away from the flock, the fold, the shepherd, and not even realize it. Then they're out there, lost.

They can't find their way home. Cows come back to the barn, horses to the stable; and did you ever try to get rid of a cat? And you've heard of homing pigeons...but never homing sheep. Sheep don't come back on their own. They have to be sought. They have to be brought. They must have a shepherd to lead them home. That's just the nature of sheep.

Worse yet, sheep are sitting ducks for predators. They have no natural defense mechanisms. They can't defend themselves.

All that is true of us as well. That's the sheep nature in us. Do you see what trouble we're in without following our Shepherd? Apart from Him, we're lost and in danger. We'll never find our way home. The Holy Spirit must lead us.

ACTION POINT How grateful we should be for our Shepherd! Because "He will feed His flock like a shepherd; He will gather the lambs with His arm, and carry them in His bosom, and gently lead those who are with young" (Isaiah 40:11). Jesus, your Shepherd, feeds you, gathers you, carries you, and leads you. What must you do? Be alert for your Shepherd's voice today. Listen and follow where He leads.

21

For thus says the Lord GOD, the Holy One of Israel: "In returning and rest you shall be saved; in quietness and confidence shall be your strength." But you would not...
ISAIAH 30:15

So many folks are all stressed up with nowhere to go. You're tense and frenetic, running around busy, in a hurry, afraid to be still. God wants His people to learn to get quiet, to lie down in green pastures and to drink from still waters.

"Be still, and know that I am God; I will be exalted among the nations, I will be exalted in the earth" (Psalm 46:10)! You may say, "How can I do that?! The world is closing in on me! I need help!"

"I will lift up my eyes to the hills—from whence comes my help? My help comes from the LORD, who made heaven and earth" (Psalm 121:1-2).

Look to your Shepherd, "casting all your cares on Him, for He cares for you" (1 Peter 5:7). The composer Bach wrote an anthem called "God My Shepherd Walks Beside Me."

In Psalm 23 we have a portrait of our Shepherd: compassionate and caring. "He will feed His flock like a shepherd; He will gather the lambs with His arm, and carry them in His bosom, and gently lead those who are with young" (Isaiah 40:11). When I was a lamb, thank God, He carried me. If He hadn't, I never would have made it. He is the courageous Shepherd. "I am the Good Shepherd. The Good Shepherd gives his life for the sheep" (John 10:11).

ACTION POINT When you are stressed, pause and remember this. Breathe deeply of the presence of God. Read Psalm 23 today. Allow His Spirit to lead you beside still waters. He has promised "...I will never leave you nor forsake you" (Hebrew 13:5). Memorize Hebrews 13:5 and Psalm 145:18, "The LORD is near to all who call upon Him, to all who call upon Him in truth."

22

For by grace you have been saved through faith, and that not of yourselves; it is the gift of God, not of works, lest anyone should boast.

EPHESIANS 2:8-9

Watchman Nee, a Chinese teacher who founded many Christian churches, once told a story of a man who was drowning. A crowd had gathered, but no one in the crowd could swim—except for one man. To everyone's shock and consternation, it appeared that man would not jump in the water and rescue the drowning man.

Finally, the swimmer jumped from the river bank, swam out, put his arms around the man, and brought him to safety. But the crowd didn't cheer the rescuer. In fact, they scolded him. One of them said, "I don't believe I've ever seen a man so much in love with his own life, that you would wait so long to save this man's life."

The rescuer explained to them, "You don't understand. I'm not that good a swimmer. Had I gone out there while this man was still fighting, he would have drowned us both. I had to wait until he was weak enough for me to save him."

ACTION POINT Are you weak enough to let God save you, or like the swimmer who was flailing around, are you still trying to do it on your own? Psalm 50:15 says, "Call upon Me in the day of trouble; I will deliver you, and you shall glorify Me." Stop flailing around. Yield to Him.

october

23

Therefore let him who thinks he stands take heed lest he fall.

1 CORINTHIANS 10:12

Edinburgh Castle in Scotland, a great fortress built high on a rocky hill, was almost impenetrable. The castle has only been captured one time, and let me tell you how it was captured: its great strength became its weakness.

They used to put sentries all around that castle—except in one place. On one particular side, there is such a sheer rock cliff that it was thought it would be impossible to attack, so no sentries were placed there. And it was from there that the enemy came and scaled that rock cliff. From there, the castle was overtaken. At the strongest point, the castle fell, because right there the guard had been let down.

God is very wise to point out to us that sometimes our place of strength can become our place of weakness.

Did you hear the story about the man who was praised for being so humble? He started a collection to build a statue in his honor. Every strength, when taken to an extreme, becomes a weakness. Think about it: Determination taken too far can become stubbornness. Enthusiasm could become fanaticism. Courage not yielded to God's control can become recklessness.

ACTION POINT Every good quality, if you become proud about it, becomes a weakness. In genuine humility, ask God to take your strengths and bring them under His control. Remember, you must willingly yield that control to God.

24

> So when this corruptible has put on incorruption, and this mortal has put on immortality, then shall be brought to pass the saying that is written: "Death is swallowed up in victory." "O Death, where is your sting? O Hades, where is your victory?"
>
> **1 CORINTHIANS 15:54-55**

Once upon a time, a little brother and sister were with their mother in the garden. As the children were playing, a large bumble bee came up and stung the little boy. He began to cry and jumped up in his mother's arms. The bee buzzed around their heads, and the little girl was frightened to death.

Soon the little boy had his tears dried, and the mother said to the girl, "Sweetheart, you don't have to be afraid of that bee."

"But he stung brother."

"Yes, but come over here and look."

And there was the stinger the mother had pulled out. She said, "See there? He left his stinger in brother and because brother was stung, you can't be stung. That bee has lost his stinger. He'll never sting anyone else again."

The Lord Jesus Christ took the sting of sin for me and for you. Death may buzz around, he may frighten you, but friend, the sting is gone because Jesus rose from the dead. "Oh, death, where is your sting? Oh, grave, where is your victory?"

ACTION POINT The old bee called "Death" may buzz around you, but it can't hurt you anymore. Jesus has taken the pain out of parting, the dread out of dying, the gloom out of the grave, and has given us a hope that is steadfast and sure. I'm coming up out of that grave. We have the promise of a resurrected body: "But thanks be to God, who gives us the victory through our Lord Jesus Christ" (1 Corinthians 15:57).

25

For now we see in a mirror, dimly, but then face to face.
Now I know in part, but then I shall know just as I also am known.
1 CORINTHIANS 13:12

I've been asked, "Will we know one another in Heaven?" Of course we will. Someone asked Charles Haddon Spurgeon this question, and his answer was classic: "We know each other here on earth. Will we be bigger fools in Heaven than we are here on earth?"

I thought about the picture we have of our little baby Phillip, whom we lost on Mother's Day, when he was just a baby. I thought of that passage of Scripture where King David's little baby died and went to Heaven. David said, "I shall go to him. He shall not return to me." (See 2 Samuel 12:23) I will go to him.

When the apostle Paul spoke about the second coming of Jesus Christ, he told the church at Thessalonica, "Then we who are alive and remain shall be caught up together with them in the clouds to meet the Lord in the air. And thus we shall always be with the Lord" (1 Thessalonians 4:17). Again Paul told them, "...that whether we wake or sleep, we should live together with Him" (1 Thessalonians 5:10b). We'll be caught up together, and then be together.

When the Old Testament patriarchs died, the Bible says they went to be with their people. "...And die on the mountain which you ascend, and be gathered to your people, just as Aaron your brother died on Mount Hor and was gathered to his people" (Deuteronomy 32:50).

ACTION POINT In Heaven, you'll know your precious loved ones, friends and family. We'll know one another in a sweeter, fuller relationship. We will not lose in the resurrection. We will gain more than we can imagine.

Beloved, now we are children of God; and it has not yet been revealed what we shall be, but we know that when He is revealed, we shall be like Him, for we shall see Him as He is.

1 JOHN 3:2

We've never seen man as he was created to be. If we saw Adam right as he came off God's assembly line, we would know just how thousands of years of sin have marred mankind.

I once read in a scientific journal that even the most brilliant person will use less than two-fifths of one percent of his brain capacity. Two-fifths of one percent—that's .004! The incredible ability God put into the human being has been dampened and disfigured by sin.

Hardly anyone reading this doesn't feel a pain somewhere right now. We're all going through the process of aging. From the crowns of our heads to the soles of our feet, deterioration is taking place.

Have you ever wished to sing or serve or pray or worship better than you do? One of these days, all of the limitations of earth will fall away. There'll be no more weakness, sighing, crying, dying, or pain. Every child of God will have the perfection God planned for us from the beginning.

"Behold, I tell you a mystery: We shall not all sleep, but we shall all be changed....For this corruptible must put on incorruption, and this mortal must put on immortality....Then shall be brought to pass the saying that is written: 'Death is swallowed up in victory'" (1 Corinthians 15:51,53,54b).

ACTION POINT Can you take this in? One day that decaying process will be reversed in an instant. "...In a moment, in the twinkling of an eye, at the last trumpet. For the trumpet will sound, and the dead will be raised incorruptible, and we shall be changed" (1 Corinthians 15:52). Instantly we will go from corruption to incorruption. One day, we will be like Jesus.

27

Be anxious for nothing, but in everything by prayer and supplication, with thanksgiving, let your requests be made known to God.

PHILIPPIANS 4:6

Prayer is our greatest Christian privilege but—we may as well admit—our greatest Christian failure. We all need to learn to pray more and to pray better. One of the reasons we don't pray more than we do, is that we have questions about prayer. We're not sure what's right and what's not, so we become uncertain. Our uncertainly leads to less prayer.

But if we're going to impact our families, nation, and world, prayer is where we should begin. Just a causal glance at the book of Acts confirms how the disciples totally depended upon prayer. Just before Jesus ascended back to Heaven, He left them with The Great Commission and told them, "Behold, I send the Promise of My Father upon you; but tarry in the city of Jerusalem until you are endued with power from on high" (Luke 24:49). True to His command, "Then they returned to Jerusalem...unto the upper room," and "...all continued with one accord in prayer and supplication..." waiting to receive the Holy Spirit. (See Acts 1:12-14.)

They didn't make a move without seeking God through prayer for His guidance. "And they continued steadfastly in the apostles' doctrine and fellowship, and in breaking of bread, and in prayers" (Acts 2:42). "'But we will give ourselves continually to prayer and to the ministry of the word,' they said" (Acts 6:4).

ACTION POINT In these difficult days when there is such need for prayer, are you making prayer a priority every morning as you begin your day? This commitment takes determination and discipline. If those who walked alongside our Lord for three years were dependent upon prayer, how much more so are we? What a grave mistake if we're casual about our prayer lives.

28

And because you are sons, God has sent forth the Spirit of His Son into your hearts, crying out, "Abba, Father!"
GALATIANS 4:6

People ask, "Should we pray when God already knows our needs? Why tell Him what He already knows? Or ask Him to do what He already wants to do?" We don't pray to impress God or to inform Him. You can't tell God anything He doesn't already know. So why are we praying?

For fellowship. We invite God into our lives when we pray. We experience fellowship with Him, becoming "...workers together with Him..." (2 Corinthians 6:1). When we pray, God gives us the privilege of administrating His affairs. Of course, He could do it without us. But what joy that God allows us the privilege of doing it with Him.

For our growth. When we pray, God is growing us. Have you ever prayed and didn't immediately receive what you asked for? What did you do? You kept on praying, but you also began searching your heart to see if something was hindering God's answer. Many times there is. God uses prayer to grow us.

For dependence. Our Father never wants us to live independently from Him. If God just did everything for us and we never had to pray, soon we would begin to take things for granted. We would cease to depend upon God.

He knows what we need before we ask, but we're told to pray and to ask—so we would have fellowship with Him, so we would grow, and learn to depend upon Him.

ACTION POINT You don't have to understand everything about prayer in order to pray. You may have valid questions about prayer, but don't let your questions keep you from praying.

October 29

> There was a certain man in Caesarea called Cornelius, a centurion of what was called the Italian Regiment....about the ninth hour of the day he saw clearly in a vision an angel of God coming in and saying to him, "Cornelius!....Your prayers and your alms have come up for a memorial before God."
>
> **ACTS 10:1-4**

Cornelius was a Gentile, a pagan, a Roman army officer, a centurion, but was one whose prayers God certainly heard. Acts 10 describes him as "a devout man and one who feared God with all his household, who gave alms generously to the people, and prayed to God always." He was an unsaved man, but God was aware of and answered his prayer.

What's the difference between a child of God who can pray in the name of Jesus and an unsaved person who prays? God has given prayer promises to the child of God that He has not given to the unsaved. But God can hear the unsaved person's prayers and have mercy upon him.

Think of it this way: Let's say a banker voluntarily gives money to a charity or worthy cause. He doesn't have to. No law says he must. It's just what he wants to do. But on the other hand, let's say I have money deposited in his bank. I can go in and write a check on my account and expect he will give me that money. Do you see the difference? In my case, it's legally owed to me, and I receive it. In the other, it's God's gift of grace.

ACTION POINT God says, "I will have mercy on whomever I will have mercy, and I will have compassion on whomever I will have compassion" (Romans 9:15). In mercy, God extends his love to us. Rejoice that God is merciful to all who call upon Him. Go before His Throne of Grace knowing that God wants to hear from you and to speak with you in prayer.

30

> Ask, and it will be given to you; seek, and you will find; knock, and it will be opened to you. For everyone who asks receives, and he who seeks finds, and to him who knocks it will be opened.
>
> **MATTHEW 7:7-8**

There's nothing in life outside the reach of prayer. For the child of God, if it concerns you, it concerns God. We sometimes try to divide life into the "secular" and the "sacred" saying, "This is the sacred. We'll pray about this. But this is the secular. I'll handle it myself."

Many years ago when Dr. Charles Stanley was the new pastor of First Baptist Church, Atlanta, the deacons and finance committee were holding a meeting. The church had been through some turmoil, and they came to a halt over a financial problem. Charles said to those around the table, "Men, let's pray." One of them answered, "Preacher, this is business. We don't need to pray about this."

Can you imagine Jesus Christ dividing His life into the sacred and the secular? Of course not. We don't divide our lives into the secular and the sacred, so what do we pray about? Everything. You might ask, "Can I pray about a parking space? That's silly; that's too small." Can you think of anything too big or too small to God? There is nothing "big" to God. Things aren't either big or small to Him. The biggest thing you can think of is small to God, and the smallest thing is important to God if it's important to you. "Be anxious for nothing, but in everything by prayer and supplication, with thanksgiving, let your requests be made known to God" (Philippians 4:6).

ACTION POINT You may ask, "Suppose there's something I want, and I know it's not God's will. Should I pray about that?" Absolutely. Pray, "Lord, there's something wrong with me. I want something You don't want. Fix my want-er." He already knows what you're thinking anyway.

31

> You are of God, little children, and have overcome them, because He who is in you is greater than he who is in the world.
>
> **1 JOHN 4:4**

Many years ago, international chess master Paul Morphy was taking a tour of Europe. He and a friend entered an art gallery. Morphy was drawn to "The Chess Players" by Moritz Retzch, a painting depicting two figures playing chess: Satan himself and a young man. They were playing for the young man's soul. Satan has just moved into position for checkmate. It's obvious now the young man has no way of escape. Pale with fear, he realizes the devil has outwitted him. All is lost. There is no move he can make.

Paul Morphy stood intently studying the chess board in the painting. His friend moved on. After a while, Morphy exclaimed, "Young man, there's one move you can make!" Morphy ran to his friend, shouting "I've found it! All is not lost!" I don't know much about chess, but I know a lot about the Word of God, and I know what that one move is. Don't you? To receive Jesus. In the warfare between Hell and Heaven, a little chorus says this about the Lord Jesus:

He signed the deed with His atoning blood.
He ever lives to make His promise good.
Should all the hosts of Hell march in to make a second claim,
*They'll all march out at the mention of His name!**

His name is Jesus.

ACTION POINT At a time when so much attention is given to Satan and his minions, understand this: Satan is a defeated foe. His kingdom is crushed. "He who is in you is greater than he who is in the world" (1 John 4:4). "Therefore if the Son makes you free, you shall be free indeed" (John 8:36). Receive Christ.There is no other way.

*Author unknown

It's better to be hated for telling the truth than loved for telling a lie.

ADRIAN ROGERS

november

1

> And Jesus answered and said to them, "Render to Caesar the things that are Caesar's, and to God the things that are God's." And they marveled at Him.
>
> **MARK 12:17**

A reporter once asked a pedestrian, "Can you tell me the two biggest problems in America?" The man said, "I don't know, and I don't care." The reporter replied, "You named them both."

Ignorance and apathy! These are days when we cannot afford to be ignorant and certainly not apathetic. Every four years, this is the time of year when we elect someone to the highest office in our land. And how important it is for followers of Christ to seek the heart, the mind, and the will of God about this and all elected offices!

There is a story that when a man visited the Continental Congress, he wanted to know which one was George Washington. The man next to him said, "George Washington will be the tall man who gets on his knees when the Congress prays." That's the kind of birth our nation had. Daniel Webster said, "Let us not forget the religious character of our origin." Our Founding Fathers wanted to infuse every area of our national life with the principles of Christianity. Our forefathers believed, as I believe, and as I hope you believe, in the separation of Church and State—but they never believed in the separation of God from government.

ACTION POINT I'm going to tell you how to vote: Go into the booth and press the button. Stop looking around and wondering what everybody else is going to do. Draw a circle on the floor, get inside that circle and say, "God, start a revival in this circle." May God help us to be Christian citizens! Father, stir our hearts, I pray. Lord, deliver us from both apathy and ignorance. In Jesus' name, Amen.

2

> Therefore, to him who knows to do good
> and does not do it, to him it is sin.
> **JAMES 4:17**

It's not a Bible proverb, but there is a wonderful proverb that says, "If gold rust, what shall iron do?"* Meaning, if those in leadership don't lead rightly, what's going to happen to the rest of us? What does the Bible say about national leadership? Proverbs 29 makes it clear: leadership should lead by setting a godly example. The Bible repeatedly warns us that our leaders should be upright—and what the consequences will be if they aren't.

Daniel confessed, "O Lord, according to all Your righteousness, I pray, let Your anger and Your fury be turned away from Your city Jerusalem, Your holy mountain; because for our sins, and for the iniquities of our fathers, Jerusalem and Your people are a reproach to all those around us" (Daniel 9:16).

Jesus said, "Render to God the things that are God's." But He also said, "Render to Caesar the things that are Caesar's." Our "Caesar" is a government of, by, and for the people. The very genius of our government is that the people participate. None other than the Lord Jesus Christ Himself teaches us to participate in government (see Matthew 22:21).

ACTION POINT Under our Constitution, the government answers to the people. It's unthinkable that Almighty God would ordain government, then have His people stay out of it. Who would that leave, then, to influence and lead? If you do not vote, you have disobeyed God's plan for His people to be involved. Get informed. Know where each candidate stands on the issue of protecting life and God's design for marriage. Then prayerfully cast your vote for those most closely aligned with God's principles for life and godliness in a nation.

* *The Canterbury Tales (General Prologue)* by Geoffrey Chaucer

3

> When the righteous are in authority, the people rejoice;
> but when a wicked man rules, the people groan.
> **PROVERBS 29:2**

Every four years, the first Tuesday in November is an important election day in the United States. When that day comes around, I trust every one of you will vote. Are you praying over your vote? Dr. Francis Schaeffer, a brilliant man, one of the foremost Christian thinkers of our time, gave us five principles to keep in mind when we vote. These have nothing to do with personalities or political parties. The principles guiding our vote should be:

- The dignity of human life
- The importance of the traditional family
- Religious freedom of speech in schools, both public and private
- Human rights and the need for justice in our world
- The compassionate use of accumulated wealth

These five ought to be in the heart and mind of every child of God. Pray over these. Then based on God's Word, make your determination. God will give you wisdom. The reason Americans have been free is because they've been people of character. Did you know that our nation was born in a spiritual revival? In 1740-1770, there was a great revival that swept across America. And out of the matrix of that revival came the American Revolution. Schools were built. Principles were instilled. Character resulted. The Declaration of Independence grew out of this. There was a rebirth of liberty. Liberty is "responsibility assumed"—not "just do your thing."

ACTION POINT Pray from your heart, "God, bless America, and God, give us space to repent. And may the ones of Your choosing be elected to lead us." Remember, "Therefore, to him who knows to do good and does not do it, to him it is sin" (James 4:17).

4

O LORD, how long shall I cry, and You will not hear? Even cry out to You, "Violence!" and You will not save. Why do You show me iniquity, and cause me to see trouble? For plundering and violence are before me; there is strife, and contention arises.

HABAKKUK 1:2-3

Like many in this nation, you may be discouraged. The book of Habakkuk was written as a song to inspire us to keep singing, despite difficult times.

Habakkuk wrote at a time of national calamity for Israel. Everything not nailed down was coming loose, and the devil was pulling nails as fast as he could. We live in a day just like it: anarchy in the nations, apostasy in the churches, apathy in many hearts, and we ask, "Why?"

Habakkuk was intensely patriotic. He loved God, God's people, and his land. Nothing he wanted had worked out. He faced the same questions we sometimes face. We stain Heaven with our prayers, we fast and pray, but things don't get better. In fact, they get worse.

Some are losing their faith not on the issue of how the world began, but on how the world is ending. They ask, "Why doesn't God do something? Where is He?"

God allowed Habakkuk to pour out his frustration about God to God Himself! What an encouragement to us: Habakkuk was frustrated, and God listened.

ACTION POINT Habakkuk wrote his book saying, "This vision is for an appointed time" (Habakkuk 2:3). I believe it was for today. He said, "Tell the minister of music not to stop singing." Don't let anything steal your song. Instead of losing heart, redirect your energy to praising God. Sing His praise. Believe His promises. Keep on praising. Keep on believing. Keep on loving. Our God reigns!

5

> For the vision is yet for an appointed time; but at the end it will speak, and it will not lie. Though it tarries, wait for it; because it will surely come, It will not tarry. Behold the proud, his soul is not upright in him; but the just shall live by his faith.
>
> **HABAKKUK 2:3-4**

Habakkuk had been praying and praying, and wondering, "Why is Heaven silent? Why doesn't God hear my prayer?" Then he realized a foundational truth for those who follow God: In such a day, the just are going to have to live by faith.

Put your faith in God, that He is king evermore. That's how you'll live in this day and age. Faith is what keeps us going in dark days. Faith sees beyond the physical to the spiritual, beyond the present to the future, beyond the temporary to the eternal. Faith does not judge by the appearance of the hour.

Don't lose your faith. If we want a better land and life, we have to live by faith. Government cannot make us better; only the Gospel of Jesus Christ can do that.

ACTION POINT In these desperate days, every child of God must get quiet in God's presence. Get centered on Him and Him alone. Listen to what He has to say. As He told the Israelites in Isaiah 30:15: "For thus says the Lord God, the Holy One of Israel: 'In returning and rest you shall be saved; in quietness and confidence shall be your strength.' But you would not..." Let's not make the same mistake.

6

> An astonishing and horrible thing has been committed in the land: The prophets prophesy falsely, and the priests rule by their own power; and My people love to have it so. But what will you do in the end?
>
> **JEREMIAH 5:30-31**

Israel's condition in Habakkuk's day was so deplorable, not only Habakkuk, but his fellow prophet Jeremiah, known as "the weeping prophet," mourned over it.

Today we have a generation of preachers, unlike Habakkuk and Jeremiah, who tell people what they want to hear rather than what they need to hear, who teach falsely, serving for gain, and the people love it that way.

What do God's people do when biblical principles are being cast aside?

- First, be assured of this: "For the earth will be filled with the knowledge of the glory of the LORD, as the waters cover the sea" (Habakkuk 2:14). One day, God is going to put His Son upon His holy hill of Zion. It has not arrived yet, but that day of reckoning is coming.
- Second, remember: God is in control. Habakkuk says, "But the LORD is in His holy temple. Let all the earth keep silence before Him" (Habakkuk 2:20). And He isn't turning loose of the reins!

When Habakkuk asked, "God, where are You?" God answered, "I'm right up here in My holy temple. There's no panic. The Holy Trinity is not meeting in emergency session. I know what I'm doing."

ACTION POINT God has not lost control. Listen to the reliability of the Scriptures. See the reign of the Savior. Know there's going to be retribution for the sinner. And rely on God's grace.

7

Though the fig tree may not blossom, nor fruit be on the vines; though the labor of the olive may fail, and the fields yield no food; though the flock may be cut off from the fold, and there be no herd in the stalls—yet I will rejoice in the LORD, I will joy in the God of my salvation. The LORD God is my strength; He will make my feet like deer's feet, and He will make me walk on my high hills. To the Chief Musician. With my stringed instruments.

HABAKKUK 3:17-19

Habakkuk ended his conversation with the Lord by expressing his frustration and dismay over his beloved land. Truly, it was God's land, for He had set apart the Hebrews for Himself centuries before.

Habakkuk had begun by asking, "Why, Lord, why?" God never did answer why. He just said, "I'm going reveal *who*: Me. I am your strength, and I will make you like a sure-footed gazelle, and you can live on your high places."

Habakkuk came to this conclusion: "I will joy in the God of my salvation. God the Lord is my strength."

ACTION POINT If you are saved, if you know the Lord, then it doesn't matter if gasoline goes to five dollars a gallon, Wall Street hits bottom, or they take away your fine house. The Bible says: "You can rejoice in the Lord your God!" Remember God's greatness. Rejoice in God's goodness. Rely on God's grace.

8

Beloved, I beg you as sojourners and pilgrims, abstain from fleshly lusts which war against the soul, having your conduct honorable among the Gentiles, that when they speak against you as evildoers, they may, by your good works which they observe, glorify God in the day of visitation.

1 PETER 2:11-12

Certain things war against the soul. The enemy is warring, strategizing, against your soul. A conspiracy born in Hell goes after your soul, the soul of your family, your church, and this nation.

You're called to live a righteous, godly life. In your heart there cannot be what the Bible calls "fleshly lust." Renounce and abstain from everything that's wrong. Embrace everything that's right.

People who are not saved love to bad-mouth the Church and ridicule Christians, and if you're a Bible-believing Christian, they especially love to lampoon you. We shouldn't be surprised, for Our Lord said, "If the world hates you, you know that it hated Me before it hated you. If you were of the world, the world would love its own. Yet because you are not of the world, but I chose you out of the world, therefore the world hates you" (John 15:18-19).

We war against unseen forces from the very pit of Hell. Peter warns all who follow Christ to be careful how we behave among our unsaved neighbors, so that even when they are suspicious of us and talk against us, in the long run they will be praising God for our good works when Christ returns. A child of God ought to be pure and clean as the driven snow.

ACTION POINT Live such a pure, honest life, that even those who hate you have to grudgingly admit there's a difference. Remember the words of Jesus in Luke 12:32, "Do not fear, little flock, for it is your Father's good pleasure to give you the kingdom."

9

Do you not say, 'There are still four months and then comes the harvest'? Behold, I say to you, lift up your eyes and look at the fields, for they are already white for harvest!

JOHN 4:35

Whatever we sow, we are going to reap. "Do not be deceived, God is not mocked; for whatever a man sows, that he will also reap" (Galatians 6:7). And if you hope to reap at all, you must get out there and sow. There will be no reaping without planting. Here in America, we are reaping blessing upon blessing because our forefathers planted.

I copied this down because I thought the writer said it well:

> *"Did we bring the Bible to these shores or did it not, rather, bring us? The breath of the ancient prophets was in the sails that drove the tiny Mayflower....The hope and faith of ancient poets, kings, and lawgivers were in the hearts of those who first sang the Lord's song in this strange land. From those beginnings until now, the Bible has been a teacher to our best men, a rebuke to our worst men, and a noble companion to us all."**

The reason America is such a great nation is not because Americans are smarter, not because the sun shines on us more, not because it rains here more, not because our soil is richer, but because our forefathers planted certain things in American soil. I'm not talking about crops and seeds; I'm talking about faith and truth and hope and charity and justice. And because of that, we are reaping a harvest.

ACTION POINT If you want to reap, first you must plant! Begin today to plant God's precepts and principles into the minds and hearts of those around you. Such seeds will yield the peaceable fruit of righteousness (see Hebrews 12:11).

*John Lawrence, *Life's Choices*, Multnomah Press, Portland, 1982

10

> For this is the will of God, that by doing good you may put to silence the ignorance of foolish men—as free, yet not using liberty as a cloak for vice, but as bondservants of God.
>
> **1 PETER 2:15-16**

What is liberty? Liberty is "responsibility assumed," not "just do your thing." Can liberty thrive in a degenerate society? No, it cannot last for long. We cannot have self-government without self-control.

As character degenerates, government must grow to cope with that societal decay. As government grows, people begin to equate security with dependence on government. So the government begins to give to the people, and the people like it. But they fail to understand that the government cannot give them anything it doesn't first take away. As government begins to take, then "give it back," we're regulated, then controlled more and more.

Dear friend, government is a watchdog to be fed, not a cow to be milked. Our Founding Fathers understood that. Wisely, they wrote into the Preamble to our U. S. Constitution what our government is actually for: to protect life and property. We can't go out as individuals and raise an army to protect our land or be vigilantes carrying out street justice. We need government for that. Government is to *provide* for the common defense, *promote* the general welfare. It did not say *provide the general welfare* or sustain it.

ACTION POINT Benjamin Franklin said, "Only a virtuous people are capable of freedom." John Adams wrote, "Our Constitution was made only for a moral and religious People. It is wholly inadequate to the government of any other." Our Republic is *by* a people of character, *for* a people of character, and only a people of character can keep it. Are you living in a way that strengthens our nation as "people of character"? Are you living according to 1 Peter 2:15-16?

11

> Now the just shall live by faith; But if anyone draws back, My soul has no pleasure in him.
>
> **HEBREWS 10:38**

In a day such as ours, we will have to live by faith. Put your faith in the fact that God is the King Eternal, as Paul wrote to Timothy: "Now to the King eternal, immortal, invisible, to God who alone is wise, be honor and glory forever and ever. Amen" (1 Timothy 1:17).

Faith in the King Eternal is the way you are going to live in this day, because faith keeps us going in dark days. Faith sees beyond the physical to the spiritual. Faith sees beyond the present to the future. Faith sees beyond the temporary to the eternal. Faith does not judge by the appearance of the hour.

Don't lose your faith. Listen to me: sin cannot win. Faith cannot fail. Faith is the only message that will see us through, and it is the only force that can change anything. I think Habakkuk 3:17-18 is the apex of faith. Dark days may come—no, I take it back. Dark days *will* come. Pretending is not going to make them go away. I refuse to be an irrational optimist, and I refuse to be a morose pessimist. I stand on the Word of God and I will live by faith. And I hope you will too. Faith doesn't live by explanations, but by promises. Faith doesn't live by appearances, but by providence. Faith doesn't live by circumstances, but by praise. Let the chief singer sing that!

ACTION POINT If we want a better land, we have to live better lives. Government cannot make us better; only the Gospel of Jesus Christ can. Decide today: "I will live by the Gospel. I will not lose faith. I will see with the eyes of faith. I will share the Gospel."

12

> Blessed is every one who fears the LORD, who walks in His ways....The LORD bless you out of Zion, and may you see the good of Jerusalem all the days of your life. Yes, may you see your children's children. Peace be upon Israel!
>
> **PSALM 128:1, 5-6**

Right now our nation is sick unto death because we have forgotten God. But listen to this, and let it burn into your soul: "The highest glory of the American Revolution was this: it connected, in one indissoluble bond, the principles of civil government with the principles of Christianity."*

Did you catch that? The principles of civil government and Christianity were linked together in an unbreakable bond. Nearly all citizens acknowledged Christian, biblical principles as the rules of their conduct.

In 1913, President Woodrow Wilson said, "America was born to exemplify the devotion to the elements of righteousness which are derived from Holy Scriptures." In March, 1931, Congress adopted "The Star-Spangled Banner" as our national anthem. Do you know what the fourth stanza says?

Blessed with victory and peace, may this Heaven-rescued land
praise the Power that hath made and preserved us a nation.
Then conquer we must when our cause it is just. And this be our
motto, "In God is our trust."

God blessed America because she was rooted in spiritual principles and truths.

ACTION POINT Pray for your nation according to 2 Chronicles 7:14—"If My people who are called by My name will humble themselves, and pray and seek My face, and turn from their wicked ways, then I will hear from heaven, and will forgive their sin and heal their land."

*John Quincy Adams' 1837 Fourth of July Address

13

Honor all people. Love the brotherhood.
Fear God. Honor the king.
1 PETER 2:17

I want to tell you, the answer to America's problems are not in the White House, the Pentagon, the Capitol, the state house, or even in the schoolhouse—but in the church house.

In our social life, we are to honor all people. In our church life, we are to love our church community. In our spiritual life, fear God. And in our political life, honor the king.

Notice it says, "Fear God." Do you know what's wrong in America today? We have a nation today where there is no fear of God. People laugh and mock at holy things. But, "The fear of the LORD is the beginning of wisdom, and the knowledge of the Holy One is understanding" (Proverbs 9:10).

Whether they be kings, governors, or presidents, my dear friend, you can honor them without venerating them or even liking them. I believe that if we would criticize less and pray more, God may change some of these people. The Bible says, "The king's heart is in the hand of the Lord, like the rivers of water; He turns it wherever He wishes" (Proverbs 21:1).

ACTION POINT Richard Halverson, chaplain of the U.S. Senate, remarked, "We're quick to criticize political leaders, but slow to pray for them." You have no right to speak against leadership in a way that's slanderous, but rather, you are to pray for leadership. Are you praying for those in authority? You really shouldn't be complaining, if you are not praying.

14

> But he who did not know, yet committed things deserving of stripes, shall be beaten with few. For everyone to whom much is given, from him much will be required; and to whom much has been committed, of him they will ask the more.
>
> **LUKE 12:48**

As Christian citizens, we must abstain from all that is wrong and approve all that is right.

It is character that produces liberty. Don't let that go past you. *It is character that produces liberty.* The reason Americans have been free is because they began as people of character.

Responsibility and character are two ways of saying the same thing. Responsibility and character are inseparably linked together with liberty. For example, a little baby has no responsibilities. He doesn't have to worry about anything. Everybody takes care of him. But he has no liberties. He does what he's told to do. He eats that pabulum and those strained beets. He is bathed and put to bed. No responsibilities, but no liberties.

As he grows in responsibility, he gets more and more liberty. There comes a time when his father will give him the car keys. But if he takes that car and acts irresponsibly, the father takes the keys and his privilege away. If he acts *really* irresponsibly, he may wind up in jail and *all* his liberties are taken away. Liberty is responsibility assumed.

ACTION POINT A republic is a government for a people with character, and only people with character can maintain it. If we lose our character as a nation, we are going to lose our liberty. And always, when there is a loss of character, there's a growth of government. If you want to remain free, you must be men and women of character, and you must raise young men and women of character.

15

For there is born to you this day in the city of
David a Savior, who is Christ the Lord.

LUKE 2:11

Therefore let all the house of Israel know assuredly that God has made this Jesus, whom you crucified, both Lord and Christ.

ACTS 2:36

Can you imagine what it meant to Mary to hear the angel say to her, "You shall call His name Jesus"? Or for those Jewish shepherds the night of His birth to hear the angels say, "...born this day in the city of David a Savior, who is Christ the Lord"?

What does that word "Lord" mean? What did it mean to these shepherds? It meant "Jehovah" to them. Jehovah, God Almighty. When the angel said, "a Savior who is Christ the Lord," the angel was saying He is co-equal, co-eternal with the Almighty.

Jesus Christ is called "Lord" far more than He is called "Savior." He's called "Lord" 747 times in the New Testament. He *is* Lord. Every so often someone says, "Well, I decided to make Him Lord." Too late for that. He is Lord.

ACTION POINT You cannot "make" Him the Lord of your life. You can only reject Him or receive Him as Lord. You can bow your knee to Him and say, "O Lord, You are the King. Therefore, I yield my heart to You." Receive Him today as your Lord. Will you submit to His Lordship?

16

> He has delivered us from the power of darkness and conveyed us into the kingdom of the Son of His love. ...He is the image of the invisible God, the firstborn over all creation. ...And He is the head of the body, the church, who is the beginning, the firstborn from the dead, that in all things He may have the preeminence.
>
> **COLOSSIANS 1:13, 15, 18**

God is Spirit—invisible, unfathomable, unapproachable. How are we going to know God? Jesus is the visible image of the invisible God. The visible Jesus makes the invisible God known.

You will know God not by reason, not by religion, not by ritual. You're going to know God only by *revelation*. Jesus Christ came to reveal God to you. You can never fully know God the Father apart from God the Son, "...who is the image of the invisible God." All of God was in Jesus Christ. He is the express image of God.

ACTION POINT Jesus Christ is there to be found. If you desire to know the very Son of God, He has said, "And you will seek Me and find Me, when you search for Me with all your heart" (Jeremiah 29:13). Seek Him in His Word, where He will reveal Himself to you.

17

All things have been delivered to Me by My Father, and no one knows the Son except the Father. Nor does anyone know the Father except the Son, and the one to whom the Son wills to reveal Him.

MATTHEW 11:27

If you want to know God, Jesus Christ has cornered the market. He has a monopoly on revealing the Father. As He says here in Matthew 11:27—it's worth repeating—"Nor does anyone know the Father except the Son, and the one to whom the Son wills to reveal Him."

Either that's true, or it's not true. Jesus has said, "Nobody knows My Father but Myself, and you can't know Him unless I introduce you to Him." Why? Because Jesus is the express image of God. You are never going to figure God out. How can the finite understand the infinite? Not by reason, but by *revelation*. Any other god that you worship is the god of your guesses, and that is a form of idolatry. You don't conjure up some god to worship him. Jesus came to reveal the Father.

"He is the image of the invisible God, the firstborn over all creation" (Colossians 1:15). The word *image* there is from the Greek word *icon*. It means an exact representation. Jesus is the icon of God. Jesus is the express image of the invisible God. See how Paul sums it up: "For in Him dwells all the fullness of the Godhead bodily" (Colossians 2:9). All of God was in Bethlehem's babe. He is the icon, the express image of God.

ACTION POINT Do you want to know what the great, invisible God is like? Would you like to know His heart? Friend, come to know Jesus Christ. He said, "...He who has seen Me has seen the Father..." (John 14:9).

...And to give you who are troubled rest with us when the Lord Jesus is revealed from heaven with His mighty angels.

2 THESSALONIANS 1:7

Are you troubled today? Listen: "And to give you who are troubled rest with us." That is, be at ease. Quit your worry. It is not over yet. The story of our age remains unfinished. If you are troubled, you need not be disturbed. "Rest with us."

You might say, "Pastor, it's so dark." Yes, it is gloriously dark, because the darkest hour of the night is just before sunrise. Our hope is not in politics, sociology, or science. The only sure hope for our world is the Second Coming of Jesus Christ. And when He's revealed, He will be revealed as the *Lord* Jesus. Today He is despised, rejected, mocked. But He is coming as Lord, to be glorified and admired.

His first coming without His second coming would be like an engagement without a wedding. The first time He came, He came to die in the sinner's place. When He comes again, He's coming to execute judgment upon those who refuse such love. When He came the first time, He came as a messenger of love. When He comes again, He is coming in vengeance as a righteous judge. The first time, He came in the greatest of humility—Deity in diapers. He is coming again as KING OF KINGS and LORD OF LORDS (see Revelation 19:16). He will no longer have a crown of thorns, but a diadem; not a cradle of straw, but a crown of glory.

ACTION POINT If you are unsaved, if you're not one of His saints, His coming will strike stark terror in your heart. But if you *are* saved, you're going to say, "Glory to the Lamb. Isn't He beautiful?" Say this aloud, if you can say it and mean it: "Lord Jesus." The most glorious fact of the future is that this Jesus is coming again.

19

But we are bound to give thanks to God always for you,
brethren beloved by the Lord, because God from the beginning
chose you for salvation through sanctification by the Spirit
and belief in the truth, to which He called you by our gospel,
for the obtaining of the glory of our Lord Jesus Christ.

2 THESSALONIANS 2:13-14

Paul tells us in 2 Thessalonians that when He comes, Jesus our Lord will reign. You will not be disappointed.

When He came the first time, there was no room for Him in the inn. When He comes again, He's coming as KING OF KINGS and LORD OF LORDS (see Revelation 19:16). When He came the first time, He came to die in the sinner's place. When He comes again, He's coming to receive the sinner to Himself.

There are two aspects of His Second Coming. First, He will come secretly *for* His bride, the Church. Then He will return *with* His bride, the Church. He is coming sweetly like a bridegroom, and then He's coming sovereignly like a King.

The unfinished story of Christmas is this: that Jesus is coming again! And Paul is telling us this: that when Christ comes again, 777 is going to take care of 666. Our Lord shall reign!

ACTION POINT In faith, look backward to a crucified Savior. In love, look upward to a crowned Savior. And in hope, look forward to a coming Savior!

20

Therefore God also has highly exalted Him and given Him the name which is above every name, that at the name of Jesus every knee should bow, of those in heaven, and of those on earth, and of those under the earth, and that every tongue should confess that Jesus Christ is Lord, to the glory of God the Father.

PHILIPPIANS 2:9-11

From the beginning of creation to now, billions and billions of people have lived on Earth. Of those, only a few have had an impact on history. And one person stands out, unique above all others. That one, Jesus Christ, attracted the largest attention, devotion, criticism, adoration, and opposition of all.

Every recorded word He spoke has been studied, sifted, and analyzed from generation to generation by theologians, philosophers, and historians. At this moment, multiplied millions around the globe in every time zone are studying what this one individual had to say.

Jesus of Nazareth taught in a tiny land called Israel 2,000 years ago. Yet His birth has divided the centuries into "B.C." (*Before Christ*) and "A.D." (*Anno Domini*, Latin for "the Year of our Lord"). He divides world history.

ACTION POINT Whether you are on death row or Wall Street, you need Jesus. He's the saving Son of God. There's no one He cannot save. There's no one He will not save. Thank God He was willing to come. If He had not, think what that would mean.

21

Let this mind be in you which was also in Christ Jesus, who, being in the form of God, did not consider it robbery to be equal with God, but made Himself of no reputation, taking the form of a bondservant, and coming in the likeness of men. And being found in appearance as a man, He humbled Himself and became obedient to the point of death, even the death of the cross. Therefore God also has highly exalted Him and given Him the name which is above every name, that at the name of Jesus every knee should bow, of those in heaven, and of those on earth, and of those under the earth, and that every tongue should confess that Jesus Christ is Lord, to the glory of God the Father.

PHILIPPIANS 2:5-11

Look at this passage once more. Under the Holy Spirit's inspiration, Paul summarized the mission, ministry and final triumph of the Lord Jesus Christ. In these seven verses, God the Father affirms Jesus is the supernatural, sinless, sovereign, sacrificial, surviving, saving, soon-coming Son of God.

This passage has it all: Christmas, Easter, the Second Coming, and His Kingship over all creation, rolled into one. The grave could not hold Him; He is Lord of both life and death. Every knee shall bow to a resurrected King.

His sandaled feet once stood on the Mount of Olives. One day those miracle feet, those pierced feet, are going to touch down again on that Mount of Olives, and the Bible says it's going to split in two at His second coming.

ACTION POINT You have a date with deity. You're going to meet Jesus Christ. He is inescapable, unavoidable, inevitable. Acts 4:12 says, "Nor is there salvation in any other, for there is no other name under heaven given among men by which we must be saved." Have you received Jesus Christ as Lord and Savior?

22

He has delivered us from the power of darkness and conveyed us into the kingdom of the Son of His love, in whom we have redemption through His blood, the forgiveness of sins. He is the image of the invisible God, the firstborn over all creation.

COLOSSIANS 1:13-15

There is One who stands head and shoulders above all others. His name is Jesus. He has received more opposition and criticism, yet more devotion and adoration, than any other human being who walked the planet.

Every recorded word He said has been sifted, analyzed, scrutinized, and debated, more than those of all the historians, philosophers and scientists of the world put together. The great historian Kenneth Scott Latourette said, "Jesus has had more effect on the history of mankind than any other of its race who ever existed."

In my humble but correct opinion, no one can call himself or herself educated who does not understand Jesus Christ! He is the purpose of creation. "For by Him all things were created that are in heaven and that are on earth, visible and invisible, whether thrones or dominions or principalities or powers. All things were created through Him and for Him" (Colossians 1:16).

What is the bottom line? "And He is the head of the body, the church, who is the beginning, the firstborn from the dead, that in all things He may have the preeminence" (Colossians 1:18). Question to you: Does Christ have pre-eminence in your life?

ACTION POINT To explain Jesus Christ is impossible. To ignore Jesus Christ is disastrous. To reject Him is fatal. Understand who Jesus Christ is. Jesus reveals the Father. Set your heart to know Him better and better each day.

23

And when they had laid many stripes on them, they threw them into prison, commanding the jailer to keep them securely. Having received such a charge, he put them into the inner prison and fastened their feet in the stocks. But at midnight Paul and Silas were praying and singing hymns to God, and the prisoners were listening to them.

ACTS 16:23-25

A lot of people are suffering—people whose bodies are being devoured by some malady, a lady with children whose husband just walked out, people whose world is upside down. They need thanksgiving more than anyone else. But it would be mockery to say, "Oh, cheer up. We'll just paint the clouds with sunshine! God's in His Heaven; all's right with the world."

God's in His Heaven, yes—but all's not right in this world. Many people are hurting. But we need to remember, the Bible says "In everything give thanks, for this is the will of God in Christ Jesus for you" (1 Thessalonians 5:18). That doesn't mean give thanks for cancer or a child who's just been run over and killed. Oh no. But in the midst of this we say, "God, You are greater than all of this. Your providence has either allowed it or brought it to pass. Lord, I'm trusting You and praising You because You're all I have. My eyes are on You. And, Lord, I praise You that You will make a way for me." This is not only an attitude that shows humility, but it shows great faith when we praise God in these circumstances.

Jesus, fully human, wept. He's moved with compassion when we suffer. He is a tender, compassionate Savior.

ACTION POINT Nothing comes to us but what He allows, and He will never, ever leave us nor forsake us. (See Hebrews 13:5.) Praise God even in the hard times. Your praise in the darkest hour brings Him even more glory. Decide that you will praise Him today.

24

> Be anxious for nothing, but in everything by prayer and supplication, with thanksgiving, let your requests be made known to God; and the peace of God, which surpasses all understanding, will guard your hearts and minds through Christ Jesus.
>
> **PHILIPPIANS 4:6-7**

Is constant, vigilant prayer and thanksgiving even possible for us human beings? Yes! Behind every command of God, such as "Fear not," "Don't be anxious," and "Be thankful," is the omnipotent power of God to carry it out. Giving thanks is one of the keys to answered prayer. Why should we ask for more when we've not thanked Him for what He's already given and already done?

There's a difference between praise and thanksgiving. Praise is reverencing God for *Who He is*; thanksgiving is recognizing *what He's done*. The two are inextricably interwoven, but they're not exactly the same. Both are absolutely necessary. The person who is not "praise-ful" will never be thankful.

Gratitude is what spoils life when it's left out. If we don't learn thanksgiving, we become self-centered, then unlovable and unloving, living in our own little world, locked up inside ourselves.

If you want your heart to sing, to be an attractive person to be around, to have your prayers answered, to have strength to endure tribulation, then you had better learn to praise and thank God. It's sad to see bitter, broken people who've never learned to be thankful. But when you're thankful, your eyes are opened and the blinders are taken off. There are so many new vistas out there. A thankful person is open to God and to others.

ACTION POINT Have you ever kept a "gratitude journal"? Get an inexpensive journal and each day write down something you're grateful for that day. By the end of thirty days, if you've been paying attention to all you have and all God has done, your journal might be full. Start that journal this week.

November

25

Depart from evil, and do good; and dwell forevermore. For the LORD loves justice, and does not forsake His saints; they are preserved forever, but the descendants of the wicked shall be cut off. The righteous shall inherit the land, and dwell in it forever.

PSALM 37:27-29

The reason many people are grumbly hateful rather than humbly grateful is that they have this belief, this conviction that no matter what, "God is fair." Let me tell you: God is not fair. God is *just*.

Fairness is a human attribute. "Fairness" implies that God owes us something, and if we don't get it, God isn't "fair" to us. Or if somebody gets more than we got, or before we get it, we grumble and pout, "That's not fair. So-and-so got more than I got."

That has nothing to do with it. Again, God is not "fair." God is just—perfectly righteous and holy. God owes us nothing, but He owes His own sense of integrity everything.

ACTION POINT People aren't going to cry out for mercy until they see that God is just. When we do, then we'll cry out for mercy. Don't complain, "I didn't get this or that." Instead say, "Lord God, You are a just God, and now I need mercy. Give me what I don't deserve: give me mercy, dear Lord, not because I have it coming to me, but because You are loving and kind."

26

Enter into His gates with thanksgiving, and into His courts with praise. Be thankful to Him, and bless His name.

PSALM 100:4

And let the peace of God rule in your hearts, to which also you were called in one body; and be thankful.

COLOSSIANS 3:15

If worry is the opposite of faith, then giving thanks is the expression of faith—in fact, the highest expression. You say, "I don't know if I have as much to thank God for as some other people." Well, the apostle Paul was in a filthy Philippian jail waiting to possibly be beheaded when he wrote, "Be anxious for nothing, but in everything by prayer and supplication with thanksgiving, let your requests be made known to God" (Philippians 4:6).

You see, God has blessed you. You may not think so, because you're measuring blessings by the barometer of health, wealth, and happiness. You say, "Oh, those are blessings!" Not always. Some people are cursed with wealth. Some people don't know how to use health. And happiness keeps some people from seeking the Lord.

My friend, let me tell you what blessings we have: "Blessed be the Lord, who daily loads us with benefits, The God of our salvation! Selah" (Psalm 68:19). God has loaded your wagon. How often? Daily! "Through the Lord's mercies we are not consumed, because His compassions fail not. They are new every morning; great is Your faithfulness" (Lamentations 3:22-23).

ACTION POINT Unthankful people are never happy people. They're always filled with bitterness, fear, negativism, selfishness and self-pity. Refuse to worry, but carry everything to God in prayer. Rejoice in the presence of the Lord. Rely upon the power of the Lord. Reflect on the provision of the Lord. Rest in the peace of the Lord. Do everything with thanksgiving.

27

Then he said to them, "Go your way, eat the fat, drink the sweet, and send portions to those for whom nothing is prepared; for this day is holy to our Lord. Do not sorrow, for the joy of the LORD is your strength."

NEHEMIAH 8:10

Rejoice in the Lord always. Again I will say, rejoice!

PHILIPPIANS 4:4

Where does your joy come from? Your job? Your health? Your friends? I hope it comes from the Lord, not circumstances. If you depend on circumstances, you can't say "rejoice always," because your circumstances could change. You might lose your job, health, friends, prestige. If you're getting your joy from your job, we can find out if we take your job and see if you still have your joy! Maybe you're getting your joy from your health. You might say, "No, it's from the Lord." If your health fails, see if you still have your joy. The only secure joy anyone can have is in the Lord.

It is to be continuous joy. It is to be conspicuous joy—it ought to show up on your face. There ought to be a sweet reasonableness that flows out of the joy of Jesus that's in your heart. I've known people who are in the deepest sorrow and pain, and yet to be in their presence is to walk away with a blessing. Isn't that true? Because they have joy! This joy is also to be continuous. And when it is continuous and conspicuous, my dear friend, it will be contagious.

ACTION POINT It is not wrong to joy in your health or your job. But that's the kind of joy that can be threatened. You need a joy which supersedes that. Psalm 16:11: says, "You will show me the path of life. In Your presence is fullness of joy. At Your right hand are pleasures forevermore." Rejoice in the Lord always—continuous joy.

28

For by Him all things were created that are in heaven and that are on earth, visible and invisible, whether thrones or dominions or principalities or powers. All things were created through Him and for Him. And He is before all things, and in Him all things consist.

COLOSSIANS 1:16-17

Colossians 1:16 states that all things were created both by Jesus and for Jesus. The word *for* in this verse is a preposition that speaks of direction. It's the Greek word for "moving in the direction of."

The western world has been invaded by Eastern religions. Eastern religions are circular; they believe everything just goes round and round. But things are not circular—this world is headed in a direction. The Bible is linear. We are moving—moving to that time when the kingdoms of this world will become "the kingdoms of our Lord and of His Christ, and He shall reign forever and ever!" (See Revelation 11:15.)

I'm told that a young man was once taking a philosophy course. The philosophy professor had a little bit of a sense of humor. He wanted to see how much philosophy these young people knew; to see how well they could think. So the final examination was one word: "Why?"

This student thought for a while, wrote one word down, and then walked out: "Because."

I would add two more words: Because of Jesus. He is the mystery of history. Why was it all made? "All things were created through Him and for Him. And He is before all things, and in Him all things consist" (Colossians 1:17). And history has a date with deity.

ACTION POINT Friend, it is all headed to Jesus. It is all for Him, for the Lord Jesus Christ. He is the key to the mystery of history. When people ask you, "What is the world coming to?" tell them: "It's coming to Jesus."

29

Then Jesus spoke to them again, saying, "I am the light of the world. He who follows Me shall not walk in darkness, but have the light of life."

JOHN 8:12

In the natural world, there is nothing as pure as light. Light can never be defiled or corrupted—no matter what it passes through or falls upon. You can let light fall on the most corruptible, putrefying, vile, loathsome, disease-ridden object; yet the light is not touched by it. It will expose it but not be contaminated by it.

Now you take water from the purest spring, but as it bubbles up and begins to flow away, it gets contaminated. But not light. Light can never by defiled, and therefore light is a wonderful picture of the Lord Jesus Christ. Jesus was in this world. He was the Light of the world. He exposed sin, but He was never contaminated by it. Jesus could touch sinners, but sin never touched Jesus.

ACTION POINT Now do you see why "light" is a perfect word to describe the Lord Jesus Christ? Compare this passage to John 1:4-5 and John 1:9: "In Him was life, and the life was the light of men. And the light shines in the darkness, and the darkness did not comprehend it....That was the true Light which gives light to every man coming into the world."

Thank the Lord Jesus today for being that pure Light who gives life to everyone who receives His offer of salvation.

30

> They fought from the heavens; the stars
> from their courses fought against Sisera.
> **JUDGES 5:20**

Military strategists are still studying Napoleon. He was a great general, but full of ego. Napoleon marched against Russia with 500,000 handpicked men. As he marched across the plains, a snowflake kissed his cheek. He brushed it off and laughed. Another came—and then a handful. And then, bushels and finally avalanches of snowflakes. Napoleon's fine horses reared and plunged and floundered in the snow. His army perished. Before it was over, Napoleon's finest lay frozen. He retreated like a whipped puppy. Napoleon had boasted, "God is on the side of the heaviest battalions." And he was right—but he forgot that God puts His battalions in the skies.

The same thing happened to one of Israel's enemies. This time, no snowflakes—but stars. The king of Canaan had kept his heel on Israel's throat for 20 years, and the king of Canaan had a general named Sisera. Sisera was a strategically gifted man, a very successful general. He had 900 chariots of iron. And Barak was the Israeli general—he had a contingent of 10,000 men. And they met in battle at the foot of Mount Tabor. Barak, who was greatly outgunned, won the battle. Sisera, who should have won the battle, lost the battle. And in Judges 5:20, a woman named Deborah explains it all in a song that she wrote, and she said, "...the stars from their courses fought against Sisera." That is, "The fight was fixed." It was over before it began for Sisera.

ACTION POINT What are your odds if you stand against the plan of God? The stars in their courses fought against Sisera and Napoleon, and they'll fight against anyone who fights against God. Get into His word. Learn His ways so He doesn't have to send the stars to correct your course. One little snowflake will do. Seek Him from the start!

Salvation is not rooted in the merit of man but in the mercy of God.

ADRIAN ROGERS

december

1

For unto us a Child is born, unto us a Son is given;
and the government will be upon His shoulder. And
His name will be called Wonderful, Counselor, Mighty
God, Everlasting Father, Prince of Peace.

ISAIAH 9:6

Seven hundred years before the first Christmas, Isaiah dipped his pen in golden glory and wrote these words about the coming Prince of Peace, the Lord Jesus Christ. "A Child is born" speaks of His virgin birth. "A Son is given" speaks of His eternality—He has been the Son of God, co-existent, co-eternal, with the Father, through the ages.

Some fifty years ago, man first stepped onto the moon. The President of the United States said, "The planting of human feet upon the moon is the greatest event in human history." I mean no disrespect to the President, but I want to say that he was totally wrong. The greatest event in human history was not when we planted human feet upon the moon, but when God's feet were planted upon planet Earth. We call that the *incarnation*—Almighty God stepped out of heaven, into this world of woe.

"In the beginning was the Word, and the Word was with God, and the Word was God" (John 1:1). Jesus is called "the Word." What is a word? A word is an expression of an invisible thought. You can't hear my thoughts, but you hear my words and therefore you know my thoughts. My thoughts are invisible, but my word makes the invisible known to you. Jesus makes the invisible God known to man. He is the very Word of God. He is God's Word to this human race. He is God in human flesh.

ACTION POINT Share this with someone you know today: on the first Christmas, God sent a package to Earth, the marvelous gift of deity wrapped in humanity. It is supernatural. Never forget this: Jesus is God in human flesh.

December

2

> And behold, you will conceive in your womb and bring forth a Son, and shall call His name JESUS....Then Mary said to the angel, "How can this be, since I do not know a man?" And the angel answered and said to her, "The Holy Spirit will come upon you, and the power of the Highest will overshadow you; therefore, also, that Holy One who is to be born will be called the Son of God.
>
> **LUKE 1:31,34-35**

Do you believe in the Virgin Birth of Jesus? Why would the Virgin Birth even be necessary? I'll tell you why.

When God created Adam and Eve and put them in the Garden of Eden, He gave Adam dominion over the Earth (Genesis 1:26). He was to rule it (Psalm 8:6-8). Yet by choosing to believe the serpent rather than God, Adam and Eve sinned and yielded their God-given authority over to Satan, the ultimate con artist. Instead of ruling as God intended, they became slaves of sin (Romans 6:16). And to everyone who came after them they passed down the same sinful nature: "For since by man came death. ...For as in Adam all die..." (1 Corinthians 15:21a,22a).

But why does that require Jesus to be born of a virgin? If Jesus had been born of an earthly father, he would have inherited the same sin nature as his natural father, a son of Adam, and been just as much a slave to sin as Adam was—and as we all are, until we are born again.

Jesus came to earth as a man, but not one with Adam's sin nature. Because the Holy Spirit came upon Mary, Jesus was born with the sinless nature of His Father, God. Our authority on Earth was lost by a man: Adam. Jesus came as a man, born of a virgin, to redeem us and win back that lost authority.

ACTION POINT Read Philippians 2:5-8 and meditate upon what Jesus Christ did for you.

3

> Therefore the Lord Himself will give you a sign: Behold, the virgin shall conceive and bear a Son, and shall call His name Immanuel.
>
> **ISAIAH 7:14**

There are people who sneer at the idea of the Virgin Birth. "Ha!" they say. "How could this happen?" As the angel said to Mary, "With God nothing will be impossible" (Luke 1:37).

Do you believe that? If you have trouble believing in the Virgin Birth, your real trouble is with God. Be reasonable: if God could make the first man without a father or mother, don't you think He could bring His Son into this world through the Virgin Birth?

If you don't believe in the Virgin Birth, you have some character problems. You would find problems with...

- *The character of Mary.* If Mary had a child out of wedlock, then Mary was an impure woman.
- *The character of Jesus.* If Jesus had not been born of a virgin, he would have been the son of Adam, and in Adam all die. Jesus Christ would have had the same human proclivities you and I have, who are by nature the children of wrath.
- *The character of the Word of God.* God's Word would be flawed if the Virgin Birth were untrue, because the Word of God clearly, plainly teaches that it happened.

ACTION POINT Think about this today: Your salvation is inextricably interwoven with the Virgin Birth. No Virgin Birth, no deity. No deity, no sinless life. No sinless life, no sacrificial death. No sacrificial death, no salvation. No salvation, you're going to Hell. Jesus came to Earth that we might go to Heaven; born of a virgin that we might be born again. Thank God for the Virgin Birth.

December 4

And she brought forth her firstborn Son, and wrapped Him in swaddling cloths, and laid Him in a manger, because there was no room for them in the inn.

LUKE 2:7

And without controversy great is the mystery of godliness: God was manifested in the flesh, justified in the Spirit, seen by angels, preached among the Gentiles, believed on in the world, received up in glory.

1 TIMOTHY 3:16

1 Timothy 3:16 says "...God was manifested in the flesh." You may not understand that. The apostle Paul said, "I don't understand it." Great is the mystery. God stepped out of Heaven and came to this Earth through the portals of a virgin's womb.

Jesus did not have His beginning at Bethlehem. When the Bible says, "In the beginning was the Word" (John 1:1), it is not talking about a *start* but a *state*. There never was a time when Jesus was not. There never will be a time when Jesus is not. He is God from everlasting to everlasting.

This little baby wrapped in swaddling clothes was the great, eternal, uncreated, self-existent Word made flesh. The little baby in Luke 2 is the mighty God of Genesis 1. "Without Him nothing was made..." (John 1:3). That baby lying in the straw with dimpled feet is the One who swung planets into space. The little boy playing with shavings in Joseph's carpenter shop is very God of very God—God manifested in the flesh.

ACTION POINT What good is it to know history and the events of history and not know Jesus? Ponder this truth: "For in Him we live and move and have our being" (Acts 17:28). He is fully God, forever God. How will this impact your worldview today?

5

> And the angel answered and said to her, "The Holy Spirit will come upon you, and the power of the Highest will overshadow you; therefore, also, that Holy One who is to be born will be called the Son of God."
>
> **LUKE 1:35**

The educated man is ignorant, the strong man is weak, and the wealthy man is poor who does not understand the true meaning of Christmas.

What good does it do us to put a man on the moon if we don't get God in our hearts? What good is it to know astronomy and not know Jesus, the Bright and Morning Star, and how to go to Heaven? What good is it to know botany and not know Jesus, Heaven's sweetest rose, the Rose of Sharon, who can perfume any life? What good is it to know history and not know that history is His story? What good is it to know the ages of the rocks, and not know Jesus, the Rock of Ages?

Jesus was not just another child. He was not just the Galilean peasant, the great teacher. He was supernatural. On the first Christmas, God sent a package to Earth. This package was a gift of deity wrapped up in humanity. What a marvelous thing this is! It's supernatural.

ACTION POINT You won't understand Christmas until you understand that this child was born of a virgin. This child is the very Son of God. Never forget this! Read the words of Isaiah 9:6-7. Let Isaiah's prophecy about this child speak to you today.

December 6

In the beginning was the Word, and the Word
was with God, and the Word was God.
JOHN 1:1

The Apostle John had lived and walked with Jesus for three years. He had seen Jesus in all kinds of situations. Now, years have passed since then. Now Jesus has gone back to Heaven, and John, an aged man, writes these words in John 1. And the Apostle John, a Jew, who would have an ingrained resistance to any kind of idolatry, said of the Lord Jesus Christ that He is fully God.

If somebody comes to your door, preaching, and does not believe that Jesus is God, he is a false prophet. "But to the Son He says: 'Your throne, O God, is forever and ever; a scepter of righteousness is the scepter of Your kingdom'" (Hebrews 1:8) Our heavenly Father has said to His heavenly Son, "Your throne is for ever and ever, and You, My Son, are God."

Everything God is, Jesus is. Everything God has, Jesus has. Everything God does, Jesus does. Jesus is God; fully God. He is not part-God and part-man. He's not all God and no man. He's not all man and no God. He is the God-man. Jesus makes the invisible God known to man. He is the very Word of God. He is God's Word to this human race. He is God in human flesh.

ACTION POINT Read John 1:1-18 today. Have you acknowledged Him, Jesus, as the One and Only?

7

Paul, a bondservant of Jesus Christ, called to be an apostle, separated to the gospel of God which He promised before through His prophets in the Holy Scriptures, concerning His Son Jesus Christ our Lord, who was born of the seed of David according to the flesh, and declared to be the Son of God with power according to the Spirit of holiness, by the resurrection from the dead.

ROMANS 1:1-4

May I ask you a personal question? Do you believe that Jesus Christ is Lord? If your answer is yes, then may I ask you another question? Is He your Lord?

Let's be more specific.

- Is He Lord of your tongue?
- Is He Lord of your time?
- Is He Lord of your treasure?
- Is He Lord of your talents?
- Is He Lord of your testimony?
- Is He Lord in deed, as well as word?

Is He truly Lord? Jesus Christ is called "Lord" far more than He is called "Savior." He's called "Lord" 747 times in the New Testament. He is Lord. Every so often someone says, "Well, I decided to make Him Lord." Too late for that! He is Lord. The question is not, "Will you make Him Lord?" The question is, "Will you submit to His Lordship?"

ACTION POINT Don't answer too quickly. Think about it: It's one thing to sing, "Bring forth the royal diadem and crown Him Lord of all."* It is another thing to mean it. Crown Him "Lord of all" in your life today.

*"All Hail the Power of Jesus' Name" — Edward Perronet, 1780

8

And when eight days were completed for the circumcision of the Child, His name was called JESUS, the name given by the angel before He was conceived in the womb.

LUKE 2:21

And truly Jesus did many other signs in the presence of His disciples, which are not written in this book; but these are written that you may believe that Jesus is the Christ, the Son of God, and that believing you may have life in His name.

JOHN 20:30-31

What is in the name of the Lord Jesus? There is wonder in His name. Do you stand in awe of the Lord Jesus Christ? Or have you become complacent? Do you not get excited when you think of Jesus? If you don't, you've lost the wonder. You have calluses on your soul.

Oh friend, Jesus is wonderful. Wonderful in His birth. Wonderful in His life. Wonderful in His teaching. Wonderful in His miracles. Wonderful in His death. Wonderful in His resurrection. And yes, wonderful in His second coming. His name is wonderful.

I heard of a man riding on a train one time, looking out the window. He was saying, "Wonderful, wonderful, wonderful, wonderful, wonderful." And the man sitting next to him asked, "Why do you think everything is wonderful?" He said, "I've been blind, and I've just had surgery, and I'm seeing things I had long since forgotten how beautiful they are. And they are wonderful to me."

ACTION POINT Friend, if Jesus is not wonderful to you, open your spiritual eyes. See just how wonderful Jesus is. There is wonder in His name.

9

For Jews request a sign, and Greeks seek after wisdom; but we preach Christ crucified, to the Jews a stumbling block and to the Greeks foolishness, but to those who are called, both Jews and Greeks, Christ the power of God and the wisdom of God.

1 CORINTHIANS 1:24

Do you need a counselor sometimes? People come to pastors and counselors for wisdom. We can counsel from Scripture, but we can't solve their problems.

We can try to lead them to the One who can solve their problems, the Lord Jesus Christ. But I don't want them dependent upon me. I want them to know Jesus. He is the Counselor.

There is wisdom in Jesus' name, because His name is *Counselor*. "For unto us a Child is born, unto us a Son is given; and the government will be upon His shoulder. And His name will be called Wonderful, Counselor, Mighty God, Everlasting Father, Prince of Peace" (Isaiah 9:6).

The Bible says, "But of Him you are in Christ Jesus, who became for us wisdom from God—and righteousness and sanctification and redemption—that, as it is written, 'He who glories, let him glory in the Lord'" (1 Corinthians 1:30).

ACTION POINT Are you going through a problem right now and you don't know the way out? You don't know what to do. Every answer seems wrong. I want to recommend my Counselor to you. His name is Jesus. Not only is there wonder in His name. Friend, there is wisdom in His name. Call upon the true Counselor.

December

10

> Therefore, having been justified by faith, we have peace with God through our Lord Jesus Christ, through whom also we have access by faith into this grace in which we stand, and rejoice in hope of the glory of God.
>
> **ROMANS 5:1-2**

The thing your heart is yearning for is peace. Jesus is called "The Prince of Peace." (See Isaiah 9:6.) The Bible says, "and the peace of God, which surpasses all understanding, will guard your hearts and minds through Christ Jesus" (Philippians 4:7). You see, God—through Jesus—came to give you peace.

Has anyone ever left you anything in a will? Jesus did. Just before He went to the cross He said, "Peace I leave with you, My peace I give to you; not as the world gives do I give to you. Let not your heart be troubled, neither let it be afraid" (John 14:27).

This is the legacy Jesus left for you. Jesus willed His body to Joseph of Arimathea for burial. Jesus gave the care of His mother to the Apostle John. Jesus yielded up His spirit to God the Father. But Jesus gave His peace to you. And there's no lawyer on earth that can break that will. It is yours. It is your throne gift.

ACTION POINT If you don't have peace, it's because you don't understand what you have in the name of Jesus. There's peace in His name. Call upon Him today. Ask Him to help you receive the peace He has provided.

11

> But while he thought about these things, behold, an angel of the Lord appeared to him in a dream, saying, "Joseph, son of David, do not be afraid to take to you Mary your wife, for that which is conceived in her is of the Holy Spirit."
>
> **MATTHEW 1:20**

Who was this Child, the one we call Jesus? There is one right answer; there are many wrong answers. Some say He was a great man. Beyond any doubt, He was, but Jesus is more than Jesus the Great. He is Jesus, the One and Only.

The late Dr. W.A. Criswell said: "To compare the greatest men of the earth, like an Alexander or Caesar or Shakespeare, with Jesus is like comparing a grain of dust to the whole universe, like comparing a molehill to Mt. Everest in the Himalayas."

Others speak of Him as a moral teacher, but as C.S. Lewis said in *Mere Christianity*:

> *"That is the one thing we must not say. A man who was merely a man and said the sort of things Jesus said would not be a great moral teacher. He would either be a lunatic—on the level with the man who says he is a poached egg—or else he would be the Devil of Hell. You must make your choice. Either this man was, and is, the Son of God, or else a madman or something worse. You can shut him up for a fool, you can spit at him and kill him as a demon or you can fall at his feet and call him Lord and God, but let us not come with any patronizing nonsense about his being a great human teacher."*

ACTION POINT Who is Jesus to you? Is He Lord, or not? You need to find out. And if He is not Lord, you must fall at His feet and make Him Lord.

December 12

> And she will bring forth a Son, and you shall call His name JESUS, for He will save His people from their sins.
>
> **MATTHEW 1:21**

One day I drove my car off the hot pavement and out into a grassy area because I knew where there was a persimmon tree. I love persimmons. But I got impossibly stuck in the mud. I got a board and tried to dig myself out. I found a piece of carpet in the woods and put that under the tires. They only sunk deeper.

I prayed, "Lord, I'm in the mud. I'm helpless here. Lord, get me out." At almost the same time, a man drove by in a four-wheel vehicle. With that mighty truck, he pulled me slowly out of the mud. I was back on solid ground. I was so grateful. I hadn't known what to do, but God sent someone who did.

That's so much like salvation. We're looking to the things of this world and sinking in the mud. We think, "I can get myself out of this." The more we try to handle it, the deeper we sink. We need someone who sees us and comes to get us out. Jesus is the Savior. He has what it takes to extricate us from the mud we've gotten into.

Back at home, I began to wash off my muddy car. That man got me out of the mud, but it was up to me to deal with the mud still on there. When I got saved, I was covered with mud. But since then, I've been having Jesus, the Water of Life, clean me up.

ACTION POINT You can struggle all you want, but you're only going to sink deeper. Stop the struggle. Surrender to Christ. You don't have what it takes to get out unless someone takes you out. That One is Jesus. His name is wonderful. He is the Mighty God, Everlasting Father, and Prince of Peace. (See Isaiah 9:6.)

13

So it was, when the angels had gone away from them into heaven, that the shepherds said to one another, "Let us now go to Bethlehem and see this thing that has come to pass, which the Lord has made known to us."
LUKE 2:15

What is the great need in the world today? Is it information? We're drowning in a sea of information. If information had been our need, God would have sent an educator. Is it technology? If technology had been the need, God would have sent a scientist. Is it money? Do you think your problems would be solved if you had more money? If money were the need, God would have sent an economist. Is the need more leisure? Maybe God should have sent an entertainer.

No. Our great need is *salvation*. So God sent a Savior.

I'm amazed (and blessed) that He sent the message to humble shepherds. Old Herod, the king, never did quite get it. He never did understand. But humble shepherds understood. Why? Because God has "hidden these things from the wise and prudent and revealed them to babes." (See Luke 10:21).

ACTION POINT Do you want to understand who Jesus Christ is today? Then lay your intellectual pride in the dust, come to Him and say, "Lord, reveal this truth to me." Sing it and follow it: "O come let us adore Him, Christ the LORD."

December 14

For unto us a Child is born, unto us a Son is given;
and the government will be upon His shoulder. And
His name will be called Wonderful, Counselor, Mighty
God, Everlasting Father, Prince of Peace.

ISAIAH 9:6

Jesus was born a king. Isaiah 9:6 says "the government will be upon His shoulder." And in the next verse, this is fleshed out. "Of the increase of His government and peace there will be no end, upon the throne of David and over His kingdom, to order it and establish it with judgment and justice from that time forward, even forever. The zeal of the LORD of hosts will perform this" (Isaiah 9:7).

This little baby was born a king, and He *is* King. We didn't elect Him, and friend, we will not impeach Him. He is King. He is Lord.

Some people will ask, "Have you made Him Lord?" You're too late for that. God has already declared Him Lord. This is Christ's sovereign nobility. He is KING OF KINGS and LORD OF LORDS (see Revelation 19:16). And if you miss that, you miss the meaning of Christmas. You have to take the cradle and the cross and the crown and put them together, or you don't have the true story of Christmas.

ACTION POINT Have you made Him Lord? No. Can you receive Him as Lord? Yes! You can bow your knee to Him and say, "O Lord, You are the King and the government is upon Your shoulder. Therefore, I yield my heart to You."

December 15

> Nor is there salvation in any other, for there is no other name under heaven given among men by which we must be saved.
>
> **ACTS 4:12**

Why did Jesus come? Luke 19:10 tells us: "For the Son of Man has come to seek and to save that which was lost." Jesus Himself said, "I am the way, the truth, and the life. No one comes to the Father except through Me" (John 14:6).

I've often said Jesus is not a good way to Heaven, and not the best way to Heaven, but the only way to Heaven. When you say that, a lot of people get their hackles up, but I still want to tell you that, apart from Jesus, there is no salvation. He is not just "one more Savior." He is the solitary Savior, the *only* Savior.

Now, if He is not the only Savior, He is no Savior at all, because He said He was the only one. And if He's not the only one, then He's a liar, and a liar is nobody's Savior.

I've got some wonderful news for you: He can save anyone. Because of the birthday of Jesus, each year you are one year closer to Heaven, one year closer to seeing His dear face. Jesus, the Son of God, left Heaven, came to this Earth, suffered, bled, died, and walked out of that grave the living, risen Savior. He's the One who sent me to tell you that He loves you.

ACTION POINT He wants to save you and He will save you today if you'll give Him your heart. If you have not already done so, do it today. Pray, "Jesus, I give You my heart. I believe You died to save me. You will save me if I trust in You. I do trust You, Jesus. I'm trusting You today."

Therefore, having been justified by faith, we have peace with God through our Lord Jesus Christ.

ROMANS 5:1

One time I was trying to witness to a man I knew well. He was what you'd call a self-made man, comfortable in his status in life. He was standing in front of his house. We had a friendly conversation, but when I broached the subject of Jesus he said, "Oh, I'm fine like I am. You see that house? It's paid for. My wife loves me and I love her. I have my retirement income. I'm doing quite well."

I said, "Sir, may I ask you a question?"

"Well, sure," he answered.

"Don't say that lightly. I want you to think, then answer me honestly."

"Of course."

"Do you have peace in your heart?"

"I told you, I'm fine."

"No, you said you would answer the question. Do you have peace in your heart?"

His chin began to quiver. His eyes brimmed with tears. "No! I don't have peace. How did you know?"

"Because the Bible says there is no peace for the wicked."

Without the saving life of Jesus Christ and the indwelling Holy Spirit, you cannot have true peace. It is only found in the wonderful name of Jesus.

ACTION POINT Do you have peace with God? If you don't know the Lord Jesus Christ, I invite you to pray a prayer like this: "Dear Jesus, I need You. I'm a sinner. I'm lost. I don't want to die in my sin and go to Hell. I trust You, Jesus. I believe You're the Son of God. You paid for my sin debt with Your shed blood on the cross. Thank You, Lord, for saving me. In Jesus' name I pray, amen."

17

Now after Jesus was born in Bethlehem of Judea in the days of Herod the king, behold, wise men from the East came to Jerusalem, saying, "Where is He who has been born King of the Jews? For we have seen His star in the East and have come to worship Him."

MATTHEW 2:1-2

Not all "wise men" are wise men. You may be a great entrepreneur, businessman, engineer, or nuclear physicist. You may be a physician, a lawyer, a gifted artist. But if you don't know Jesus, you are not truly wise. There is a kind of wisdom that's not wisdom at all—the wisdom of this world. "PhD" may stand for "Phenomenal Dud" if you don't know Jesus.

Omar Bradley, a great American five-star general, once said, "We're living in a time when our achievement, our knowledge of science, has gone far beyond our power to control it. We have too many men of science and too few men of God. We've brought about brilliance without wisdom, power without conscience. We're living in a time of nuclear giants and spiritual pigmies."

Well said. What is real wisdom? First, wise men will seek Jesus. Tell me what motivates you, tell me the consummate ambition of your life, and I can tell you clearly whether you're wise or not just by what you seek.

The Apostle Paul summed up his life in one sentence: "For to me, to live is Christ, and to die is gain" (Philippians 1:21). The source, the substance, the subject, the satisfaction of his life was Christ.

ACTION POINT Put your life in a sentence like this—"For me, to live is Christ." Honestly consider that. Is it true of your life?

18

And when they had come into the house, they saw the young Child with Mary His mother, and fell down and worshiped Him...

MATTHEW 2:11A

And you will seek Me and find Me, when you search for Me with all your heart.

JEREMIAH 29:13

Are you seeking Jesus? Is that the burning ambition of your life? You might say, "Well, I come to church." I'm not talking about that. Think about these men from the East. Do you know where "the East" was? They were from Babylon—300 miles across the Syrian Desert! Think of the distance and difficulty.

Christmas cards picture them coming on camels. I don't know how they came, but I know how they didn't come: by plane, bus, car, or motorcycle. I know where they didn't stay: at the Holiday Inn.

And they came in spite of danger. It was the time of King Herod, insane with jealousy and rage, who had his own wife and three sons murdered. These men, in the face of that danger, said, "We have come to seek Jesus Christ." Wise men will seek Him in spite of the danger.

Wise men who seek Him will see Him. When they came into the house, they fell down and worshipped Him. It is worth it to seek Him, because when you seek Him, you will see Him. "And you will seek Me and find Me, when you search for Me with all your heart" (Jeremiah 29:13). They searched for Him, found Him and saw Him.

ACTION POINT Do you have a desire to know Him? To love Him? To serve Him? Is something drawing you to God? What is drawing you is Someone—the Holy Spirit. Thank God for the ministry of the Holy Spirit!

19

> I will be found by you, says the LORD, and I will bring you back from your captivity; I will gather you from all the nations and from all the places where I have driven you, says the LORD, and I will bring you to the place from which I cause you to be carried away captive.
>
> **JEREMIAH 29:14**

Three things drew the wise men to Jesus:

- The ministry of the Spirit
- The message of the Scripture
- The miracle of the star

Who put in their hearts the desire to find the Christ child and worship Him? The Holy Spirit. Do you know why we seek Him? Because first He went seeking us. First John 4:19 states, "We love Him because He first loved us."

Do you know why I love the Lord Jesus? Because God in grace and mercy put a desire in my heart to seek after Him. The Bible says that by our nature, our flesh, none of us would seek after God—no, not one (Romans 3:11), and that would have included these wise men.

They didn't come to Him because they were smarter than other men or because they were so intellectual. They were wise, and that wisdom caused them to be yielded to God. That's why God the Holy Spirit could work in their hearts and draw them to Jesus.

ACTION POINT Do you have a desire to know Him? To love Him? To serve Him? Do you find something drawing you to God? Remember His promise: You will find Him when you search for Him with all your heart.

december

20

They fought from the heavens; the stars from
their courses fought against Sisera.
JUDGES 5:20

You know, even the stars have to obey our Lord. In the Old Testament, the Bible says the stars in their courses fought against Sisera. He was a general whose army had 900 chariots going to war against God's people. Imagine—900 chariots! But God sent such a tremendous rainstorm that his chariots bogged down and he was defeated.

Later when they wrote a song to celebrate the victory, one of the stanzas says "the stars in their courses fought against Sisera." His kingdom came tumbling down. And ultimately Herod's kingdom came tumbling down too, for Herod stumbled over a star—the Star of Bethlehem.

Listen to me, the whole Universe is against the man who is against God. But the whole Universe lines up behind the man who seeks God. Whatever is necessary, God will do it to get the hungry heart to Jesus. If you want Him, God is a God of might and miracle.

ACTION POINT Some of you may be reading this by divine appointment because you've been wanting to find the Lord. God has guided you here. Thank God for the miracle of the stars. Bethlehem's star was there to guide those wise men. It tells me that whatever is necessary, God will guide your hungry heart if you want to know the Lord Jesus Christ. Are you ready to receive Him today? Are you willing?

21

And when they had come into the house, they saw the young Child with Mary His mother, and fell down and worshiped Him. And when they had opened their treasures, they presented gifts to Him: gold, frankincense, and myrrh.

MATTHEW 2:11

Many people think these three gifts were just random; something incidental. Oh, no! It's something fundamental. And they weren't random trinkets—these were treasures that didn't occur by happenstance. They carry deep significance. They were planned.

Why these specific gifts? They are highly symbolic.

- *Gold* speaks of Christ's sovereign dominion—He was born a King, and the Bible speaks of kings wearing a crown of gold. "For You meet him with the blessings of goodness; You set a crown of pure gold upon his head" (Psalm 21:3).
- *Frankincense* speaks of His sinless deity—He is God in human flesh. Frankincense was used in burning incense.
- *Myrrh* speaks of His sacrificial death—He was born to die that we might live. Myrrh was used to embalm the dead.

He is a king; they brought gold. He is God; they brought frankincense. He is a Savior; they brought myrrh.

ACTION POINT Now that we know this, how should it instruct us today? Because He is a King, He has my wealth. Because He is God, He has my worship. And because He died, He has my witness. All that I am, all that I have, all that I do, belong to this One. That is wisdom. That's what a wise person will do. Do some soul-searching today. Are you really wise?

The king shall have joy in Your strength, O Lord; and in Your salvation how greatly shall he rejoice! You have given him his heart's desire, and have not withheld the request of his lips. *Selah*. For You meet him with the blessings of goodness; You set a crown of pure gold upon his head.

PSALM 21:1-3

Consider the first of the wise men's gifts: gold. In this passage of Psalm 21, David is speaking of a king. Kings wear crowns of gold. When the wise men brought gold, they were saying that they recognized the Child of Bethlehem as a King. They even asked, "Where is He who has been born King of the Jews?" (See Matthew 2:2.) He is destined to reign. He has sovereign dominion. Gold symbolizes His kingship.

You may ask, "Well, how am I going to crown Him?" Crown Him the way they did—with gold. If all of your wealth is not submitted to the Lordship of Jesus Christ, you've not recognized Him as your sovereign king. He has a right to all you own. You say, "It's mine." If He is not Lord of everything you have, He's not your Savior. His throne is not a duplex.

ACTION POINT How will you serve Him? One way is to serve Him with your wealth. As the saying goes, "He has no hands but our hands." Serve Him by showing His love to those in need. He requires your absolute surrender to His lordship. He is the king.

23

And the LORD said to Moses: "Take sweet spices, stacte and onycha and galbanum, and pure frankincense with these sweet spices; there shall be equal amounts of each. You shall make of these an incense, a compound according to the art of the perfumer, salted, pure, and holy. And you shall beat some of it very fine, and put some of it before the Testimony in the tabernacle of meeting where I will meet with you. It shall be most holy to you. But as for the incense which you shall make, you shall not make any for yourselves, according to its composition. It shall be to you holy for the LORD.

EXODUS 30:34-37

Not only did the wise men bring gold; they brought frankincense and myrrh also. Frankincense symbolizes His sinless deity; myrrh, His sacrificial death.

Incense was a sweet perfume to be burned in worship—the worship of God alone. Frankincense represents the beauties, the fragrance, of the Lord Jesus Christ our Intercessor, and His intercessory prayers for us. Its fragrance speaks of the love and mercy of God.

Myrrh, in contrast, was used to embalm the dead. When the Lord Jesus Christ was being buried, they poured spices and myrrh into His grave clothes. "And Nicodemus, who at first came to Jesus by night, also came, bringing a mixture of myrrh and aloes, about a hundred pounds" (John 19:39).

In these gifts of the wise men to the young child Jesus, we see His sovereign dominion, sinless deity, and sacrificial death. He was born to die.

ACTION POINT Give, worship, witness, serve. Give to Him—He is King. Worship Him—He Is God. Serve Him—He is your Savior.

December

24

God is our refuge and strength, a very present help in trouble.

PSALM 46:1

Let your conduct be without covetousness; be content with such things as you have. For He Himself has said, "I will never leave you nor forsake you."

HEBREWS 13:5

Some people feel so alone over this holiday season. One Christmas Eve, I went to talk to a person who was hurting. I said, "Why don't you call a friend?" She said, "I don't have a friend." I said, "Oh yes, you do." And I told her His name. It is the One who said, "I will never leave you nor forsake you" (see Hebrews 13:5).

Greek scholars tell us that sentence has five negatives in it. Now we say that a double-negative is bad English, but evidently it wasn't bad Greek. Here's what it literally says: "I will never, no not ever, no, never leave nor forsake you."

Famed research analyst Dr. Abraham Maslow said, "The truth is that the average American does not have a real friend in the world." And psychiatrist Alfred Adler said, "All human failures spring from a lack of love." People need someone to love, and they need to be loved. Without it, their lives are full of fear and frustration. Hebrews 13:5 tells us we can face a new year with the certainty of His provision and with His companionship in our hearts and lives.

ACTION POINT Who do you know that might need a call from a friend today? A new widow? An empty-nester? A stay-at-home mom? Make that call.

25

And she brought forth her firstborn Son, and wrapped Him in swaddling cloths, and laid Him in a manger, because there was no room for them in the inn.

LUKE 2:7

And suddenly a voice came from heaven, saying, "This is My beloved Son, in whom I am well pleased."

MATTHEW 3:17

While he was still speaking, behold, a bright cloud overshadowed them; and suddenly a voice came out of the cloud, saying, "This is My beloved Son, in whom I am well pleased. Hear Him!"

MATTHEW 17:5

Jesus never had an "identity crisis." "Jesus said to him, 'I am the way, the truth, and the life. No one comes to the Father except through Me'" (John 14:6). Jesus never said, "I am one way to God." He didn't say, "I am a life." Jesus said, "I am *the* way, I am *the* truth, I am *the* life." And God the Father says, "He is My dear Son."

In John 8:58, Jesus said, "Before Abraham was, I AM." Not "I was," but "I AM." He is the great I AM. He didn't have His beginning at Bethlehem. He never had a beginning. He has always existed. The One who created the Universe not only has this whole world in His hands, but also has the past, the present, and the future in His hands. People ask, "What is the world coming to?" Answer: "It's coming to Jesus." "All things were made through Him" (John 1:3), and all will climax in Him.

ACTION POINT Take a moment to worship Jesus! "Sing, choirs of angels, sing in exultation, sing, all ye citizens of heav'n above; glory to God, all glory in the highest; O come, let us adore him, Christ the Lord!"*

*"O Come All Ye Faithful" — John Francis Wade

december

26

...and to give you who are troubled rest with us when the Lord Jesus is revealed from heaven with His mighty angels...

2 THESSALONIANS 1:7

...when He comes, in that Day, to be glorified in His saints and to be admired among all those who believe, because our testimony among you was believed.

2 THESSALONIANS 1:10

Christmas is not the end of the story! It's not yet finished, for the Jesus who came the first time is coming again, and Christmas is not complete without the Second Coming of Jesus Christ. The incarnation without the coronation would be like east without west, like an engagement without a marriage.

You may have thought this was a good Christmas for you—but, friend, the best is yet to come! The Heavenly Father has so much more in store for us when Jesus comes again. We get all wrapped up in the little baby in the manger, then we go beyond the birth of the baby, saying, "Yes, He came to die for our sins" (thank God He did that), but I want to remind you that the First Coming of Jesus and the Second Coming are linked together.

The Christmas Story in Luke 1 and 2 speaks not only of the Jesus who redeemed, but also of the Jesus who reigned—not only of the Jesus who came the first time, but also of the Jesus who is coming the second time to sit upon the throne of His father David, to rule over the house of Jacob forever and ever.

ACTION POINT Imagine for a moment what your life would be like without the Resurrection, the Rapture, and the Second Coming of Jesus. The most glorious fact of the *past* is that Jesus came the first time. The most glorious fact of the *future* is that Jesus is coming again. The one sure hope of this jittery old world is the Second Coming of Jesus Christ.

december 27

[God] has in these last days spoken to us by His Son, whom He has appointed heir of all things, through whom also He made the worlds; who being the brightness of His glory and the express image of His person, and upholding all things by the word of His power, when He had by Himself purged our sins, sat down at the right hand of the Majesty on high.

HEBREWS 1:2-3

Two thousand years after His birth, there is never one minute on Earth when millions of people are not studying what Jesus Christ said. Think about it: He is a person who lived in a tiny land 2,000 years ago, yet His birth divides the centuries from "B.C." to "A.D. "

He never wrote a book. Yet libraries could be filled with the volumes written about the Lord Jesus. He never painted a picture, yet the world's greatest art, music, and literature have Jesus Christ at their center. He never traveled far from His birthplace, yet His testimony has gone around the world. He only had a handful of followers and a ministry of only three short years, yet 2000 years later, we still say, "Jesus, Your name is wonderful."

He had no formal education, yet colleges, universities and seminaries are built in the name of Jesus Christ. To know Him is to love Him. To love Him is to trust Him. To trust Him is to be radically, dramatically, eternally transformed.

Human speech is too limited to describe Him, the human mind too small to comprehend Him, and the human heart can never completely, totally absorb who Jesus Christ is: God, manifest in the flesh.

ACTION POINT If you want to know God, come to know Jesus. John 1:18 says, "No one has seen God at any time. The only begotten Son, who is in the bosom of the Father, He has declared Him."

December 28

> Peace I leave with you, My peace I give to you; not as the world gives do I give to you. Let not your heart be troubled, neither let it be afraid.
>
> **JOHN 14:27**

One of the wonderful names of Jesus is "The Prince of Peace." Isaiah prophesied that He would be called "The Prince of Peace." Jesus holds the key to peace, whether it's personal peace in your heart, domestic peace in your home, or eternal peace in Heaven.

The angels told the shepherds that His coming was "good tidings of great joy," for His incarnation meant "peace, goodwill toward men."

Certainly there is a need for peace. But look around. What's happened to the promised peace? It was postponed when the world rejected and then crucified the Prince of Peace whom God had sent.

There will be no peace on Earth until the world that rejected our Savior receives Him again in power and glory. The only true hope for peace for the Church, the nation, the world, and the individual is the Second Coming of Jesus Christ.

ACTION POINT This Christmas, do you have peace with God, or is the war still going on? The only way you can have the peace Jesus made is to surrender to Jesus. He has fought and won the battle. He has made peace through the blood of His cross. But that peace does you no good until you bow to Him in total, absolute surrender and lay down your sword of rebellion at His feet. Once you have that peace *with* God, then you can have the peace *of* God.

December 29

Now Thomas, called the Twin, one of the twelve, was not with them when Jesus came. The other disciples therefore said to him, "We have seen the Lord." So he said to them, "Unless I see in His hands the print of the nails, and put my finger into the print of the nails, and put my hand into His side, I will not believe."

JOHN 20:24-25

At Bethlehem, a bright star pointed the way to Jesus. But there is a darker side to Christmas. Consider the scars of the Lord Jesus...they are not incidental. They are so fundamental that Jesus carried those scars with Him to Heaven.

Think about it: the only man-made things in Heaven are the scars of Jesus Christ. When He returned to Heaven, He took some souvenirs of His visit with him...the scars in His hands and side, keeping them as a lasting memorial through all eternity.

When Jesus comes again, one of the ways we'll know Him is by the scars on His hands and feet. Zechariah 13:6 says, "And one will say to him, 'What are these wounds between your arms?' Then he will answer, 'Those with which I was wounded in the house of my friends.'"

ACTION POINT Imagine our risen Savior on the throne of His glory. See in His hands the print of the nails, because He bears them for all eternity. See those nail-scarred hands reaching to you right now. Put your hand in that hand and say, "Save me, Lord Jesus. Thank You that You came to Earth as a man and suffered in order to save me." Pray it and mean it.

December

30

For You have delivered my soul from death,
my eyes from tears, and my feet from falling.
PSALM 116:8

I believe the holidays are the loneliest time of the year. Everywhere, people are told they are supposed to be happy, and they realize they're not. They see everybody else acting happy, and they feel so lonely. I'm speaking today to women whose husbands have walked out on them, to children whose fathers have forsaken them, to men whose wives have left them, and to others who feel abandoned and forsaken.

Yes, believers can experience loneliness. Death, divorce, desertion, even travel, can make you lonely. Success can make you lonely. You often hear, "It's lonely at the top." Old age makes you lonely. You can be lonely in a big crowd. You can be lonely in a mall. Loneliness is one of the chief maladies of our age, but God promised, "I will never leave you nor forsake you" (See Hebrews 13:5). What that literally means is, "I will not abandon you. I will not give up on you. I will not leave you a helpless orphan. You will not be forsaken."

What I am saying, my dear friend, is that when I am discouraged, His presence sees me through. When I am lonely, His presence cheers me up. And when I am worried, His presence calms me down.

ACTION POINT When you are tempted—and you will be tempted this coming year—His presence will help you out. Begin now to practice the presence of the Lord as you enter this new year. The thing that helps keep us all straight is to know that Jesus Christ never leaves us and never forsakes us. Have the contentment of His provision, the companionship of His presence, and the confidence of His promise.

december

31

Therefore He says: "Awake, you who sleep, arise from the dead, and Christ will give you light." See then that you walk circumspectly, not as fools but as wise, redeeming the time, because the days are evil.

EPHESIANS 5:14-16

We stand on the threshold of a new year. And if you are like I am, you make resolutions that go in one year and out the other. We determine we're going to do this or that or not do this or that. And then at the end of the year we look back and see we've failed to some degree to keep our resolutions.

But that doesn't mean we shouldn't resolve again, by the grace of God, because I have wonderful news for you: The God we serve is the God of grace, the God of forgiveness, and the God of beginning again. Don't forget it! He is the God of a new start. He is the God of the second chance.

God's two great gifts to you are *Jesus* and *time*. God has given you time to work, time to serve, time to love, time to laugh, time to labor. But like any gift, how you use it is up to you. See this day and every day as a gift from God. Time is not something that you own. God is the creator, the possessor of time. The difference between people is not that some people have more time than other people, but that some people are better stewards of the time that God has given them.

ACTION POINT See this time as a provided opportunity; as something that God has given you and wants you to awaken to. I am a steward of the time that God has given me, and one day I will have to answer to God for what I did with this day and every day that God has given me. There are 24 hours or 1,440 minutes or 86,400 seconds in the day—and every instant is a precious gift from God.

notes

notes

notes

notes

notes

notes

notes

notes

A**drian Rogers**, one of America's most respected Bible teachers, faithfully preached the Word of God for 53 years—32 of those years as senior pastor of the historic Bellevue Baptist Church near Memphis, Tennessee.

He wrote 18 books and over 80 booklets giving strength and encouragement on subjects such as marriage, prophecy, evangelism, and the Christian walk.

In 1987 he founded Love Worth Finding Ministries to communicate the glorious Gospel of Jesus Christ with millions around the world. The message of God's love continues today, and as he so aptly put it, "Truly, the sun never sets on the ministry of Love Worth Finding."

WILL YOU SUPPORT LOVE WORTH FINDING?

This ministry is funded primarily by gifts from Christians committed to sharing God's Word with lost and hurting people from all walks of life.

If this resource has been a help to you, please consider joining with us to bless others with the Gospel of Jesus Christ.

lwf.org/give

PO Box 38300 | Memphis TN 38183-0300 | (901) 382-7900

CPSIA information can be obtained
at www.ICGtesting.com
Printed in the USA
LVHW042258041221
705236LV00003B/3

9 781613 147672